New Frontiers of Slavery

FERNAND BRAUDEL CENTER
STUDIES IN HISTORICAL SOCIAL SCIENCE

Series Editor: Richard E. Lee

The Fernand Braudel Center Studies in Historical Social Science will publish works that address theoretical and empirical questions produced by scholars in or through the Fernand Braudel Center or who share its approach and concerns. It specifically seeks to promote works that contribute to the development of the world-systems perspective engaging a holistic and relational vision of the world—the modern world-system—implicit in historical social science, which at once takes into consideration structures (long-term regularities) and change (history). With the intellectual boundaries within the sciences/social sciences/humanities structure collapsing in the work scholars actually do, this series will offer a venue for a wide range of research that confronts the dilemmas of producing relevant accounts of historical processes in the context of the rapidly changing structures of both the social and academic world. The series will include monographs, colloquia, and collections of essays organized around specific themes.

VOLUMES IN THIS SERIES:

Questioning Nineteenth-Century Assumptions about Knowledge I: Determinism
Richard E. Lee, editor
Questioning Nineteenth-Century Assumptions about Knowledge II: Reductionism
Richard E. Lee, editor
Questioning Nineteenth-Century Assumptions about Knowledge III: Dualism
Richard E. Lee, editor
The *Longue Durée* and World-Systems Analysis
Richard E. Lee, editor
New Frontiers of Slavery
Dale W. Tomich, editor

New Frontiers of Slavery

Edited and with an Introduction by
Dale W. Tomich

FERNAND BRAUDEL CENTER
STUDIES IN HISTORICAL SOCIAL SCIENCE

SUNY
PRESS

Cover photo courtesy of Dale W. Tomich

Published by State University of New York Press, Albany

Printed in the United States of America

For information, contact State University of New York Press, Albany, NY
www.sunypress.edu

Production, Ryan Morris
Marketing, Kate R. Seburyamo

Library of Congress Cataloging-in-Publication Data

New frontiers of slavery / edited and with an introduction by Dale W. Tomich.
pages cm. — (SUNY series, fernand braudel center studies in historical social science)
Includes bibliographical references and index.
ISBN 978-1-4384-5863-2 (hc : alk. paper) — 978-1-4384-5864-9 (pb : alk. paper)
ISBN 978-1-4384-5865-6 (e-book) 1. Slavery—Case studies. 2. Slaves—Case studies. I. Tomich, Dale W., 1946–

HT861.N49 2015
306.3'62—dc23 2014048846

10 9 8 7 6 5 4 3 2 1

This volume is dedicated to

Stanley J. Stein and in memory of Barbara H. Stein

CONTENTS

TABLES

Introduction

Dale W. Tomich

This book examines nineteenth-century slavery from a distinct conceptual and historiographical perspective. Conventionally, slavery has been understood as a uniform phenomenon. Although slavery in different countries exhibits particular national variations, these are fundamentally regarded as different iterations on the same thing. These iterations are viewed as independent of one another, and the goal of comparative study is to disclose variations between independent national cases. In this context, slavery is generally regarded as archaic, backward, and incompatible with a modern economic, social, and political order. Consequently, the "great transformation" of the nineteenth century signaled the universal crisis of slavery; the emergence of free markets, modern industry, modern forms of the nation-state, abolitionism, and liberal ideology are taken to have inevitably destroyed chattel slavery throughout the Americas.

In contrast, the perspective adopted here regards slavery in the Americas as part of the modern world-economy. It calls attention to the interrelation and interdependence of slave systems as part of a larger socioeconomic whole; that is, particular instances of slavery are understood as constituted and reconstituted within processes of the capitalist world-economy. Hence, modern slaveries are not viewed as uniform and homogeneous, nor are they seen to be directly comparable with one another outside of world-economic processes. Rather, they are treated as distinct local responses to world-economic transformations. This perspective opens a new analytical and interpretive approach to the crisis of slavery in the nineteenth century. It emphasizes the differentiation, heterogeneity, and specificity of particular slave systems as part of the political, economic, and social transformations of the world-economy. Most importantly, it distinguishes between the redeployment of slave relations in new zones of commodity production and the simultaneous crises of older zones of colonial slavery, which I have elsewhere analyzed as the formation of the second slavery (Tomich 2003, esp. pp. 56–71). In complex and contradictory ways, slavery and bonded labor are disclosed as spatially and temporally heterogeneous and, at the same time, as integral aspects of the "great transformation," modernity, and capitalist development.

These "new frontiers of slavery" differ from the older zones of colonial slavery. They emerged after the Haitian Revolution and the destruction of colonialism as the organizing framework of the Atlantic world. They presuppose and are part of the historical transformations of the world-economy marked by the developments noted above: free markets, industrial capitalism, independent nation-states, abolitionism, and liberal ideology. The distinctions between the older colonial slavery and this newer "second slavery" are expressed in the relations between masters, slaves, and freed people, in the local society and at the level of the world-economy itself.

The chapters in this book explore the "new frontiers of slavery" by addressing a variety of conceptual and substantive historical problems within this framework. They emphasize in new ways the importance of Atlantic slavery for the formation of the modern world-economy as they indicate new perspectives on old problems and raise new questions for research. This project was initiated at a conference, "O Século XIX e as Novas Fronteiras da Escravidão e Liberdade," held in Rio de Janeiro and Vassouras, Brazil, in 2009 under the sponsorship of the Universidade Federal do Estado do Rio de Janeiro, Rio de Janeiro, Brazil; the Universidade Severino Sombra, Vassouras, RJ, Brazil; the Universidade de São Paulo, São Paulo, Brazil; and the Fernand Braudel Center, Binghamton University, Binghamton, NY. We would particularly like to thank Keila Grinberg, Ricardo Salles, and Rafael Marquese for their efforts in organizing this event. The conference brought together scholars from Europe, Brazil, the Caribbean, and the United States. Several of the papers in this volume are from this conference, while others are the result of subsequent discussion of these themes and problems.

No one participating in a conference on slavery held in Vassouras could help but feel the presence of Stanley Stein. His classic work *Vassouras* (1985) is still the necessary reference for Brazilian coffee plantation slavery and remains a model for scholars of slavery throughout the Americas. Everyone participating in the project feels in his intellectual debt. This volume is dedicated to him and his late wife Barbara Stein with respect and admiration.

Works Cited

Stein, Stanley. 1985. *Vassouras: A Brazilian Coffee County, 1850–1900: The Roles of Planter and Slave in a Plantation Society.* Princeton, NJ: Princeton University Press.

Tomich, Dale. 2003. *Through the Prism of Slavery: Labor, Capital, and World Economy.* Lanham, MD: Rowman & Littlefield.

Vassouras Yesterday and Today

Revisiting the Work of Stanley J. Stein

Dale W. Tomich

In 1957, the publication by Harvard University Press of the book *Vassouras: A Brazilian Coffee County, 1850–1900* by Stanley Stein, originally a doctoral thesis, initiated the distinguished career of this work. The first Brazilian edition was published in 1961 by Editora Brasiliense under the title *Grandeza e Decadência do Café*. The 1957 edition was republished in 1970 by Atheneum as part of the series Studies in American Negro Life. In 1985, Princeton University Press published a commemorative edition with a new preface by the author and 39 images, including iconography from the nineteenth century and unpublished photos by Stein, made during the period of his fieldwork. Finally, in 1990 Nova Fronteira published the Portuguese translation of this last edition in Brazil. Over the course of more than fifty years, this work by Stanley Stein has established itself both as an obligatory reference for the history of slavery and coffee in Brazil and as a classic of Brazilian and North American historiography.

Intellectual Framework: History and the Social Sciences

Why has a doctoral dissertation retained such importance for more than half a century? To better understand the historiographical richness of Stein's work, I would like to emphasize some of the intellectual influences in the conceptualization of the project and in its execution that contributed decisively to the depth of the book. A discussion of these influences is especially important because an explicit theory is absent from its pages and because of the apparently descriptive character of the work. To many, thc analytical perspectives through which Stein structured his project appear outmoded. Nonetheless, a careful reading of how Stein constructed *Vassouras* reveals that the book still has great value for contemporary historical reflection.

The very title of the book, *Vassouras: A Brazilian Coffee County, 1850–1900*, calls attention to the key elements of its theoretical and analytical framework. First, the title identifies the object of the work as the county of Vassouras. The book is conceived as the analysis of a community. The term "county" (*município*) delineates Stein's unit of analysis and determines the architecture of the book. That is to say, the book is not constructed around the relations between masters and slaves, but rather around broader relations among all of the groups that form this community. Stein's focus on the county of Vassouras indicates the impact of "community studies," which were highly influential in the social sciences in the United States during the 1940s and 1950s and which inspired the construction of the research project. In a revealing interview granted to the Brazilian historian José Carlos Sebe Bom Meihy at the end of the 1980s, Stein remarked that *Vassouras* was intended as a contribution to community studies: "Therefore, I think that it is appropriate to suppose that my work is integrated in a general historiographical trend that evolved from a technical and methodological debate in North America on community studies" (Meihy 1990: 85).

The importance of "community studies" in Stanley Stein's work is testimony to his broad interdisciplinary approach to historical work, even while a graduate student. Stein, a graduate of the City College of New York in 1941, began to study the history of Latin America in the Department of History at Harvard University under the supervision of Charles Haring after having served in the Navy during the Second World War. In the interview with Meihy, Stein recalled: "while still a student at Harvard I decided not to be trained only in political history. The most important courses for me were in anthropology and sociology" (Meihy 1990: 84).

(The other course that was essential for him was Arthur Schlesinger's course on North American cities, emphasizing the importance of material culture in historical development.)[1] Stein's interest in the social sciences permitted him to conceive of history in way that was open to interdisciplinary influences. The perspective allowed him to go far beyond the predominant political history of that era to engage economic and social history.

In Stein's dialogue with the social sciences, anthropology played a fundamental role. At that time community studies had a strong presence in anthropology and offered useful models of analysis, especially for students of Latin America. Stein recounts: "Anthropology at that time was in a strong phase of community studies and had developed techniques that made possible exciting results. . . . Moreover, with regard to community studies there existed a significant number of excellent works done in Mexico, resulting from research done on that country since the Mexican Revolution. Some of these studies were by authors such as Ralph Beals, Robert Redfield and the last member of this group, Oscar Lewis. . . . Following the methodological evolution of this group suggested to me a way of studying Brazil" (Meihy 1990: 84). In Stein's words, "anthropology functioned as a type of introduction to social history" (Meihy 1990: 84). (It is worth remembering that he was formed as a historian decades before the social history revolution of the 1960s and 1970s.) At the same time, he followed the methodological development of anthropological research on Mexican communities in order to form his project of social history. Anthropology, then, offered him not only a new object of research, but also a new methodological approach. Influenced by anthropologists such as Beals, Redfield, and Lewis, he defined the object of his research as the history of a Brazilian microregion, a type of study of Brazil that was not common at that time.

The delimitation of the scale of analysis to a particular microregion offered obvious practical advantages for a dissertation based on primary sources. Stein recalls, "Following this path, that is, taking a community as my point of departure, it was not necessary to elaborate a monumental thesis, a gigantic explanation of the entire country, nor of the continent, and this was at least prudent for a foreigner who was beginning Brazilian studies" (Meihy 1990: 84). On the contrary, this strategy permitted intense research on diverse themes in the local archives within the period of time available to a young researcher. From the onset of the project, Stein sought to break with the use of general sources such as travelers' accounts that were common in Brazilian historiography. The availability of local sources was a fundamental factor in the choice of Vassouras as the focus of research.[2] As Stein recounts, "I was not interested in returning to the same old sources such as travelers' accounts that invariably resulted in general analysis. . . . This practice, used since the nineteenth century, had already been worked over, almost always producing generic and repetitive histories. I wanted to do something new. My challenge was to reflect on important documentation and combine it with the living memory of persons of the time. I sought a passage between recorded history and experiences that could still be captured" (Meihy 1990: 87). In fact, *Vassouras* is distinguished by its trail-blazing exploration of the municipal archives and the records of the public notaries (*Cartórios Públicos*), characterized by Stein in the preface to the first edition as "the richest and perhaps the most neglected repositories for historians, economists, anthropologists, and sociologists" (Stein 1985: ix).

Anthropology influenced Stein in another way. Even while he was planning the project, Stein was concerned with the problem of "gaining access to the 'voice' of the slaves on the big coffee plantations, recreating their world, and particularly finding the forms or expressions of resistance and accommodation" (Stein 2007: 39). Two sources inspired his aspiration to interview former slaves or the descendants of slaves in Vassouras: on the one hand, the projects of interviews with former slaves and the descendants of slaves carried out in the 1930s by Fisk University and by the Federal Writers Project, parts of which had been published in the book *Lay My Burden Down*, edited by Peter Botkin (1945); on the other hand, the work of Melville J. Herskovits and his studies of the acculturation of Africans in the New World.[3] Herskovits's importance for Stein's work was not limited to the innovative theoretical perspectives on the experience of Africans in the Americas that he introduced, but also encompassed new research techniques.

Barbara Hadley Stein met Herskovits for the first time in Bahia in 1941–1942, in the course of her own research. Before traveling to Vassouras, Stanley and Barbara Stein met with Melville Herskovits and his wife Frances at Northwestern University in Evanston, Illinois, to learn interviewing techniques.[4] During that visit, Herskovits showed them some recordings of black music made in the course of their field research in the Caribbean, Brazil, and Africa. This experience made Stanley Stein aware of the technical possibilities for recovering voices and memories (in this case, a big, heavy tape recorder borrowed from the U.S. embassy) that were realized in his recordings of *jongos*[5] (Lara and Pacheco 2007). (In this context, we must also call attention to Stein's use of photography to document aspects of work and material culture in the course of his research in Vassouras.) Through his contact with Herskovits, Stein utilized anthropological techniques to obtain nonwritten documentation and extend the range of sources available to historians (Stein 2007: 39–40). Stein's conception of the project combined anthropological field research with work in the archives: "Thus I established two approaches to documentation: the officially registered data and the informants, the bearers of the memory of process. I think that I established a path between the two blocks of sources and then was able to elaborate more pertinent links [between them]" (Meihy 1990: 86).

Community Studies and Plantation Society

Community studies were widespread in North American sociology between the 1920s and 1980, above all because of the importance of Robert Park and the Chicago School in the social sciences. For the group that formed around Park, the concept of "community" is an instrument to analyze the impact of modernization on rural and urban cultures. An imprecise concept, "community" refers in general to small-scale collectivities—rural populations or urban enclaves, neighborhoods, or subcultures. Frequently it is associated with positive traits such as solidarity and familiarity as well as unity of purpose, interest, and identity (Rabinowitz 2001: 2387).

In general, there are two theoretical approaches to community studies. The first, which is perhaps more common today, is based on fundamental sentiments of identity, belonging, or both, independent of the geographical distribution of the members of the group. The analysis of "imagined communities" proposed by Benedict Anderson (1983) offers a good contemporary example of such "communities of sentiment." This type of study is geographically diffuse and ambiguous from a spatial perspective. It includes extensive communal relations, but in general is limited to sets of singular ideas, values, and beliefs and does not deal with complexity. It is possible that communities of sentiment can exist in a given locality, but typically they extend beyond locality (e.g., nationalism, Catholicism, etc.). From this point of view, local communities can have little importance. On the other hand, within a given locality, isolated, unique, and homogenous communities of sentiment generally do not exist. Rather, multiple communities coexist, interact, and even collide with one another (without mentioning the social and material conditions of life that unify the community). From this latter perspective, given collective sentiments are interpreted by means of complex interactions that establish particular and defined local contexts.

The second approach to community studies is older and typical of the period in which Stein wrote *Vassouras*. It emphasizes the territorial base of community and treats groups within a defined locality. This approach to community studies seeks to understand the complexity of diverse relations and processes that form a given community in space as a totality (Redfield 1989: esp. 1–16). We should mention here that the concept of "totality" does not refer to an empirical whole, but rather to a methodological construction that can be conceptualized from diverse perspectives. This conception, nevertheless, calls attention to the importance for the formation of community of ecology and geography as well as social structures, relations, and organization that go beyond sentiments and cultural values. It treats these elements as parts of a whole and analyzes the relations among them to reconstruct the relevant historical contexts. Thus, this approach to community studies offers a method for understanding the dense, specific interconnections of the relations forming the community, and is not restricted to the more general field of regional or national studies.

Vassouras is constructed in accordance with this second conception of community. However, its emphasis on spatial unity, social solidarity, and identity of interests and common values—elements inherent in the concept of community—required Stein to reformulate it to account for the historical character of his object of inquiry. To analyze the county of Vassouras as a community, Stein had to address three specific problems. First, he had to identify the limits of a community based on a monocultural agro-export economy that was dependent of the African slave trade. Second, he had to account for the distinct socioeconomic and cultural inequalities, divisions, and conflicts that characterized a slave plantation society. Third, in the context of the divisions in the slave-based society of Vassouras, he had to identify the elements and mechanisms that integrated it as a community.

Faced with the heterogeneous, ambiguous, and poorly defined elements of a slave society based on coffee monoculture, it is important to call attention to the influence of Charles Wagley on Stein's work.[6] In Stein's words, "It is important to remember, nevertheless, that in 1947 I was interested in *plantation* economy and society, not in slavery itself, much less in the comparative history of slavery or in slave agriculture in the New World. In other words, my attention was drawn to what the anthropologist Charles Wagley once appropriately called '*plantation America*'" (Stein 2007: 36).

Within the field of community studies, Wagley was one of these responsible for the formulation and popularization of the concept "plantation society" as a subtype of community (Wagley 1957). Wagley treated the plantation not as a unit of production, but as a type of society. Identifying the characteristic aspects of "plantation society"—monoculture, rigid class divisions, multiracial societies, weak community structure, the presence of small peasant proprietors, and matrifocal families—Wagley elaborated a general typology to treat the common elements of the "cultural sphere" of "plantation America," which included the U.S. South, the Caribbean, and Brazil, extending from Maryland to São Paulo. Wagley's purpose in constructing this typology was to avoid research that was conducted in "too local terms" and to promote a more comparative perspective (Wagley 1957: 11–12).[7]

Construction of the Research Project

With the typological approaches of anthropology and sociology to "community studies" on the one hand, and "plantation America" on the other hand, the problem confronting Stein as a historian was to reconstruct the "plantation society" of Vassouras as a historical community, formed within specific relations and processes.

Stein's interest in developing a research project on Vassouras was motivated by his interest in Brazilian economic history and, above all, by the history of coffee. As he recently stated, "My objective was to examine a theme that has been present in the history of Brazil since the beginning of the sixteenth century—the successive cycles of export-oriented growth. First around sugar, then tobacco, then gold, and, from the beginning of the nineteenth century, coffee" (Stein 2007: 35). This emphasis on the importance of economic cycles and on coffee indicates the influence of Brazilian authors on Stein's thought. He cites the significance of his readings of Roberto Simonsen, Paulo Prado, Sergio Milliet, João Normano, Caio Prado Júnior, and the fifteen volumes on the history of coffee by Affonso Tauney, as well as Gilberto Freyre and the novelists Monteiro Lobato and José Lins do Rego (Stein 1985, 2007). It would not be an exaggeration to say that the situation that was current in Brazil in the 1940s also influenced the young historian: "*Vassouras* was deeply influenced by that Brazilian nationalistic current critical of perennial export-oriented plantation agriculture with and without slave labor, that had confined Brazil to the condition of '*país esencialmente agrícola*' ['essentially agricultural country'] and prevented the formation of an industrial base" (Stein 1985: xii–xiii).[8]

Under these influences Stein conceived his study of the Paraíba Valley by making use of the concept of "coffee cycle." In his words, "That full cycle could be seen in a geographical area first fully developed and ravaged by coffee producers, the middle and upper Parahyba Valley" (Stein 1985: xii). The coffee cycle—from its beginning, to its apogee in the middle of the nineteenth century, until its decline around 1900—established the temporal limits of the period that he examined. In spite of the importance given to the concept of the coffee cycle, Stein rejected the possibility of writing a general history of coffee or of treating the history of the Paraíba Valley as if it were the history of Brazil, or even a simply "local" history of a coffee community. On the contrary, he opted to integrate the history of a particular "plantation society" with the history of the coffee cycle of the second half of the nineteenth century. "Barbara and I," Stein recalled in a recent memoir, “discussed the various options for developing the research and decided to examine a coffee society in a specific area of Brazil, insofar as possible analyzing it with the hope of being able to see it from within and from without” (Stein 2007: 36).

However, for Stein this desire to see the coffee community “from within and without” could not be realized by simply juxtaposing “internal factors” and “external factors.” Rather, inspired by the French *Annales* school, he sought to write “total history”: “There was one final influence on the research and writing of *Vassouras*. From the outset, there was the intention, perhaps overly ambitious, to produce a holistic study of a coffee plantation community along the lines of what was then termed the ‘new history’: to recreate a sense of ambiance as would a human geographer integrating soil, topography, climate, and man; to detect networks of community through the lenses of the social anthropologist; the achieve a historian’s perception of factors and processes over time” (Stein 1985: xii). The project of reconstructing the “total history” of the community of Vassouras in the nineteenth-century coffee cycle required empirical research, methodological reflection, and theoretical rigor. Stein reflects, “This thematic definition, however, was neither mechanical nor easy. On the contrary, it followed a course that combined my intellectual development and my training with the situations encountered in the field” (Meihy 1990: 84–85).

The relevance and the analytical value of the project deepened with the reconstitution of the relations that integrated the community of Vassouras with the coffee cycle and with broader historical processes. The theoretical innovation of the book resides in the reconfiguration of the concept of “cycle” by means of a dialectical analysis of the relation between the movements of the world market and the local economic, social, and political forces that produced them. To achieve this, Stein broke with the understanding of cycles then current in Brazilian social sciences. Taking the local community as his point of departure, Stein reconstituted its links with processes that operated at more varied scales. “To approach community, it is sufficient to choose a representative area, investigate it through a prism that is of interest and has ample expression. And that is what I did. . . . The general framing came about from the insertion of the product of historical analysis, the past of the community, into the larger context of the economy on an increasing scale, suggesting the passage from the local to the regional, from the national to the international. . . . It was, so to speak, the reverse [of what] was done in terms of Brazil, where histories were general, almost always" (Meihy 1990: 84–85). By means of this methodological procedure the study specifies its object in space and in time. It implies not only the reconstruction of the community, but also the locality as a historical phenomenon. As Stein declared in the preface of the first edition of *Vassouras*: "The aim of this analysis of the plantation economy and society in Vassouras, a community of the Parahyba Valley of south-central Brazil, is to examine at the local level the effect of the changing world economy upon Brazilian institutions" (Stein 1985: vii).

In contrast to general studies, Stein's method discloses the complex spatial-temporal totality of historical relations and processes that constitute the coffee cycle. On the one hand, Stein specifies the particularities of the community of Vassouras within broader networks of relations—local, regional, national, and, at the limit, global. On the other hand, this community is a specific element in the formation of these same networks, illuminating, from this point of view, the processes that form broader scales.

The Architecture of Vassouras

As has already been stated, there are various ways to think of community as a totality. Stein's approach to this question determines the architecture of the book, that is, the mode of presenting the work and its analytic structure.

Stein begins his analysis of Vassouras by examining the ecological unity of the community. He establishes this unity by reflecting on the impact of coffee on the environment and on the formation of the community. From this perspective, he emphasizes the physical and material aspects of coffee cultivation in the context of the particular geography of the valley and of the county of Vassouras. He implicitly distinguishes between the ecological system and the productive system, demonstrating how the specific geographical and environmental conditions were transformed by the introduction of coffee. Even in the 1940s, Stein was sensitive to the destruction of the Atlantic rainforest and how the intense exploitation of the environment resulted in a migratory agricultural system and fragile base of prosperity. On the other hand, analysis of the ecological-productive unity of the Vassouras coffee community was complemented by discussion of the world market. At this stage of the analysis, Stein highlights growing European and, above all, North American demand for coffee, the importation of the slave-labor force, and the sources and movement of credit. In this way, the analysis of the development of the Vassouras coffee community is framed within the external conditions and limits determined by nature and by the world market.

The material conditions and processes of production form the organizing thread of the analysis of ecological-productive unity of Vassouras. To establish this unity and the specific characteristics of the community, Stein traces the expansion of coffee cultivation in the county and documents the concentration of land and the formation of coffee plantations beginning in the decade of the 1820s. He calls attention to material conditions, including the scale of production, the patterns of cultivation, agricultural practices, and the transportation networks. In this way, beyond carefully describing the material culture and architectonic aspects of the plantations, he discloses the routines and rhythms of work that were operative on the coffee plantations. Finally, he interprets changes in the material and social conditions of production as indices of the growth of coffee cultivation.

From the perspective of the material conditions of coffee cultivation, Stein reconstructs the social unity of the community—its specific structure formed by the diversification and reintegration of various social strata that are related to one another through the coffee economy, at the same time that these strata are seen as diverse and even conflicting. The concentration of land meant the marginalization of squatters, the economic, social, and political domination of the great planter clans, and the appearance of non-rent-paying tenants (*agregados*) as a significant social group. In this context, Stein examined the demand for labor on the coffee plantations and the various categories of labor available to satisfy it. He proceeded to analyze the impact of the international slave trade and the internal slave trade on the county to appraise the changes in the demographic composition of the slave population during the coffee cycle. Reconstructing in this way the complex and heterogeneous social structure of the community, Stein addresses the necessity of establishing its social limits. For that purpose, he examines the commercialization of the product, local provisioning, and the transport networks to identify groups such as mule drivers and commission agents who operate on the margin of the community, but who in their turn link it to the external world. In effect, their activities defined the social frontier between those within and those without. (Obviously, the circulation of goods, products, and credit followed national and international circuits that went beyond the limits of the community.) After distinguishing the diverse groups by their economic roles, Stein treats the community in terms of "free" and "slave" as well as other social categories that simultaneously integrate and divide the community.

Thus, only after establishing the unity of diverse material and social factors does Stein address the relation between masters and slaves. It is important to note this strategy carefully, because despite the importance of the master-slave relation for determining the character of the Vassouras community, it is itself formed within an already established complex of historical relations and processes. The agency of both masters and slaves was formed through specific material conditions and social relations. Grounding his analysis in concrete historical conditions, Stein turns toward the exploration of the classical themes of community studies done by anthropologists. He examined the interrelations and interactions between masters and slaves, and reconstructed the patterns of life on the plantations as well as typical biographies, values, and beliefs. The path he followed reveals the violence of domination in slave society, the forms of slave resistance, and the social and cultural practices that maintained the integration of the community despite the fundamental antagonisms between master and slave and that, at the limit, permitted the formation of communities within the community (Redfield 1989: 113–31).

Conclusion

Grounded in specific spaces and temporalities, Stanley Stein's *Vassouras* is not a general history (Mintz 1959: 557); at the same time, it is "more than a local history" (Wagley 1958: 420). The book is a rich source of data and perspectives, and for this reason it is open to various possible readings. Reflecting the changes of interest and perspective over the last fifty years, the book was read as a critique of Gilberto Freyre's interpretation of Brazil's slave past, as a contribution to the analysis of Brazilian economic dependence, as a source for historical comparisons between the Paraíba Valley and the west of São Paulo, as a methodological model for local agrarian history, and as an interpretation, model of research, and source of information for the culture and memory of the enslaved population (Lara 2007: 53–67).

Each of these readings finds a legitimate basis in Stein's book. Nonetheless, they are all partial. I would like to argue that the great value of his work lies in his "apprenticeship in total history," that is, in his reconstruction of the material, social, and cultural processes and relations that formed a slave plantation society in the coffee cycle of the nineteenth century. The richness of his analysis of this concrete totality focused on the community of Vassouras permits all of these partial readings. More important, however, is what it reveals with regard to the interrelation of historical phenomena that are not taken in isolation. In Stein's perspective, each historical process is realized within a broad complex of relations that form the communities and interact with other such processes. The density of such diverse interdependencies and interactions establishes the specific context of historical processes and thus deepens our comprehension of them. Recalling the words of English historian E. P. Thompson, "history is a discipline of context and of process: every meaning is a meaning-in-context, and structures change while old forms may express new functions or old functions may find expression in new forms" (Thompson 1977: 256). Stein's methodological approach clearly offers such an interpretive movement within a dynamic historical whole.

To conclude I would like to mention two other questions implicit in Stein's work that perhaps are relevant for contemporary historical studies—that of representation and that of scale. For Stein, as for anthropologists, the value of local community studies is that they represent "microcosms" of more general processes (Stein 2007: 37–38; Redfield 1989: 103, 105). Reflecting larger worlds, Stein's focus on community thus permits the realization of more concrete analyses that are closer to lived experience and human agency than is generally possible in macrohistorical studies. Nevertheless, it is necessary to pay attention to the contribution of Italian microhistory. As Giovanni Levi emphasizes, automatic mechanisms through which social actors align themselves with structural changes and transformations do not exist. These processes present problems for historical analysis. According to Levi, reduction of scale represents an experimental and analytic method capable of revealing previously unobserved factors. By means of this process, microhistory seeks to discover previously anomalous or unobserved events that reveal the incoherencies in an apparently unified order (Levi 1991: 107). In this way microhistorians open a space to reflect on communities in broader contexts.

On the other hand, we can interpret *Vassouras* from the opposite perspective. Stein's focus is the community, which he wants to analyze "from within and from without." In spite of his reconfiguration of the concept of "cycle," his notion of "without" remains an abstact and general conception of the world market. Changing the unit of analysis to world-economy, it becomes viable to consider the plantation community as the object of inquiry within broader processes. Thus, it is possible to place the local plantation community of Vassouras within the processes of expansion of the world-economy and the reformation of the world geographic and economic division of labor. From such a perspective, the similarities between the Paraíba Valley coffee zone, the cotton South of the United States, and the Cuban sugar zone are evident. Seen in this way, the analysis of Vassouras reveals not the linear repetition of an archaic slave system and plantation regime threatened by economic, social, and political modernity, but rather the formation of a new productive space in which the reconstitution of the slave system and the plantation economy occured within the framework of an integrated world market, marked by the expansion of industrial production, by the political independence of Europe's former colonial possessions in the New World, and by the ascension of liberal ideologies, which include both national and international abolitionism—in other words, the creation of a new frontier of slavery. From such perspectives, Stanley Stein's *Vassouras* still has much to teach us.

Notes

1. Stanley Stein discusses his experiences before beginning his historical studies at Harvard in Meihy 1990: 81–82.

2. "In Vassouras I found, in the Archive of the Municipal Council, several boxes of documents under the stairs, together with old and dusty personal belongings. In the city there were three Public Notaries, and after I visited them the decision to study that community was relatively immediate. Finally, Vassouras, a great producer of coffee, had abundant documentation and made possible good conditions for work and family life. . . . It was during this period that I precisely defined my intention make a socioeconomic community study, covering the passage of coffee from its beginning up to what I thought would be the end of its presence, between 1900 and 1910. . . . Then my family and I hurried to move to Vassouras, where, with only a few interruptions by trips to Rio de Janeiro to finish research, we lived from December 1948 until November of '49. Having lived such a long period in Brazil, I can say that I felt well adapted and even partly Brazilianized" (Meihy 1990: 85).

3. "Nor could an apprentice social historian fail to be stimulated by the fresh perspectives on the black process of acculturation and the black experience in general in the New World and Africa in the works of Melville Herskovits—*The Myth of the Negro Past*, *Dahomey*, and *Trinidad Village*" (Stein 1990: xii).

4. "[W]hen we went to Vassouras to gather testimonies from people, I always remembered what they said to me, in essence, in the first place [that I should] never take notes in front of people and, second, [that] I should visit the informants and speak with them in their surroundings, not in mine. . . . Following such suggestions, after having established my contacts, I was careful to meet and converse with them in the fields. I prepared beforehand a long series of questions, and with them in mind, I went to their homes and we conversed. . . . After the interview, I sat down and wrote my notes. I then typed them, making a sort of diary that later, my wife organized by themes. . . . This gave me a base of information from which to reconstruct what the lives of Blacks had been during the time of slavery" (Meihy 1990: 87).

5. Impromptu rhymed verses sung at slave festivals (*Caxambú*). Also slave work songs (Stein 1985: 298, 297).

6. Anthropologist and Latin Americanist specializing in Brazil, Charles Wagley was professor of anthropology at Columbia University from 1946 to 1971. By chance Wagley and his wife Cecilia were on the same boat when Stanley and Barbara Stein travelled to Brazil in 1948 to do their research in Vassouras. Stein already knew Cecilia's mother, Dona Belinha, and even lived in her house on his first trip to Brazil in 1942 (Meihy 1990: 82–83).

7. "Within the framework of the culture sphere of Plantation-America there are innumerable 'variables' which make comparison both possible and promising. . . . It is precisely in this projection of the cultural variation—whether inherited from Europe, derived from variations in the local natural and sociocultural environs or from distinctive developmental trends—against the common feature of the cultural sphere and in the seeking out of significant relationships that we can use the comparative method to help us build a science of society and culture" (Wagley 1958: 12).

8. "I arrived . . . in Brazil, in 1949, at the height of the 'O Petróleo é Nosso' [The Petroleum is Ours] campaign. It was all very interesting, full of enthusiasm, dynamic, and contagious! . . . It fed my desire to know more and understand better the important themes of the social debate, the vivacity of that culture. . . . Logically, such matters involved aspects of the debate over the role of agriculture, which sharpened my curiosity even more. Finally, it was a period in which the effects of the colonial agricultural past could be weighed and one could reflect on the importance and relevancy of agriculture in a phase that began with modern industrialization. . . . This was a rather attractive and vivid mosaic for someone who came from abroad with the intention of doing historical studies that in some way intersected all these themes" (Meihy 1990: 85).

Works Cited

Anderson, Benedict. 1983. *Imagined Communities: Reflections on the Origins and Spread of Nationalism.* London: Verso.

Botkin, Benjamin A., ed. 1945. *Lay My Burden Down: A Folk History of Slavery.* Chicago: University of Chicago Press.

Lara, Silvia Hunold. 2007. "*Vassouras* e os sons do cativeiro no Brasil." Silvia Hunold Lara and Gustavo Pacheco, orgs., *Memória do jongo: As gravações de Stanley J. Stein: Vassouras, 1949.* Rio de Janeiro: Folha Seco; São Paulo: CECULT, 45–67.

Lara, Silvia Hunold, and Gustavo Pacheco, orgs. 2007. *Memória do jongo: As gravações de Stanley J. Stein: Vassouras, 1949*. Rio de Janeiro, Brazil: Folha Seco; São Paulo, Brazil: CECULT.

Levi, Giovanni. 1991. "On Microhistory." Peter Burke, org., *New Perspectives on Historical Writing*. Cambridge, UK: Polity Press, 93–113.

Meihy, José Carlos Sebe Bom. 1990. "Como um todo a comunidade brasilienista não se mostrou passiva: Entrevista com Stanley J. Stein," *A Colônia brasilianista: História oral de vida acadêmica*. São Paulo: Nova Stella, 79–101.

Mintz, Sidney W. 1959. "Vassouras. A Brazilian Coffee County, 1850–1900, by Stanley J. Stein." Book review in *The Economic History Review*, n.s. 11(3): 557.

Rabinowitz, Dan. 2001. "Community Studies: Anthropological." In *International Encyclopedia of the Social & Behavioral Sciences*, edited by N. J. Smelser and P. B. Baltes. Vol. 4. Amsterdam: Elsevier, 2387–89.

Redfield, Robert. (1960) 1989. *The Little Community and Peasant Society and Culture*. Chicago: University of Chicago Press; Midway Reprint.

Stein, Stanley J. 1957. *Vassouras: A Brazilian Coffee County, 1850–1900*. Cambridge, MA: Harvard University Press.

———. 1961. *Grandeza e decadência do café*. São Paulo: Brasiliense.

———. 1970. *Vassouras: A Brazilian Coffee County, 1850–1900*. New York: Atheneum.

———. 1985. *Vassouras: A Brazilian Coffee County, 1850–1900: The Roles of Planter and Slave in a Plantation Society*. Princeton, NJ: Princeton University Press.

———. 1990. *Vassouras: Um município brasileiro do café, 1850–1900*. Rio de Janeiro: Editora Nova Fronteira.

———. 2007. "Uma viagem maravilhosa." S. Hunold Lara and Gustavo Pacheco, orgs. *Memória do jongo: As gravações de Stanley J. Stein: Vassouras, 1949*. Rio de Janeiro: Folha Seco; São Paulo: CECULT, 35–42.

Thompson, Edward P. 1977. "Folklore, Anthropology, and Social History." *The Indian Historical Review* 3(2): 247–66.

Wagley, Charles. 1957. "Plantation America: A Cultural Sphere." *Caribbean Studies: A Symposium*, edited by Vera Rubin. Seattle: University of Washington Press, 3–13.

———. 1958. "Vassouras. A Brazilian Coffee County, 1850–1900, by Stanley J. Stein." Book review in *The Hispanic American Historical Review* 38(3): 420–22.

Agency and Transnational Perspectives on the Constitution of Waged, Unfree, and Free Labor

The Role of Mobility in the Nineteenth Century*

Yann Moulier Boutang

I would like to address three points that, in my view, constitute clusters of related problems that are central for a retrospective balance sheet of the "long" nineteenth century (1789–1914): first, the question of agency or the spaces of freedom and servitude in the emergence of industrial capitalism; second, the question of transformation inferred from the hypothesis of Atlantic space and not just the Atlantic economy in relation to "national," "nationalist," or "imperialist" approaches to slavery and then transnational migrations under contract (coolies); and finally, the question of the invention of the free labor market, that is, a hidden text of liberation from slavery reinscribed in a public text of the free labor market.

These three questions inform the agenda of my own research as presented in my book *De l'esclavage au salariat* (Moulier Boutang 1988) in a renewal of the

*Translated by Dale Tomich.

well-known question of the freedom of subjects "from" and "in" history. This question, consigned to oblivion by triumphant historical and dialectical materialism, which buried the question as "idealist and petit bourgeois," has returned in the form of the question of the "agency" and "empowerment" of marginalized social subjects for the past fifteen years in history and in political science, especially with regard to dominated groups such as women (Pollack 2000: 75–89). Many currents of thought, other than the very structuralist long-term *mentalités* approach of the *Annales* School, have contributed to the rehabilitation of a collective and historical subjective dimension. These include a heretical tradition of Marxism (Italian "workerism" [Moulier Boutang 1998]) in relation to Eurocentric history, the heretical position of the postcoloniality of power (Mignolo 1997, 2012, 2001; Quijano 2000: 215–32), and currents from feminism to subaltern and minority studies (Scott 1985, 1992) that have posed the question of liberation and not simply that of exploitation, criticizing severely the preceding current of orthodox Marxism.

Nothing better raises the question of freedom in history than the ascension and abolition of modern slavery. In the genesis of that capitalism, which appeared with the industrialization of the large factory (1750–1840), the enigma of the emergence of capitalism from the ruins of feudalism is partially resolved by the decline of the early forms of capitalism and by the emergence of the absolutist state, which presides over the formation of mercantilism—but only partially. In its trajectory, capitalism has known two bifurcations that have projected it to a world scale, and, through the narrow spectacles of the western European peninsula, present a two-sided Janus-face: the arrival of wage labor at the front door, and the appearance of transatlantic slavery and eastern serfdom at the service entrance. The nineteenth century is the hinge of this movement.

The nineteenth century appears as the century of closure for the social institution and economic system of plantation slavery.[1] After the Saint Domingue insurrection of August 22–23, 1791, after the abolition of the slave trade by the first and only world naval power in 1807, after the insurrection in Jamaica that precipitated the abolition of slavery by the United Kingdom, the die was cast. The nineteenth century is the century of the irresistible abolition of modern slavery and serfdom. Nicolas de Condorcet on the eve of the French Revolution (Condorcet 1781) and Lincoln on the eve of the War of Secession had envisioned a transition of more than ninety years to abolish slavery. These figures were appalling for the slaves (they represent almost five generations), but they are not far from reality on a world scale, since between 1791 and 1888 (Cuba) and 1890 (Brazil) the abolition of Atlantic slavery occurred on that order of magnitude.

A phenomenon that lasted for more than 500 years, slavery—from the first slave sale under the sponsorship of the king of Portugal in Lagos in 1444 to the abolition of slavery in Zanzibar in 1907—required 100 years to come to an end. The "long nineteenth century" from 1791 to 1890 virtually coincides with Karl Polanyi's "Great Transformation" (1815–1914). Slavery presents the negative proof of the Polanyian thesis of the embeddedness of "social" and "political" rationality in the madness and chaos of the utopia of the self-regulating market. Slavery, like modern servitude, constitutes a pure labor market, the only one that has really existed, but it was only able to survive as a mode of economic exploitation at the cost of a monstrous deformation of society (the quasi-apartheid that the first colonial slavery of Saint Domingue had attained on the eve of the Revolution).

A priori, the whole history of capitalism seems to be muted by a beautiful, tranquil teleology: that of the emergence of democratic freedom with exceptions in the form of residual pockets. However, the violence of the events that accompanied not only the decline of the institution of slavery but also the establishment of the regime of forced labor (colonial *corvée*, international migrations under contract, the installation of the regime of the internal passport in South Africa, deportation to Siberia[2]) prevents history from unfolding as the realization of the idea or of the concept of liberty.

Just as there is no tendency for capitalism to necessarily move toward a market system as the space of confrontation between independent small producers (the vision of the socialist Léon Walras, who stood for the complete abolition of inheritance),—the entire history of capitalism shows that on the industrial plane and on the financial plane it tends toward monopoly—there is no internal necessity that would drive capitalism only by means of the extortion of work from the worker who is dependent on the free wage, on freedom.

In contrast, what I call the "march toward freedom"—not in the sense of Michelet; we shall see what meaning other than the Hegelian or idealist one to give to this term[3]—allows us to account for the history and the historical economy of institutions, the mechanisms of control, as well as the forms of resistance and the conflicts that shape the particular creases and twists in the formation and destruction of slavery. The paradox that we wish to explain is that the invention of free labor and the wage-earning class, as much in its microeconomic juridical codification as in its global traits, arises from the very interior of the march toward freedom by slaves and serfs, both medieval and modern. To give this notion of the "march toward freedom" a "historically determined" content, we first examine the old question of the freedom of subjects in history at the margins of autonomy and empowerment.

The Question of Freedom of Agency and Empowerment

History has long had to choose between two models to explain the rise of capitalism and the genesis of free wage labor. The first, the structural or technologically determinist model, explains the transition from the plantation economy (from the apogee of the slave system relying on the slave trade, i.e., Saint Domingue on the eve of the French Revolution), to the system built on sharecropping (Brazil in 1840), and then the European international migrations (to the Paulista region of Brazil and the United States around 1870–1890) by the mutations of the composition of products in world commerce (the passage from tobacco to sugar in Cuba, or from sugar to coffee in Brazil), and by innovation of the railroad, which permitted the size of sugar mills to grow and the industrialization of the harvest. According to this approach, the incapacity of the slave system to absorb this technical modernization and globalization made it progressively obsolete. Or, for another variant, it's obsolescence was due to its incapacity to ensure a sufficient rate of accumulation, competitive with industrial capitalism based upon free wage labor. This type of "explanation" raises the following problems: (a) its very mechanical character; (b) its limited capacity to explain trajectories that deviate totally from the supposed ineluctable decline of slavery; (c) the expulsion of every subjective factor, of the historical ruptures (the "long" nineteenth century was fertile with revolutions, counterrevolutions, civil wars) of the economic and infrastructural sphere; and (d) its inability to account for counter-truths. With regard to the last-mentioned point, the problems of the slave economy of the United States South on the eve of the War of Succession were not an insufficient rate of accumulation or an insertion into world commerce that was too modest, but rather the inverse. The plantation economy was extroverted. It accumulated capital even if that capital was absorbed by finance. In comparison to the deformed agrarian capitalism that Kostas Vergopolous has analyzed for the Turkish Empire, one could even argue that plantation slavery is hypercapitalist, that in terms of the return on capital, it perfectly well sustains comparison with the most modern terms of free labor capital. Its Achilles' heel lies in its social instability and internal politics and in the overbidding occasioned by confrontation of colonial powers shaken off by decolonization.

The model of "abnormal" slavery, backward in relation to the modern development of capitalism and condemned as such, is not incompatible with politics and with the history of institutions and mentalities (*mentalités*). Thus, from this perspective, the abolition of slavery does not proceed from what happens on the "shop floor" of the plantation, from its social history (in a class struggle transposed to the plantation), but rather from its political history (the confrontations of colonial powers), and from the ideological struggles of the abolitionists (most often whites). A shared complementarity exists between the two models of technological determinism and political abolitionism. On the one hand, the realm of economic necessity is posited with its iron laws and the development of the fully realized productive forces of capitalism in its baggage (in fact, the structuralists and economists are Hegelians without knowing it). On the other hand, the capacity of the agent-subjects to make history, and to enjoy very relative margins of freedom, is to be found in the political and ideological superstructures. The margin of action left to the freedom of the actors or the subjects is reduced to the coming to consciousness of an inescapable destiny, *amor fati*, for the dominated. (These historians are ultimately economistic and even more mechanistic than the economists themselves.)

Here are found all of the bad antimonies of historical reason that Kant qualified as *dialectical reason*. The freedom of the agents in history is only an illusion of scale. The agents can only slightly accelerate or retard the path of necessity, but never redirect it by dealing a new hand. Men do not make history, they are in history (Althusser 1973). Althusser himself has remarkably noted that one of the singular characteristics of Stalinism is to have allied one of the crudest economisms (that of the development of the productive forces) with the exaltation of a heroic subjectivity (that, for example, of Stakhanov). The latter only accelerates industrialization and constitutes a figure of it, and is thus a "ruse of history."

The partisans of slavery also serve themselves from this historical necessity. They never cease to invoke it, for their own benefit, of course. But what is even stranger is that the partisans of "gradual" abolition employ similar arguments. Condorcet recognized the unsustainable character of slavery as a principle, but remained committed to the impossibility of economically despoiling the slaveholders in a single blow and destroying the economy. Others appeal to the immature character of the slaves in relation to the condition of liberty. (The argument is reprised for the rejection of voting rights without a property qualification.)

The epistemological reef of the technologist perspective is a genuine functionalist understanding of history. Even Fogel and Engerman's *Time on the Cross* (1974) does not escape. The work has the merit, beyond its naïvetés, notably a methodological individualism that overshoots the mark, to knock flat the thesis of the backwardness of the slave system and its noncapitalist character as well as that of the premodern and peasant mentality of the slaves (i.e., the vision developed by Frederick Law Olmsted [1856]). The labor system of the industrial gang was forged on the southern plantation. Large-scale slave agriculture was more productive than the agriculture of free peasants. But this paradox never goes beyond a functionalism of accumulation. That these neoclassical theorists should have returned to a determinism of capital accumulation without the critique that one still finds among the Marxists is not surprising. It is the spontaneous ideology of the economists. Robert Fogel may have realized it, since twenty-five years later their response to the deluge of criticisms of *Time on the Cross* reintroduced a radical reevaluation of the subjective abolitionist movement, that is, of political ideas (Fogel 1989). But there is no bridge whatsoever between the social-economic level of the slave mode of exploitation and the ideological and political sphere, but rather a radical delinking. Between Fogel and Engerman (1974) and Fogel (1989), the revision is stupefying. One could almost speak of recantation or of schizophrenia. Those accustomed to what has become political economy will be less astonished. It is now common that the technical positions of those economists who are the most neoclassical in their discipline coexist without difficulty with positions that, since it is a question of sociology, a Pierre Bourdieu would not have refused without seeing that in the real and transdisciplinary space, the positions are incompatible. In the realm of science they are positivists and individualists. In the realm of sentiments they are structuralists and critics of *mentalités*. Better yet, such an economist on the "left" makes calculable general equilibrium models while fervently supporting a pure Stalinism.

The problem is that one exchanges technological and economic determinism for another determinism, that of abolitionist reason in history. I believe that one could address a similar critique to the monumental work of Robin Blackburn (1988, 1997), which nevertheless departs from presuppositions radically opposed to those of Fogel and Engerman. Overevaluation of the ideological sphere and the diplomatic history of states, which is the sole realm of freedom, and the double underevaluation: of the contradictory elements of the so-called economic sphere and of what James Scott refers to as "infra politics." (This infra politics, whose terrain is the confrontation between the public text and the hidden text, could be drawn closer to the little perceptions of Leibnitz.) Hybrids such as revolts within the mode of production and social instability in politics occupy a ready-made niche, the niche of perpetual checks or of subalternity—"subaltern" not in the sense of *subaltern studies*, but "subaltern" in the sense of detail that has no importance other than being decorations in a plot that is played out elsewhere and is determinant.

Now, I recall a phrase from Nietzsche that is paradoxically completely enlightening for the historian who would restore the tremulousness of time and the vacillation of trajectories. The philosopher said (I cite from memory) that in order to know how things necessarily happened as they have, we look to the Romans; in order to understand how they should have happened otherwise, we look to the Greeks.

The "general laws of history" inevitably draw us toward necessity, repetition, resemblance, and determinism that are either Laplacian (total predictability) or partial, thus statistical. The nonrepeatable character of events that the German historical school defends pulls to the side of singularity, but in the same stroke dissolves the references to repeatable structures, which for it no longer serve any purpose.

In this way one obtains a conception of freedom as the pure impossibility of correctly predicting complex historical processes (but also blocking them, because if there is not foresight, there is no possibility of intervention), or rather a certain margin of action within limits, whether they are economic or political (the well-known gap of the economists who separate the possibility of determining behaviors from the single incitation or of the political scientists who content themselves with advancing the decision-making of agents without claiming to determine the content of their action). The only freedom left to agents *in* history would be to accelerate or resist the trend, to a *fatum* (whether it is the law of accumulation or the reason of the strongest imperialist).

Nonetheless, the accent placed by historians and political scientists of societies based on domination, such as those that are regulated by slavery as the central principle, on the dynamics of movement through the theme of agency and empowerment deeply revisits these great antimonies. The theme of agency and of empowerment appeared first with regard to the situation of women and the analysis of transgressions of the law. It has flowed from more than twenty years of feminism that has attacked not only the question of suffrage but also gender roles and domination in daily life. At bottom it interrogates the conditions for the emergence of subjects who, taking hold of their destiny, acquire the faculties to express themselves or to act. But these themes are rapidly extended to situations other than those of transgressions of the law, as they recall the principle from the seventies that "the private is political." This current of thought cannot be separated from the transformations that are also found in the postcolonial school that is associated with the British Indies or Spanish Latin America. The work of historians of the poor, the *lumpenproletariat* held in such contempt by the classic worker's movement in Europe, has also contributed to the alteration of the dividing lines that determine what is political and worthy of the historian's attention. The *Annales* School has reintegrated culture and society at the heart of history, but it did so only by separating them from event history. Everything that concerns changes in comportment reveals the tectonic movement of plates and is imperceptible through the lens of the event and institutional rupture.

The displacement toward governmentality and micro powers (and thus the daily administration of populations on the model of the ecclesiastical pastoral) made by Michel Foucault (and put into practice by Michelle Perrot and Arlette Farge) has reintegrated questions of domination at the heart of analysis, without rejecting the question of exploitation, but rather conferring a new pertinence on it, a relevance *hic et donc.*

The study of slavery and situations of colonial domination has experienced a parallel movement. Some important stages in the study of slavery from the point of view of the subjects themselves, from the formation of a complex society full of movements in every sense of the word, have, in my view, included not only Eugene Genovese's *Roll, Jordan, Roll* (1974) (more than his *The Political Economy of Slavery* [1967]) and George Rawick's *From Sundown to Sunup* (1972), but also Gilberto Freyre's *Casa-Grande e Senzala* (1933). These three works are very different in their method and their postulates, but they have all led to the same result: restoration of the dimension of a society subject to the whole gamut of conflicts (from total and overt rebellion to silent flight) to the understanding of the slave plantation economy, which is conventionally viewed as the site where exploitation and domination reign unchallenged, but also as a place without density. Above all, they have permitted reconstruction of the links between the transformations of institutions, laws, the functioning of the economy, and movements that appeared to go in all directions. What has exploded in splinters is the idea of a submissive society without the presence of a living alternative.

In the case of peasants, of untouchables, of Amerindians, there has been this same rehabilitation of the space of movements and contestation that has a meaning, an orientation. The contractual model of democracy originating with Hobbes and Locke founded a threshold (property) over which politics does not enter because nothing passes that is not the order of repetition of the identical, thus nothing that could interest the historian of the event and ruptures or the historian of the representation of interests and deliberative procedures to resolve conflicts of interest.

In pushing beyond the "residual" conception of subaltern, dominated spaces of freedom that are immediately consigned to historical insignificance (sent back to the ethnology of cold societies), several heuristic principles become clear:

- The economic is politics in concentrated form, to cite Lenin *cum grano salis*: it is necessary to repoliticize the economic, which presents itself in the text as the epitome of the natural. Consider in particular that the daily economic functioning of the plantation presents a variety of problems that at once touch on the control of the poor over territory (mobility), the acceptance of discipline in production, and the governance of the inevitable community that finds itself generally denied because the empowerment that it confers on its members is considered subversive (and justly so).

- The "political," like the "ideological," the "religious," and the "cultural," are not as they present themselves. They are no longer "natural." They are constructed and constitute a procedural issue (independently of their substantive content).

- Exploitation and domination must not be confused with one another (Foucault); in the same way, domination and submission must not be confused (Tronti 1966, 1971; Scott 1985).

- Historical sources that privilege the written traces are tainted with many fundamental biases. First, they are the basis of legitimation of the dominant strata and power. Outside of exceptional circumstances (open rebellions), they deny the spaces of freedom and movement of antagonistic subjects. In the case of rebellion, the subjectivity they reveal is monstrous, criminal. Alternately, the black is foolish, mute, a child or demonic, excessive in everything. Nonetheless, all of this is very well known. Thus the work of the historian here is concerned with slavery. But for the workers' movement, for women, for the untouchables, for all the minorities, it is the same thing. It is to defy the sources by reading between the lines, relying on oral history (the compendium of the last witnesses to slavery), for that which reveals the mechanism of the scenes that the commentators and directors do not know. All of this is not to say that one cannot make use of sources even if they are strongly biased, as Peter Linebaugh's work (1992) on the 5,000 capital executions in eighteenth-century London well demonstrates.
- The role and importance of defection, flight, and withdrawal (the *exit* effect) must also be reevaluated. Although these often do not appear overtly, they are all the more important in situations of domination where open protest (*voice*) has little chance of success, and at the same time, because they have an immediate economic impact. Because of their quotidian massified character, these behaviors (to which can be added absenteeism and worker sabotage, nonparticipation in the institutional sphere of industrial capitalism viewed in its totality as a repressive apparatus) fashion a repressive juridical apparatus, but also incitements that would otherwise be neither comprehensible nor measurable in their finality and in their real dimensions.

If we return more specifically to the transformation of plantation economy-society and the institution of slavery, we will see that these principles lead to the most wonderful discoveries: those of the formation of a free peasantry in the Caribbean (Mintz, 1974) or the squatters' movements in Africa (Cooper 1980). These guiding principles, even if they have not been theorized, have also served to formulate Dale Tomich's hypothesis of a second slavery after the Haitian revolution and the first abolition. The institution of slavery survived for so long in the nineteenth century because it could adapt and make use of new technologies, free European migrations (see the example of Cuba [Moulier Boutang 2002]), and increase the paths to manumission and the percentage of manumitted, while quickly blocking the roads to liberation exploited by the slaves (the breaches in interracial relations, the peasant breach of access to property and to the market) to weaken the slave system. To recognize this is also to recognize the macroeconomic and political impact of agency and the empowerment that is legible at the micro level. It is to reevaluate the proper balance of determinant factors. It is to remedy the principle fault of the history of *mentalités*, because microbehaviors surely include transgressions. The manner of emptying the repressive apparatuses of their venom does not distance us from the most eventful history, but rather allows us to interpret facts that enter only very approximately into that framework, to reconstruct as events phenomena that for official historiography often only function to conceal or to dilute.

One might say to me that all of this is practically accepted. But I would like to hammer the message home and show that, in the apprehension of the transformations of the slave system during the globalization of the second capitalism, industrial capitalism, and the full and complete integration of the second slavery in the formation of the proletariat and the working class of the South, two methodological principles have appeared. The first, which arouses strong polemic, is the hypothesis of an Atlantic *history* and not simply an Atlantic *economy*. The second, which I argued in my thesis, is that of the reintegration of slavery as the missing link between medieval European liberation and the modern liberation of the wage-earning classes. It is no longer a question of understanding modern slavery and servitude as a bizarre bifurcation, an anomaly, backward or degenerate, but rather as the *primitive accumulation of the working class and of the wage-earning classes*. And the link that runs between these two principles is that of mobility.

The Contribution of Atlantic History to an Active Conception of Movements

The idea of an integrated economy on both sides of the Atlantic comes from the economists. Observing British and American economic growth during the nineteenth century, particularly the cycles of building and railroad construction, Brinley Thomas, in his foundational work on international migrations ([1954] 1973), adds to the extremely classical idea of the dependence of labor and population migrations on the economic cycle the more revolutionary idea of a single economic space in spite of national divisions since the independence of the United States. Instead of explaining the migration to the United States originating in Britain by the depressed conjuncture in the United Kingdom (the *push* factor), he puts the emphasis on the role of the American conjuncture (the *pull* factor) and demonstrates that this approach better accounts for the fluctuations of migrations and migratory waves. Thus, beyond the simple international commercial space, he recognizes the outline of an underlying world market that makes the construction of Pacific railways have a consequence on Wales comparable to the demand for labor on the London docks. Naturally, this idea of an integrated economy puts a halt to the widely documented but trivial acknowledgement of the interdependence of European metropoles and their colonies. However, the slave trade causes a third term to appear in this binomial. The triangular character of commerce integrates commodities and "pieces of ebony," and thus introduces the commodification of human labor. (I will even say the productive force of labor since, in the vocabulary of physiocrats and plantation owners, the value of a slave was measured in pounds of sugar or tobacco well before Ricardo measured the workers' labor in liters of wheat, and the value of an estate or plantation was measured only by the number of slaves—reducing landed rent to an unaccountable quantity.)

However, this integrated economy is still treated as an appendix to the study of international commerce. It leads to the opposition of a North Atlantic to a South Atlantic, which lessens the value of European interdependencies (the changes of the relations of force established in the ancien régime, which were still more unstable until 1815), but also intra-Caribbean circulation and circulation between the Antilles and mainland North and South America.

The emphasis put on the slave trade in the systemic dynamic of slavery has progressively emerged from a framework that is still too narrow. The systematic study of this crucial link in thc plantation economy, such as that which has led Luiz Felipe de Alencastro (2000) to examine the sixteenth to the eighteenth centuries, emphasizes not only the functionality of this commerce for the plantation system, but also its importance as a source of private profit and fiscal resources for the colonial Portuguese state. The financial profits made from the trade or from the *Asiento* by Portugal along with other powers, together with the growing indebtedness of the plantations, form a globalized system at the beginning of the nineteenth century. The slave system breaks at both ends of the chain (in Africa and in America) because the conditions of the circulation of labor change. The abolition of the slave trade, progressively established by England beginning in 1830, in spite of the strong resistance to its application in Brazil and Cuba, modified the conditions of mobility of slaves within the slave regimes of the Americas. In particular, it altered the rate of circulation of slaves from one plantation to another, their fixity, and thus their conditions of labor and tolerance or repression of "petit" or "grand" marronage. The so-called "internal" history of Africa also can no longer be separated from the vicissitudes of the trade. Rather, we are beyond the idea of a single economy integrated only at the level of international exchanges. But the most important aspect of this conception of a more deeply integrated economy is the almost brutal disappearance of the source of *indentured* servants and the *redemptioners* (familial migration) from continental Europe from about 1815–1817, the development of international migrations under contract coming from the countries of the (global) South, and the free migrations coming from Europe. The flow of free human circulation accelerated. Cost-free migrant labor became increasingly accessible. For that reason, it was even less suitable for one-sided contracts that forbid breaking the contract because of the debt that had been contracted. Meanwhile the cost of an imported slave continued to rise. But these flows also permitted large-scale political operations by the colonial authorities: In Cuba, for example, after the first war for independence, which was a failure, the black population, which had been becoming the majority because of the rapid development of the sugar industry, was decimated and the Spanish government developed the intense immigration of white settlers from Galicia, who contained the black minority below 40 percent of the population (Moulier Boutang 2002). The administration of the sharecropping *colonato* in Brazil (Moulier Boutang 1998: 461–524), the marginalization of the flow of the black populations to the U.S. South before and after the War of Secession, and European migration to the industrial North are part of the large-scale operations, during which internal migrations were not desired by the authorities (because they correspond to the movements of liberation of the slaves or free immigrants), and mobility on a transnational scale completely reshuffled the deck.

But it is necessary to speak of a human and therefore a social economy more than of an integrated economy in the Atlantic. The works of Marcus Rediker and Peter Linebaugh (2000; see also Rediker 2007) attempt to reconstruct an analytical framework of revolutionary subjectivity that goes beyond a single national or international framework. They are thus led to emphasize the hybridity of categories, the relations among slaves, the free and the freed, the blacks and the whites, and *sang-melés*, African-born (*bossales*), and creoles (Moulier Boutang 2003: 201–19). The pipeline of the slave trade, and the Atlantic exchanges that cannot be separated from it, make men, culture, and ideas encounter one another. Thus, "pieces of ebony" are very different from the commodities that economists are used to manipulating and for whom slaving authorities wish to reduce the spaces of subjectivity and contestation.

Presently there certainly exists a limit in the working agenda of Atlantic history that is not that usually evoked in academic discussion (and not only a reproach for approximation, lack of nuance, and anachronism [Guasco 2003]). This limit resides in an asymmetry in accounting for the interior history of colonial America in relation to the slave trade and the plantation economy and that of the interior of Africa in relation to the trades (principally the Atlantic) and its links with Europe and the Indian Ocean (Coquery-Vidrovitch 2009). Nevertheless, the program of research of Atlantic history includes an extremely rich principal in the approach of the second slavery (Tomich 2004). The world-economy cannot be grasped as a dynamic system by beginning from its points and then constructing the relation between these two or three fixed points (nodes). In fact, it is the relation (the edges) that determines ex post the essential characteristics of the nodes. The relation between the three zones (Africa, the Americas, and Europe) constitutes the object and the definitional matrix of the properties of each node. In the successive globalizations that the world has known, the local and the punctual is determined in its dynamic by the global. Revisiting the relations between the three nodes (Africa, the Americas, and Europe), recent contributions have underscored the importance of the Atlantic Ocean as a true milieu per se.[4] The global is manifested in the *local*. But the local incorporates the relation. It cannot be grasped independently of it. Dale Tomich proposes to treat industrial accumulation in the nineteenth century in the same manner. It is necessary to read it through the prism of slavery that is coextensive with free labor, with the free wage-labor and the logic of large-scale industry and its technological changes. In this sense, slavery in the nineteenth century does not constitute the monstrous external other, the shameful sickness thereof, but rather one of the components of its inner frontiers capitalism (Berlin 1998: 5).[5]

To conclude, I would now like to come to terms with the reintegration of slavery as the missing link of medieval European liberation and the modern liberation of the *salariat*.

The Invention of the Salariat: Agency and Empowerment in the Second Slavery

I have tried to show how modern slavery and servitude, in their rise, apogee, and decline, do not constitute an anomaly or degeneration, but the *primitive accumulation of working class and of the salariat*. The thesis of the primitive accumulation of capital as a social relation that is found in Marx presents a major disadvantage of which I will speak below (Moulier Boutang 2005: 1069–92). Prehistory has no history. By the same token capitalist accumulation and free wage labor appear without one being able to trace their genesis. The explanation of the initial capital of the money-owner (one wants to instead speak of the money-owning state) can be made on the basis of despoliation (the *enclosures* and proletarianization) or direct plunder (the war booty of Sir Francis Drake), but the construction at the heart of the relation of the exploitation of human labor in the *salariat* cannot be conjured up with the same trick. To what does the primitive accumulation of the *salariat*, the proletariat, the working classes correspond?

I propose to displace a certain number of principles to answer that question. First, to put at the center of the birth of capitalism not money, not profits, but the specific subjugation or subordination of labor as dependent labor, as opposed to labor on its own account. Then to consider that the labor contract drawn against remuneration in diverse forms (in kind, in money) immediately encounters problems of realization or execution. The principle of resistance to work has been to break the contract and take flight. Control over breaking the labor contract was most clearly posed in the late Middle Ages, when peasants and urban laborers (*journaliers*) engaged in a struggle of liberation from ancient slavery or feudal serfdom by attaining the use of, and then formal property in, land, a house, and the instruments of production.

The second point I wish to make is the increasing importance of constraint in the execution of the labor contract contrary to our retrospective and anachronistic vision of the contract, which often makes the latter appear as an instrument of the consolidation of rights and justice even though it had a disciplinary character (Steinfield 2001: 31).[6]

The relation of subordinated labor governed by a "free" contract, in contrast to the more restricted contract administered through the usages of corporations, becomes the object of flight. Such flight is the principle characteristic of the problem posed by the poor in the ancien régime. Beyond the whip and the hot iron, deportation was the principle instrument for enforcing the subordinated labor contract and controlling mobility by fixing the poor in a given territory through the invention of poor laws that distribute aid.

If the attempt to employ subordinated labor already encountered multiple resistances in Europe, in the colonies it appeared to find a solution that quickly proved inadequate, with the institution of indenture (engagement in subordinated labor for a determined period pledged against the debt contracted for the voyage). Indenture was insufficient because of the availability of lands not controlled by the authorities (even if these lands were seized from the Amerindians). The pawning of the individual to protect against defection from his subordinated activity in the plantation economy results in flight as a response. The generalization of indenture for life for blacks redefines both domestic slavery (those slaves working in the master's house) and slaves working in the fields. It is organized on a large scale. This holds for the ascent of modern slavery from 1440 to 1690. But to control, in its turn, the flight of slaves, the plantation economy was going to learn by the eighteenth century to mobilize technology and to organize work in a manner to exploit women and children (before the exploitation of the latter in the great Manchester factories). It was faced with considerable insubordination (Aptheker 1943), to which it reacted by increasing the size of plantations, by hardening the apparatus of control on the slave-trading ships, militarizing them more and more, but above all, by hardening the apparatus of control in society as well. But, alongside the repressive apparatus, elements of communal autonomy (the slave quarters, the exercise of a syncretic religion) grew with the increase in the number of slaves and with the ascension also of a *métisse* or free black population. Beginning with the Haitian Revolution, the first slavery was on the defensive. But its sunset was also the dawn of industrial capitalism, of the rural exodus, of the birth of the great industrial capitalist firm, of the organization of labor and the administration of the labor supply, of free transatlantic migrations, and of the contract migrations of colonized peoples. Finally, within slavery, it is not so much the classic period of 1670–1780 that is interesting. Rather, it is the rise of slavery's institutionalization *before* and its long sunset afterward with the hybrid, intermingling, codetermination of the two variants of dependent labor, the one not waged and not free, and the other salaried and located at the heart of industrialization, as well as the second wave of European globalization with the construction of the second colonial empires.

Dale Tomich is right to advance the hypothesis of a second slavery after the first abolition. The mutation of the institution of slavery operates under the impact of a demographic rationing (the severe restriction of the trade after 1808) and of a political rationing. The specter of Haiti, repeated by the terrible revolt in Jamaica during the Christmas holidays of 1831 (the Baptist War) led the principal fortresses of slavery (the U.S. South, Cuba, and Brazil) to reorganize and strengthen the system. The replacement of Saint Domingue, which had produced half of the world's sugar supply, furnished the economic occasion. But the 12,000 white planters expelled in a few weeks from the north of Saint Domingue reorganized themselves in the east of Cuba and in Louisiana. Certain of slavery's transformations, produced largely by the necessity of repressing maroon secessions and the incessant rebellions, had been sketched out in Brazil since the eighteenth century, with the formation of troops of police largely from the free colored population, with control over the religious confraternities. In short, the notion of control of a whole territory and no longer a single plantation went hand in hand with the systematic formation of a national guard, very much directed against the possibility of a general uprising of the slaves, rather than an exterior enemy of foreign powers.

Questions of mobility are always found at the heart of the spaces of agency and empowerment of the slaves. The duration of *petit marronage* (less than six months) is an index of the power conquered by the slaves at the heart of a given slave society. The attenuation of racism (though not its elimination) by tolerance for interracial sexual relations and also the growth of a *métisse* population, but also tolerance for informal *quilombos*, which do not seek liberty like the republic of Palmares but content themselves with fulfilling irreplaceable economic functions that shelter them from repression and destruction, signal an equally uncertain status for slavery. The development of cultivation of provision grounds or interstitial cultivation on the plantations, the right to sell the product of the latter, to accumulate savings, and the percentage of manumission in its different forms (including self-purchase) are testimony to a rise of the power, of the capacity, of slaves to act and speak. The underground railway in the United States, which permitted flight to the nonslave states, is similar to the flight from plantations in the state of São Paulo for the port of Santos.

In chapter sixteen of my book (Moulier Boutang 1998) I call attention to the birth of a market for free and salaried labor by hired slaves who were rented out by their masters. In this way, the masters tried to regularize the absenteeism of the labor force and to control the slaves' paid labor for other owners and, even more importantly, self-hire (*escravos de ganho*) in the cities. Masters who were incapable of supporting their slaves released them, so that they could find work and give the masters a part of their gain. When Rio became the imperial capital, the slaves invented jobs as maintenance workers, water carriers, and dockworkers, beyond their more traditional but no less fundamental role in the domestic economy. Thus, by its very scale, flight or desertion produced necessary adaptation by the system, and its evolution laid the foundation for the free *salariat*. When slave masters rehired their own runaway slaves in Santos, the institution of slavery could be seen to be dying. On a more general plane, it could be said that the formal characteristics of the free labor contract, that is, its indeterminate duration, which excludes not only the purchase of the body of the laborer but also the purchase of a predetermined period of labor time (as in the indenture contract), are results of the constant struggle of slaves and *engagés* to weaken bodily restraint of subordinated labor, to empty it of its effective content.

The regime of mobility is one of the most solid criteria for the scope of agency or of empowerment. In the case of a subordinated worker, whether formally free or partially or totally constrained (from slave to peon passing through familial assistance), freedom and the margins for maneuver are found in the absence of obstacles to self-mobility (including particular forms of self-mobility that consist of remaining in place, of setting oneself down, settling). The degree zero of the power to act is forced mobility or forced fixity (serfdom, slavery). This is why the first demand for freedom from Magna Carta up to the Bill of Rights of 1689 or to the American and French constitutions is the freedom to come and go, to not be arbitrarily detained.

The bourgeois tradition defines freedom as the property of an individual proprietor, therefore, suffrage is based on property qualification (consider the debates at Putney between the Independents and the Levelers during the English Revolution). But the quest for property by the poor, the proletarians, the serfs, the slaves, corresponds to the conditions that permit or consolidate this self-mobility. The possession of a good, of money, of self, of a family, of a child, of a roof, are to be interpreted in relation to the question of the control of mobility that itself arises from proletarianization (the question of the possession of self, of the means of production, of access to the market and to money) and the fixing of dependent or subordinated labor. The principal directions of freedom that are found in labor, depending on the moment when it is generalized and becomes the heart of capitalist accumulation, are the following:

- Relation with the means for production (tools but also family or clan relations)
- Relation with self; the inalienable right to the autonomy of one's own capacity to reason and body as an active part of the making of mercantile transactions
- Access to the market: this clause has been largely underestimated in the definition of the real content of the freedom of the free *salariat*
- Deterritorialization that escapes the assignation to residence or to the interior or exterior passport

In the case of the mutation of slavery into labor under contract (the coolies) or into free wage labor, it is in these four directions that the agents of history become collective subjects of a transformation.

Notes

1. Orlando Patterson emphasizes the necessity of distinguishing between societies where slavery occupies a marginal and very limited place (for example, the system of janissaries or eunuchs) and societies where it forms the pivot of society because it is the spinal column of economic activity (1982).

2. For a systematic inventory of these forms of forced labor see Moulier Boutang (1998), but also Miles, (1987), Brass, (1999), and Tinker (1974).

3. Pierre Dockès (1982) is the decisive work.

4. The concept of Atlantic economy as a cultural system has been illustrated by M. Rediker (1987). D. Tomich has discussed the reception of this concept.

5. "On mainland North America, as in the Americas generally, slaves worked. New World slavery did not have its origins in a conspiracy to dishonor, shame, brutalize, or reduce slaves on some perverse scale of humanity—although it did all of those at one time or another. The stench from slavery's moral rot cannot mask the design of American captivity: the extraction of labor that allowed a small group of men to dominate all" (Berlin 1998: 5).

6. Robert Steinfield (2001) shows that the close association of the work book, surveillance, and repressive measures until the end of the nineteenth century have been shared by various forms of "free workers," servants, indentured labor, and slaves.

Works Cited

Alencastro, Luiz Felipe de. 2000. *O trato dos viventes: Formação do Brasil no Atlântico Sul, séculos XVI e XVII.* São Paulo, Brazil: Companhia das Letras.

Althusser, Louis. 1973. *Réponse à John Lewis.* Paris: François Maspero.

Aptheker, Herbert. 1943. *American Negro Slave Revolts.* New York: Columbia University Press.

Berlin, Ira. 1998. *Many Thousands Gone: The First Two Centuries in America.* Cambridge, MA: Belknap Press Editor.

Blackburn, Robin. 1988. *The Overthrow of Colonial Slavery, 1776–1848.* London: Verso.

———. 1997. *The Making of New World Slavery: From the Baroque to the Modern, 1492–1800.* London: Verso.

Brass, Tom. 1999. *Towards a Comparative Political Economy of Unfree Labour: Case Studies and Debates.* London: Frank Cass.

Condorcet, M. J. A. Nicolas de Caritat. 1781. *Réflexions sur l'esclavage des Nègres.* Neufchatel, Switzerland; Société typographique. *http://classiques.uqac.ca/classiques/condorcet/reflexions_esclavage_negres/condorcet_reflexions_esclavage.pdf.*

Cooper, Frederick. 1980. *From Slaves to Squatters: Plantation Labor and Agriculture in Zanzibar and Coastal Kenya, 1890–1925.* New Haven, CT: Yale University Press.

Coquery-Vidrovitch, Catherine, 2009. "Slavery in Africa and the Atlantic World in the Nineteenth Century" ("L'esclavage en Afrique et l'Atlantique au XIXe siècle"). Unpubl. paper delivered at Seminário Internacional: O século XIX e as novas fronteiras da escravidão e da liberdade, Universidade Federal do Estado do Rio de Janeiro (UNIRIO), Rio de Janeiro Universidade Severino Sombra (USS), Vassouras, August 10–14, Rio de Janeiro, Brazil.

Dockès, Pierre. 1982. *Medieval Slavery and Liberation.* Chicago: University of Chicago Press.

Fogel, Robert W. 1989. *Without Consent or Contract: The Rise and Fall of American Slavery.* 4 vols. New York: W. W. Norton.

Fogel, Robert W., and Stanley Engerman. 1974. *Time on the Cross: The Economics of American Negro Slavery.* 2 vols. Boston: Little Brown.

Freyre, Gilberto. 1933. *Casa-grande e senzala.* Rio de Janeiro, Brazil: José Olympio.

Genovese, Eugene D. 1967. *The Political Economy of Slavery: Studies in the Economy and Society of the Slave South.* New York: Pantheon.

———. 1974. *Roll, Jordan, Roll: The World the Slaves Made.* New York: Pantheon.

Guasco, Michael. 2003. "The Many-Headed Hydra, by P. Linebaugh & M. Rediker." Book review, "H-Net Review in the Humanities & Social Sciences," June. *http://www.h-net.org/reviews/showrev.php?id=7645.*

Linebaugh, Peter. 1992. *The London Hanged: Crime and Civil Society in the Eighteenth Century.* Cambridge, UK: Cambridge University Press.

Linebaugh, Peter, and Marcus Rediker. 2000. *The Many-Headed Hydra: Sailors, Slaves, Commoners, and the Hidden History of the Revolutionary Atlantic.* Boston: Beacon Press.

Mignolo, Walter. 1997. *The Darker Side of the Renaissance: Literacy, Territoriality, and Colonization.* Ann Arbor: University of Michigan Press.

———. 2001. *Capitalismo y geopolítica del conocimiento: El eurocentrismo y la filosofía de la liberación en el debate intelectual contemporáneo.* Buenos Aires, Argentina: Ediciones del Signo.

———. 2012. *Local Histories/Global Designs: Coloniality, Subaltern Knowledges, and Border Thinking.* Princeton, NJ: Princeton University Press.

Miles, Robert. 1987. *Capitalism and Unfree Labour: Anomaly or Necessity?* London: Tavistock Publications.

Mintz, Sidney W. 1974. *Caribbean Transformations.* New York: Columbia University Press.

Moulier Boutang, Yann. 1998. *De l'esclavage au salariat: Économie historique du salariat bridé.* Paris: Presses Universitaires de France.

———. 2002. "Le fonctionnement de l'économie de plantation esclavagiste à Cuba (1790–1868)." *Revue Tiers-Monde* 43 (171): 555–77.

———. 2003. "La fin de l'esclavage: Haïti et les modèles de transition abolitionnistes." In *Rétablissement de l'esclavage dans les colonies françaises, 1802: Ruptures et continuités de la politique colonial française, 1800–1830: Aux origines d'Haïti,* edited by Y. Bénot and M. Dorigny. Paris: Maisonneuve et Larose, 201–19.

———. 2005. "Formes de travail non libre: 'Accumulation primitive: Préhistoire ou histoire continuée du capitalisme?' " *Cahiers d'Etudes Africaines.* Paris, Editions de l'EHESS, Special Issue: "Esclavage moderne ou modernité de l'esclavage?" nos. 179–180: 1069–92.

———. 2007. "Introduction." Antonio Negri. *Politics of Subversion: A Manifesto for the Twenty-First Century*, re-edited (orig. 1989). Minneapolis: University of Minnesota Press.

Olmsted, Frederick Law. 1856. *A Journey in the Seaboard Slave States: With Remarks on Their Economy.* New York: Dix & Edwards; London: Sampson Low.

Patterson, Orlando. 1982. *Slavery and Social Death: A Comparative Study.* Cambridge, MA: Harvard University Press.

Pollack, Shoshana. 2000. "Reconceptualizing Women's Agency and Empowerment: Challenges to Self-Esteem Discourse and Women's Lawbreaking." *Women & Criminal Justice* 12(1): 75–89.

Quijano, Aníbal. 2000. "Coloniality of Power and Eurocentrism in Latin America." *International Sociology* 15: 215–32.

Rawick, George. 1972. *From Sundown to Sunup: The Making of the Black Community.* Westport, CT: Greenwood Press.

Rediker, Marcus. 1987. *Between the Devil and the Deep Blue Sea: Merchant Seamen, Pirates, and the Anglo-American Maritime World, 1700–1750.* Cambridge, UK: Cambridge University Press.

———. 2007. *The Slave Ship: A Human History.* New York: Viking.

Scott, James C. 1985. *Weapons of the Weak: Everyday Forms of Peasant Resistance.* New Haven, CT: Yale University Press.

———. 1992. *Domination and the Arts of Resistance: Hidden Transcripts.* New Haven, CT: Yale University Press.

Steinfeld, Robert J. 2001. *Coercion, Contract, and Free Labor in the Nineteenth Century.* Cambridge, UK: Cambridge University Press.

Thomas, Brinley. (1954) 1973. *Migration and Economic Growth: A Study of Great Britain and the Atlantic Economy.* 2nd ed. Cambridge, UK: Cambridge University Press.

Tinker, Hugh. 1974. *A New System of Slavery: The Export of Indian Labour Overseas 1830–1920.* London, UK: Oxford University Press.

Tomich, Dale W. 2004. *Through the Prism of Slavery: Labor, Capital, and World Economy.* Lanham, MD: Rowman & Littlefield.

Tronti, Mario. 1966, 1971. *Operai e capitale.* Torino, Italy: G. Einaudi.

The Discovery of Progress in Cuba

Machines, Slaves, Businesses*

José Antonio Piqueras

The transformation that began in the west of Cuba in the 1790s meant that attention was increasingly paid to the nearest sugar plantation models, which had become a reflection of progress and an example to follow. At the hands of the most illustrious plantation owners and their most distinguished thinker, the experience of the eighteenth century, revitalized from the mid-1760s onward, then adopted a true perspective and took on a coherent direction toward the horizon of development, which was unmistakably associated with the notion of the island's prosperity. Prosperity was understood to be the generation of wealth, and those responsible for driving that wealth were the sugar plantation owners from Havana. They had an advantage over all other groups, and in particular over the merchant-moneylenders, tobacco farmers, and stock farmers, and over the interests of the colonial bureaucracy and the Royal Navy.

*This work has been written as part of the research project HAR2009-07037/HIST, funded by the Spanish Ministry of Science and Innovation; translated by Paul Edgar.

Imbued with a combination of physiocratic ideas and the corresponding *liberal mercantilism* that characterized the economic thinking of European colonial powers during the last third of the eighteenth century (Llombart 1992: 117–18), Francisco Arango y Parreño, who represented Havana in Madrid from 1788 to 1794 (González-Ripoll Navarro 2001), was able to express in a clear and well-argued manner the interests of plantation owners, who had ample support within Havana city council. He did this with such skill that these interests were presented so as to concur with those of the Crown, in other words with the tax revenue which the island's progress would provide for the Royal Treasury in the medium to long term.

According to the large number of *Aranguist* exegetes and historians, the genius from Havana rose to prominence at an early age and achieved two accomplishments in a short space of time. First, he persuaded the Crown of the advantages of his ideas, changing Spain's colonial policy toward Cuba. Second, following two months' seclusion, he produced a masterpiece on liberal economic theory. With regard to the first point, other works have contextualized the circumstances surrounding the royal concessions of 1789–1793 (freedom to import African slaves, concessions regarding the importation of tools and utensils) based on two elements. First, physiocratic projects and others concerning the reassessment and reform of monopolistic mercantilism had been maturing in the Court for a long time, and in 1787 became a government bill in the form of the *Instrucción Reservada* prepared by José Moñino, Conde de Floridablanca (the secretary of state), which in the years to follow had the support of several of Carlos IV's ministers. Second, Arango's aspirations were shared by the empire's most active elites, as can be seen from statements made by their respective representatives in the Court, which were very similar to those made by Arango. In a sphere of government dominated by inertia, fear, and opposing interests, the king listened to the divergent opinions of those he included in his Council of State Secretaries. As ministers fought to impose their points of view, seeking the support of the representatives of overseas elites became part of the method of governing. It was enough to insinuate to these colonial representatives that certain requests (which they themselves suggested) would receive their support, but to achieve their objectives with the least resistance from their adversaries, it was preferable for the minister to cede the initiative to the subjects from overseas instead of making the case themselves (Piqueras 2009).

His *Discurso sobre la agricultura de la Habana y medios de fomentarla*, which Arango addressed to the Spanish Crown in 1792, was less an example of theory than a paradigmatic example of applied economics and a masterpiece of political economics. Without a shadow of a doubt, *Discurso sobre la agricultura* laid the foundations for the modern slave plantation (Tomich 2003). In other words, the text presented and argued the bases of the development of sugar production and manufacturing in line with the new times and with *progress*, despite the fact that the word itself was not used in the document at all. The notion of progress was, however, apparent in certain production methods and in a general understanding of the integration of factors of production, goods, and consumption.

Progress (a malleable notion) referred in the first instance to the progress of advanced nations, which offered a model to follow, aimed at increasing the prosperity of the mother countries and the most willing and intelligent colonists. "All the Representative's attention must go toward promoting and increasing the happiness of his homeland," was the order that Arango received from his predecessor when he took up the position in 1788 (Arango y Parreño 2005, 1: 77–78). And this he did, writing reports and making various different requests, following the direction taken in previous years. However, the news he received from European countries led to a more ambitious project. On the one hand, he observed the trend of growing sugar consumption associated with an expanding consumer market, resulting from the evolution of prices and habits in the context of social change. In England, consumption had increased by 50 percent per capita during the previous half century. People had become accustomed to consuming sugar, and demand had multiplied. With good reason, sugar was to become the natural accompaniment, in the form of sweet calories, to the British Isles' refreshing drink par excellence and a replacement for beer and other more expensive (and nutritious) foods among the working classes (Mintz 1996: 160–63). Second, Arango observed the effects that technology, science, and the organization of activities as a business had on producing greater quantities and increasing profitability (Tomich 2009).

Discourse of the Method

Discurso sobre la agricultura was a reasoned exposition of the obstacles that had to be overcome to ensure Cuba's prosperity. It also contained, as we mentioned previously, a project aimed at acquiring the knowledge necessary to set the island's economy on the road to prosperity. And that knowledge had to be sought abroad. Thus, Arango proposed that two envoys be authorized to embark on a fact-finding mission. To avoid any difficulties or suspicion, he suggested that the true objective be kept secret and that they pretend to be travelers or smugglers (Arango 2005, 1: 174). The minister of finance between 1791 and 1796, Diego de Gardoqui (who in 1790 had headed the "branch for the supply of Negroes" of the Indies Royal Treasury and Trade Administration) actively promoted the venture (Pezuela 1863, 1: 32).[1] Gardoqui had personal experience in overseas trade and had negotiated with delegates of the thirteen colonies to ensure Carlos III's assistance in their struggle for independence.

England and France held the keys to the future of Cuba. "It is a question of transferring to our soil the advantages that have provided foreigners with their greater knowledge, of providing means to spread this and create further knowledge that perpetuates this and other possible benefits," wrote Arango (2005, 1:173). In his opinion, comparisons could be made between four particular situations, which could be summarized as in table 3.1:

Table 3.1. Opposing Concepts in *Discurso sobre la agricultura*

THEM	US
Innovation, advances	Inertia, backwardness
Superiority, high profits	Depression, low profits
Knowledge, tools, improvements	Ignorance, errors
Foreign countries	Havana

Source: Based on Arango (2005, 1: 144–226).

It is important to bear in mind that the increase in the number of sugar plantations during the second half of the eighteenth century was the continuation of the previous model. Despite being bigger, the new plantations had the same structure, the same uses and procedures, identical technology, and the same concept of labor. Cuba's total exports in 1780 (6,724 tons) were lower than those of Grenada and the Grenadines (8,664 tons), which had been acquired recently from the French. Cuba's exports were also lower than those of St. Kitts (8,807 tons) and Guadeloupe (7,898 tons in 1767), and similar to those of Suriname (Deerr 1949, 1: 197–99, 212, 236; Fraginals 1978, 3: 43). None of the Cuban sugar fortunes were comparable to those of magnates from Saint-Domingue at that time.

Having stated the objectives, Arango explained to the Court that the envoys would "go to cities in France and England where Negroes are bought and sold directly and where the machines and tools required for farming in America are manufactured. They will attempt to discover the prices of all the devices in these factories, find out why they are beneficial and whether they are made in the colonies; they will make an accurate report of the customs tariffs applied in both kingdoms . . . ; they will make a detailed report of the way in which slave expeditions to the coast of Africa must be carried out in order to discover their advantages" (Arango y Parreño [1792] 2005, 1: 173).[2]

When referring to *progress*, as a stage or an objective, Arango and his contemporaries from Havana used the word as a dynamic verb instead of a noun: they used the verb *progresar* (to progress) in the sense of advancing. To progress implied moving in a particular direction with a clear objective. This objective was the happiness of the island, with the "island" understood to be the predominant society and its corresponding hierarchical order. Happiness was not, however, a frame of mind but rather the extent to which this was associated with material well-being, with a more comfortable and pleasurable life as a result of increased wealth, improved efficiency, the reward for effort and sacrifice: all the things that allowed access to as many of the advantages of modern civilization as possible from the main urban centers—which at that time were the cities of Europe, and shortly afterwards, the cities in the east of the United States. The richest and most advanced cultures brought with them new, modern customs, almost always after developing new scientific techniques and ideas applied to manufacturing and agriculture. The notion of progress, of advancement, had many different aspects. The ability to multiply a fortune if a series of factors was available was one of them, but was by no means the only one. In the realm of everyday activities it was noticeable that certain customs, which had developed into habits, had become a sign of backwardness. If they were wisely introduced, certain innovations and advances could provide agriculture and manufacturing with increased profits.

The notion of progressing or advancing toward happiness represented a double abstraction. Happiness, in the sense that it satisfied requirements, was an achievable aim that was preferentially accessible to one sector of the population. Limited accessibility was a constant feature of unequal societies, yet that did not prevent the idea of happiness from being projected, by way of an illusion, as an open possibility to the rest of the population, because its re-creation allowed it to be adapted to the social conditions. The tangible profits of the sugar industry led large sectors of the middle classes and other indirect beneficiaries to close ranks around the proposals of the plantation elites for almost a hundred years. In another sense, in a society based on slavery, there were enormous differences between master and servant: the objective of human happiness, the direction toward which progress was heading, was difficult to share if, as was assumed, it depended on the expansion and amplification of slave sugar plantations and therefore created a whole series of radically opposed material, social, and moral interests. The national history of societies with a past of slavery gives rise to this legacy, which makes it difficult to integrate the memory of the past, and makes it necessary to highlight at each step the inequality of the experiences that the creators and bearers of the ideology of progress, such as Arango, mystified and hid behind extraordinary results.

The advantages enjoyed by foreign colonies were the result of certain economic conditions (which included technical aspects) and political conditions (including the system of taxes and tariffs). Progress was also understood to encompass the knowledge of nature, the application of established knowledge (science), and the creation and use of practical technology. It represented a profound change, both in society and in the way of life, a higher stage of civilization. The idea originated during the Scottish Enlightenment, which was the first to conceive the evolution of civilization in terms of successive, superior phases. *L'Encyclopédie* systematized and spread this evolutionary sense of the concept, and its entries and illustrations offered an up-to-date vision of modernity (see the entry for *sucrerie et raffinerie*).

Postrevolutionary thinkers took up the task of offering a rational order and providing explanations not so much for the events experienced (perceived by the majority of them as the work of a maelstrom triggered by passions) as for the substitution of the previous social and political regime, which was conceived in a coherent and unitary sense (*society*), by another different regime, which was no less unitary and interrelated. They were successive phases of a social order that, once free of revolutionary excesses, undeniably offered advantages insofar as the next stage was superior to the last. The generation that experienced the major upheavals of the Atlantic revolutions, the modernization of thinking, and the industrial revolution were strongly influenced by the climate of change. The phenomenon fits perfectly within the time span of Arango's life (he was born in 1765 and died in 1837).

Progress in the nineteenth century was no longer conceived of as moral advances "of the spirit"; rather, it became a material, cultural, and social concept (see Nisbet 1981). Why, asked Goethe (quoted in Derry and Williams 1987: 408), were the English in relation to the Prussians "more advanced than us at everything"? Progress was also a political concept in two senses: (1) the adoption of political forms considered appropriate to modern times, that is, the promotion of measures that removed the obstacles that hindered private free initiative, in place of monopolistic impositions by the State; (2) the existence of representative governments born of national sovereignty. In modern nineteenth-century colonialism, attitudes toward politics, backed by the mother country and like-minded colonists, became a secondary aspect of social life, replaced by the administration and creation of wealth. Cuba was, in this sense, an outstanding early example, following the antecedent of Saint-Domingue and the tensions that arose during its two brief constitutional phases (1810–1814 and 1820–1823).

In his request to the Crown in 1792, Arango acknowledged that:

> The project . . . is, in my view, *the only one which can release us from the desolation* we are suffering because of the *superiority of foreign knowledge.* With a *more lively trade in Negroes* as a result of the two decrees which I indicated, and with permission to *enter all farming tools and machinery*, with regard to these two points we will be more or less at the level of foreign nations.
>
> My word is not the only guarantee of the *superiority of foreign enlightenment.* Read the substantial memoirs written by a Spanish traveler about the French colony of Saint-Domingue and which D. Ignacio Gala published in this letter in 1786 and it can be seen that the only Spaniard who has taken up the pen on this subject takes pains to expose the *backwardness of* our colonies' *knowledge* with regard to that of Guárico. (2005: 162, 207, emphasis added—JP)

In 1832 he again took up the subject when he stated that "The plantation owners . . . admit that . . . their production would increase by up to a quarter if use was made of the animals, machinery, farming and chemical procedures which are common in Europe" (Arango y Parreño 1832: 272).

Since authorization for the journey took almost two years, the French leg of the expedition (to France and Guárico) was cancelled because hostilities broke out in 1793. Instead, plans were made to extend the visit to the British colonies in the West Indies, taking advantage of the recent alliance with England. The objective was to acquire "a deep understanding of the way in which all cane fruit, coffee, cotton and indigo etc. is grown, and of the different machines used . . . , of everything which helps to know what the foreigners do from the moment of seeding . . . until the fruit is packaged and put on display in urban stores." Arango's journey with the Count of Casa Montalvo between March 1794 and February 1795 took them to Portugal, England, Barbados, and Jamaica. During eleven months, they received exhaustive training in economic and social organization (González-Ripoll Navarro 2002: 85–102).

The report presented agricultural technology and science, specialized labor, and the organization of labor as the panaceas of progress in the sugar industry.

The Advances of Others: Never-Ending Progress

With regard to scientific and technological development, Arango made a clear distinction between farming and manufacturing. With regard to the first, he said: "There is no need to walk through the fields of Havana to know that nobody has any knowledge or that nobody even knows the names of practical subjects like Natural Physics, Chemistry or Botany; but even without these aids, one only has to stop to see the different state of one type of agriculture and the other" (Arango 2005, 1: 152). "They plant the canes in a different way; they gather the harvests of several grains on the land itself, and there are many other differences which I shall avoid boring you with here" (Arango 2005, 1: 153).

Even in 1828 and 1829, he still recommended the *urgent* creation of a School of Chemistry.[3] Not until a Spaniard educated in Paris, José Luis Casaseca, settled in Cuba were advances made in that direction. What is more, Casaseca was knowledgeable about machinery and to a considerable extent his recommendations inclined the sugar planters toward Derosne-Cail machines. Finally, he passed on his knowledge to his pupil, Álvaro Reynoso (Moreno Fraginals 1978, 1: 221).

Arango highlighted examples of Cuban backwardness in the manufacturing process. The other colonies used:

1. A varied driving force that did not depend on animal traction, but instead used water and wind power

2. Iron grinding mills

3. Horizontal rollers, which offered better performance and were harder wearing

4. Reverberatory furnaces, the Jamaican train, which offered advantages in terms of fuel consumption

Arango was truly dazzled by mechanization. He regarded machines as a powerful tool and a perfect metaphor for human beings, society, and the State. The word *machine* appeared to gradually take hold of him: "Everyone knows that economising on human labour involves substituting it with machines or beasts, and that time and experience help to perfect machines" (Arango y Parreño 2005, 1: 153). He also made reference to "the political machine of my homeland" in 1812 (Arango y Parreño 2005, 2: 115).

It is clear that before embarking on his journey to England, he was aware of the possible advantages offered by a strong steam-powered engine. Scientific publications provided news about this and some engines manufactured by Boulton & Watt that had been installed in Spain since 1775.

For him, applying that driving force to farming and processing was the key to the future of agriculture. "[In Cuba] there are no windmills or watermills and nobody even knows what they are, whereas in foreign colonies, in addition to these being very common, *habitations* which due to their location cannot have them use well-built iron sugar mills; the levers or driving beams are placed almost horizontally and this allows them to mill a larger amount of cane in the same space of time" (Arango 2005, 1: 153).

In the neighboring colonies, technology was also used during the other stages of production: "To boil the sugar cane broth they use reverberatory furnaces which save vast expenditure on firewood since it is enough to use dry sugar cane *bagasse*; meanwhile in Havana there are still doubts about whether these reverberatory furnaces are a better idea than spending nine-tenths of the value of the crops on cutting down and ripping up a whole forest of trees for every sugar harvest" (Arango 2005, 1: 153).

And with regard to the refining process, in comparison with the traditional drying rooms, he reported that in foreign countries the operation was carried out "with fire produced by stoves designed for that purpose" (Arango 2005, 1: 154).

Arango focused his attention on the British colonies and attempted to hold them up as a model. He showed an interest in the type of cane and took samples from Tahiti, which he then lost after he returned. Time would show that his decision to focus on the British colonies was correct. He observed the plantation methods, the use of irrigation, the improved cutting conditions, and the production levels that could be achieved through the combination of water and wind power in the sugar mills, both of which were preferable to animal power—which, however, still prevailed in the neighboring colonies. Arango had most definitely been seduced by machinery before embarking on his journey.

Arango and Montalvo went further afield. In England, they were amazed by and became familiar with the steam engine, thinking that it could be used for milling. Montalvo decided to commission the construction of such an engine in accordance with the wishes of his son-in-law, the Count of Jaruco, Joaquín de Santa Cruz y Cárdenas, whom he kept informed of each stage of the developments. The aim was to produce more with less investment per productive unit, to increase profits even if that initially involved considerable investment in equipment, labor, and employing technicians. It also involved purchasing slaves. When the travelers returned to Havana in 1795, Arango was reluctant to provide a detailed report of his expedition, as requested by the Royal Consulate. He only provided an outline of the route taken and presented a verbal summary of the journey in several sessions. However, in one of these meetings he announced the project for the machine he had commissioned to drive sugar mills and he presented "a small model and several diagrams which showed the workings of the machine" (Arango y Parreño 2005, 1: 258). Everyone was satisfied.

On this journey that revolved around mechanical progress, the person chosen to carry out the work commissioned in England was, paradoxically, the Spaniard Agustín de Betancourt. He was an engineer from the Canary Islands who had been head of the School of Civil Engineering in Madrid, had lived in Russia, and settled in Bristol. In England, Betancourt had managed to gain access to detailed information on the technology developed by Watt before the patent expired. He was in charge of manufacturing the device for Arango (González-Ripoll Navarro 2002: 91; Egorova 2011a: 189–213, 208; 2011b: 31–48).

The task set was actually not so simple. To persuade the authorities and gain support, Arango sent an official letter addressed to the minister Gardoqui, which exaggerated the results of the informative expedition and highlighted one of the main achievements: "We will also be the first ones to bring the most powerful agent known to industry across the Atlantic, so that those who do not have ready access to water can use the steam pump to drive their mills and forever abandon the costly, uncertain and weak resource of mules and oxen" (Carrillo y Arango 1862: 70).In fact, the English had tested steam-powered mills in Jamaica in 1768, and there are explanations and diagrams of various prototypes applied to different phases of the manufacturing process.[4]

The steam engine was installed in a sugar plantation belonging to the Count de Jaruco, Arango's patron during his stay in Madrid. In his eulogy written in 1837 on request of the *Sociedad Patriótica*, Anastasio Carrillo, the trustee's nephew, wrote the following about the machine: "It worked with some regularity although it did stop quite frequently and *the machine had to be abandoned due to the lack of a skilled operator*. For many years that misfortune robbed us of the benefits of the most admirable discovery of our era" (Carillo y Arango 1862: 70, emphasis added—JP).The machine was put in operation in January 1797 but stopped working and was removed after only a few weeks. It was not until 1817, twenty years later, that a steam mill brought from England and set up in Matanzas in Juan Madrazo's sugar plantation started to work (Moreno Fraginals 1978, 1: 207). This frustrated outcome takes nothing away from the visionary nature of Arango and his friends. It simply forces us to take into consideration the period and avoid confusing an experiment or faith in the power of new technology with its practical, profitable application.

It is important to bear certain technical factors in mind when evaluating the subject of mechanization in reasonable terms. Not until 1784 could the primitive steam engines produce the regular rotary movement required to power the transmission system. In addition, high-pressure steam was not used until after 1802, and it was difficult to couple the vertical machines to the mill, a problem later solved with horizontal machines like those taken by Fawcett in 1817. On the other hand, the production of machines was fairly limited while Watt still had the patent, with some twenty machines being built each year. In around 1803 it is calculated that there were no more than a dozen steam engines in the New World, in the United States. Depending on the industrial sector, the use of steam to replace windmills or waterwheels did not bring significant advantages (Derry and Williams 1987: 409, 469). This point was mentioned by Moreno Fraginals, who added that in terms of the efficiency of sugar mills, there was no actual difference between the new equipment and mills driven by animal power, or at least not until the 1840s, when iron rollers became more widespread in horizontal mills and when their weight and rotation could take advantage of the horsepower provided. The advantage of steam brought immediate savings in oxen (from fifty to eighty yokes) and slaves to handle them. In contrast, it meant hiring qualified staff, who had to be brought from abroad (Moreno Fraginals 1978, 1: 210).

In general, the availability of machine operators was a chronic problem. When mechanization became more widespread, there was not usually a surplus of operators in the sugar mills, and there were no extra workers to replace those who were ill or had left. Neither did the operators have sufficient knowledge of mechanics to ensure the maintenance and repair of the machines. We have found several examples of such cases around 1882. Throughout the century we have also found that a large proportion of machine operators were foreign, which contrasts with employees in the sawmills and urban industries, although it is true that the appliances were less complex. This question brings us back to the controversy surrounding slavery and mechanization, always a latent issue during that period and in historiography. In short, maintenance of the machinery caused numerous setbacks, and until the middle of the century, it was common for sugar mills to have a mill driven by animal power to which they resorted if the steam-powered mill broke down.

The sequence of events that marks the advances made on the island of Cuba is a *continuum* of major landmarks. In terms of sugar mills, these were steam mills, the Jamaican train, the Derosne system, condensers, etc. The signs that marked modernity in production and communications were steamboats, railways, the telegraph, etc. As we know, steamboats and railways were specific solutions to the extremely deficient network of pathways that linked the sugar fields to the loading stations and linked the main cities to each other. The network of roads, which was frequently requested, received scant attention from the authorities and also came up against the difficulties involved in building and maintaining such a network in a country the physical and environmental conditions of which made any project very expensive (Saco 2001, 1: 168–241). The solution was left in private hands, converting requirements into a business opportunity and postponing public works for a century. One form of progress deterred another more basic form. Progress does not always move in a straight line.

Returning to the subject of technical progress and the conditions of its acceptance, Moreno echoed the introduction of the Jamaican train in the boiler room, in which all the evaporators were fed by a single source of heat provided by the fuel of the first. This led to energy savings and the alternative use of *bagasse* and brushwood, something that was delayed in Cuba due to the plentiful supply of wood (Moreno Fraginals 1978, 1: 88).[5] The so-called Jamaican train or French train had been tested in the sixteenth century in Saint-Domingue together with the Spanish train, which had a source of combustion in each boiler and allowed for faster heating. It was actually the availability of resources and their economy that at one time or another led the different systems of evaporators to pass as advances. Progress is not univocal.

Moreno criticized historians for the fact that in terms of the Jamaican train, they passed off as an innovation something that was actually a return to an old solution when it was imported to Cuba in around 1780 and slowly became more widespread during the following decades. Incidentally, he described Alejandro Oliván as a "fraud of the worst kind who knows nothing whatsoever about sugar growing." The latter's recommendations, which were presented in 1831, delayed the introduction of modern industrial equipment to Cuba for twenty years. Oliván recommended the Jamaican train with open boilers as opposed to the system of vacuum evaporation and concentration (Moreno Fraginals 1978, 1: 217–19). The problem is that the reproach was unjust, even though Oliván was quite possibly the greatest fraud ever to have visited the island, and not just in terms of sugar-growing techniques.[6] It is important to bear in mind that the vacuum evaporation and concentration system had been tested, but the experiments were not successful until Derosne completed his machine in 1831 and took it to Guadeloupe in the years that followed. Oliván traveled to Paris in 1830 and it was therefore impossible that he was aware of the patent.

Oliván presented his conclusions in Cuba to veritable experts from the sugar industry. Arango did not raise any objections. Had the intelligentsia of the sugar industry lost all their knowledge, all their information about what was happening on the neighboring islands, all their intuition as men of progress? The plantation owners followed Oliván's recommendations and installed the double train of boilers and animal filters in none other than Arango's sugar mill, La Ninfa. The pioneers of 1794 adopted a primitive system forty years later. Is that not strange?

This is the same dilemma as the one regarding decisions about the mechanization of the manufacturing industry, as Hobsbawm highlighted for industrial England. It is essential to raise the profit threshold enough that it is worth investing in expensive machinery that brings net improvements to productivity. The adoption of technology is also a question of customs and the need for time to adjust, and both factors discourage investment. Inertia, which works against progress, leads people to continue what they are familiar with and what more or less works. Arango wrote about Tomás Guilti in this respect, saying that "he has always been brave enough to endure the moaning of his countrymen and the losses which always accompany the initial trials, and in the end he has managed, with the help of a French economist, to increase the production of his sugar mill by twenty-five percent" (Arango y Parreño 2005, 1: 195).

In 1846, practically half of the fifteen largest sugar mills had installed the Derosne train and the rest still used the Jamaican train (García de Arboleya 1852: 133–34).[7] Technical progress was gradual and at times slow, but it set a relentless trend. The incorporation of stream-driven mills was the condition required to introduce iron grinding mills; vacuum condensation then transformed the manufacturing process.

They were the conditions for the great sugar revolution and the premise for the consolidation of slave labor in modern times.

Preparing the Sugar Revolution: Slave Labor, Business, and the Colonial Condition

Among the aims set for the envoys sent to examine the progress of other nations, *Discurso sobre la agricultura* highlighted the fact that the machinery required an extra element: "[T]hey will do everything possible to be accompanied by as many operators as they see fit in order to carry out the initial trials and share this new knowledge among operators from Havana." To meet their objective, "the envoys will have the power to make the most beneficial agreement with them; in this case they must proceed with the utmost care and maturity, both in their choice of operators and in the terms used when formalising the contract, the first clause of which shall be the obligation to share their knowledge with a certain number of young professionals" (Arango 2005, 1: 174).

As can be seen, the young man from Havana planned to hire salaried technicians whom he hoped could be placed in charge of the most skilled processes. Arango considered that the *agricultores* (a Hispanicized expression used to refer to the sugar plantation owners or planters) "cannot work on their own; they need skilled workers and subordinates to carry out their wishes." He wondered where they could be found, and before answering the question, explained the case of the Count of Casa Montalvo and the Count of San Juan de Jaruco, in Madrid at that time. They could illustrate "untold instances of this fact with regard to reverberatory furnaces; convinced of their advantages, the former brought a specialist from Guárico and despite demonstrating them in their sugar mills, which are the biggest in Havana, and despite the due acknowledgement which their skills and judgement deserve, few have followed the example, even though everyone knows that every foreign sugar mill has them" (Arango 2005, 1: 195).

Just like the skilled workers they intended to hire in Europe, the "specialists" from Guárico (sugar-mill technicians) were obviously free, white workers. As mechanization progressed, Arango *racialized* the various functions in the sugar mill.

Enlightened thinkers had proclaimed the virtues of vocational schools and the benefits of freely offering information to the public about advances in agriculture through periodicals and discussion sessions. Experiments involving the latest ideas by the boldest sugar-mill owners led to the creation of *jardins d'acclimatation*, and the new manufacturing processes were tested on their estates. Although the plantation owners were reluctant to reveal the secrets of their skilled sugar experts, they did agree to share with their neighbors the results of their experiments with different varieties of sugar cane and with the different devices acquired abroad, just as they shared the risks and profits of slave expeditions. The former belonged to the realm of competition, whereas the latter were one of the factors required to increase the island's sugar production, on which they hoped to construct society and establish themselves as a social class.

However, not everything depended on differences in the access to and use of technology. In the instructions given, Arango stated that "They [the envoys] will also pay equal attention to the system used to divide the labour of their slaves." The distribution and control of functions refers to the organization of production from a business point of view. And he added that they: "[will examine] their authority over slaves, any disputes which have occurred in this regard and the effects of each one at a certain time; their method of governing them economically." Reference is made here to the authority and governance not of labor, but of laborers who were the property of the plantation owners. At the same time, the interest in economic management seeks to reconcile this with profitability: costs and production. That was the objective. It was the essential concept of the productive model that Arango expressed so brilliantly on the eve of the *second slavery* (Tomich 2009: 139–40). All the fascination with modern technology and the introduction of the productive system hid the most decisive and immediately applicable revolution in sugar plantations, namely the organization of slave labor and the regime of authority over slaves.

On beginning his journey in 1793, Arango was aware of the modest results obtained in Cuba from the license to import slaves directly from Africa. Increasing trade required capital and organizational experience. Instead of waiting to acquire such experience and knowledge, which would take time, Arango had the idea of importing it from those who best knew how to do it. How did the Portuguese ship owners operate? How did they manage to move such a large volume of resources to Brazil? And what about the British, who had established companies with at least as much capital as the most notable companies of the period? Why continue importing an overwhelming proportion of male slaves to form an instantly available workforce? Instead, why not seek a certain degree of balance with at least one-third female slaves and thus aspire to more through natural vegetative growth? In Barbados, he was surprised by the high number of female slaves. "The Barbadian experience," wrote Gloria García, "had a profound impact on Arango and transformed his vision of labour in the plantation, in addition to his understanding of the operation of the slave regime" (García 2005: 30).

In Jamaica, he managed to gather together the Cubans who were involved in smuggling Negroes from the Windward Isles, and he encouraged them to take more women. However, his ideas were met with jeers and objections. The cost of the crossing was the same, but the price paid for a female slave in Cuba was lower. The logic of the slave trader was implacable. The logic of the plantation owner, which was guided by the idea of prosperity and progress in the medium to long term, demanded reductions in the costs of replacing the labor force in the future. Attention also had to be paid to one of the requirements that the mother country had in fact imposed, namely the analysis of the causes that had led the prosperous colony of Saint-Domingue to become a dreadful disaster. Arango thus considered that the creation of family-based slavery offered the advantage of fulfilling the first expectation while improving the submissiveness of the slaves and the reducing the likelihood that they would attempt to run away. Ignored in Jamaica and by his countrymen, he began his experiment on his own sugar plantation, La Ninfa. It is not known whether or not he managed to obtain the desired results.

There was still a lot to learn about trading African slaves, and Baker & Dawson, the company that had been awarded previous contracts, could continue to show them how the factors operated, how to negotiate with ship owners and captains, and which transport conditions entailed the least possible loss.

What else did the most advanced nations have? Arango was aware that specialists had fled from Saint-Domingue, and in Jamaica he convinced several of them to move to Cuba to take up their activities once again. In fact, the engineer Esteban La Fayé, who arrived from Haiti in 1790, introduced the sugar mill with horizontal rollers, a system that was quickly adopted. However, in the years that followed, Arango systematically ignored the experience of the French planters who arrived from the neighboring island, most of whom had settled in the east of Cuba. They had developed the most productive *habitations* known at that time, and several of them recreated such complexes in the region of Santiago. Yet in around 1800, Santiago was practically a different country, and it did not appear later to become part of the history of Cuba's sugar and slave industries, according to the reports available. In 1803, Arango traveled to Guárico to witness the end of a world that had become an opportunity to launch Cuba and a cautionary bad example in social, but above all, in political terms. Arango contrasted the model of the good, compassionate slave owner with the example of the despised owner who was the author of his own misfortune (Piqueras 2010: 139–56). However, despite being based on the intensive exploitation of labor, the Franco-Dominican slave regime had managed to organize the use of land and to produce sugar efficiently.

Arango observed the progress being made. And among the things he observed, there were also situations that should preferably be avoided or that should be avoided at all costs. We are not referring here to the Navigation Acts, which he mentioned but failed to comment on and which gave the British merchant marine a monopoly in trade with the colonies; by contrast, he did mention the low customs tariffs paid on agricultural produce when it was exported. We are instead referring to sugar refineries. Arango visited one in England and was amazed by the installations and by the whiteness of the end product. In Cuba, sugar was called "white" even though it was not white, but a pale color. The country, he argued, would benefit by introducing the refining stage, which would increase the value of its exports. However, he considered the way in which the English had separated their possessions to be an error: The colonies did not have refineries, so the raw sugar was transported to the mother country to finish the process. In addition to the costs of loading and transportation, during the voyage the casks continued to leak sugar cane syrup, wasting an eighth of the load, and in addition, wasting the molasses, since there were no distilleries for the production of rum (Arango y Parreño 2005, 1: 245). It was an example of the colonial division of industry, which Cubans did not understand or preferred to ignore. Very soon, the "reintegration of the world sugar market" (Tomich 1990: 21–32) under British control and the industrial development of the United States demanded that same international division of production and the refining phase would be monopolized by new parent companies.

In Arango's line of reasoning, there was little competition between the mother country and the colony, since at the time of writing Spain had very few refineries, although the number was sufficient for the country's limited consumption of sugar cane. In this respect, he urged their installation, together with the initial phases of the manufacturing process in the sugar mill in Cuba, where the only thing that needed to be done was "to add three boilers, some earthenware moulds to filter the sugar and twelve or fourteen more Negroes." With regard to the costs, he compared England with Jamaica, adding that "here, a year's wages cost almost as much as the lifelong slavery of a black" (Arango 2005, 1: 245). The cost of a slave in Jamaica was £50, almost 600 pesos.

The proposal had a coherence ahead of its time and it foreshadowed the new colonial status he envisaged for the island: the sugar industry would remain entirely in the island's hands, although there was no objection to allowing the incorporation of Spanish merchants in the Peninsula; the producers should be free to export to conquer new markets, even if they had to grant concessions to the purchasing countries in terms of tax privileges for their vessels and to grant certain advantages to ships flying the Spanish flag. Concessions also had to be granted on the importation of equipment required for agriculture and the sugar industry; and low duty levels had to be established for staple foods whose supply from the mother country was insufficient or pushed up the price too much. Spain would have to be satisfied with tax revenue from customs duty: the more sugar was produced and exported and the higher the value, the more tax revenue would be received. It was, on the other hand, revenue that was easy to collect, a flow of funds that could be used to further the projects required by the island's economy and society and to bolster the royal treasury. Cuba could become a veritable treasure island for the treasury of the mother country if the proposed prosperity materialized. As soon as the intendant, Alejandro Ramírez, had put the treasury in order, the results were glaringly obvious and Cuba began to provide what it had never provided in the past: net proceeds and a balance against which orders of payment could be made, something that played an important role in the Spanish government's accounts during the 1830s.

A second table of opposing concepts applied to the world of the sugar plantation can be made by combining the different factors analyzed in *Discurso sobre la agricultura* (table 3.2, page 70).

After 1815, when sugar prices stabilized on the London market at the end of the revolutionary and Napoleonic wars and the double bonus of the Haitian Revolution and the disputes that conditioned Atlantic trade between 1796 and 1807 were lost, Cuban plantation owners made every effort to introduce the technological advances announced in 1792, which until that time had only been the subject of a small number of trials. Sugar had to be produced more efficiently and in larger quantities, since there was a large and growing foreign market. This meant fully adopting the concept of business and paying careful attention to performance, which in turn meant paying careful attention to the balance between costs and profits. On the other hand, the mass importation of African slaves and changes in their administration began around 1796. From the beginning of the period of free trade in Africans in 1789 until 1816, some 124,000 Africans were shipped to Cuba. During the five years that followed, the figure rose to 100,000 (Eltis et al. 1999).

Conceived in this way, progress on the island meant prosperity. It was a markedly hierarchical form of prosperity, first and foremost for the plantation-owning

Table 3.2. Opposing Applications in *Discurso sobre la agricultura*

	FOREIGN COUNTRIES	CUBA
Agriculture	Scientific cultivation: selection of plants +chemicals + farming tools	Ordinary farming
Manufacturing	Machinery	Artifacts
Driving force	Hydraulic, steam	Animal
Mill rollers	Iron	Wood with copper cladding
Reverberatory furnaces	Jamaican train	Spanish train
Skill level	Salaried technicians	Hired workers and certain special slaves
Production	Integrated process: planting, harvesting, manufacturing, packaging, warehouse, market	Phases with little coordination
Supply of labor	Direct from Africa, en masse	Subject to treaties and contracts with intermediaries
Replacement of labor	Trade and reproduction (percentage of female slaves)	Trade
Organization	Division of labor	Indifferent use of labor
Slaves	Economic governance	Simple control
Slavery	Productive, plantation	Productive + urban (servants, manumission)
Business	Performance, costs profits	Earnings, yield on capital invested

Source: Based on Arango (2005, 1: 144–226).

classes. In this respect, it laid the foundations for territorial, autonomous development that left production and trade in local hands. It *Cubanized* them, which was a specific form of "patriotism," of boosting the homeland's progress. Taxation, however, which had become an umbilical cord joining Cuba to the mother country, was reserved for Spain; together with that was bureaucracy. And with the latter came the ability to make political decisions regarding concessions to the economic interests of the Peninsula. On this point, it would be difficult to place pressure on the government in Madrid to obtain advantages. Intra-imperial trade favored control by traders from the Peninsula, together with their legions of employees. Arango's project for progress was, in all respects, unmistakably colonial, colonialist, and it tied Cuba to its condition as a colony. It introduced rationality and provided the division of functions in the mother country–colony axis, which to provide the expected profits, the dreamed-of happiness, had to avoid any violent upset of the status quo. This could be improved through agreements and new administrative and even political concessions, although in around 1803, with all eyes set on Haiti, Arango warned of the risk of a local assembly being elected by the main plantation owners. During his trip to Jamaica in 1794, Arango took an interest in the local system of government, but his conclusions never took the form of recommendations until 1811, when he rescued the idea in order to restrict the application of the liberal constitution drawn up in Cadiz. On the other hand, the campaign against slavery (which was on the increase when he visited London in 1793), together with the English and American abolition of the slave trade in 1807, shifted to a different level the political problem of the catastrophe that a nonnegotiated break with Spain would entail. Cuban slave traders, in need of Africans, required the international, political, and naval protection of the mother country to continue trading. After 1821, this dependency became much more important. The Spanish colonial government was aware of this. So was Arango (Piqueras 2012: 222–27).

In short, progress was all those things, in particular the last chapter mentioned above, which revealed the accumulation of produce and, as a result, of profits and capital, or to be more exact, the transformation of merchandise into money.

In both public and private life, the use of money in turn reveals the fruits of progress.

Notes

1. Regarding the position of de Gardoqui, see José Antonio Escudero (2001, 1: 513); for his effect on the reforms in *Actas de la Junta Suprema de Estado*, see Appendix 2 of the same book (2001, 2: 763–79); see also Piqueras (2009).

2. All the quotations in this work are our translations—JP, PE.

3. Arango y Parreño ([1829] 2005, 2: 330–32), extension of a letter from the previous year.

4. The model had been patented in London in 1767 by John Stewart, who published it in *A Description of a Machine or Invention to Work Mills, by the Power of a Fire-Engine, but Particularly Useful and Profitable in Grinding Sugar Canes*, a book which, according to Moreno, could be found in Nicolás Clavo's library in Havana, where Arango would have consulted it. See also B. W. Higman (2001: 149–51), which explains other adaptations promoted on the island, none of which worked on a regular basis.

5. On the abundance of firewood and its low price, see Reinaldo Funes Monzote (2004: 149ff.). Funes highlights that savings in wood as a result of the Jamaican train were, however, later balanced by a higher demand for firewood to heat the steam boilers and the Derosne train, which in turn required more cane to maintain a high output, to the detriment of the forests (2004: 127).

6. In 1838, Oliván could be found maneuvering to substitute Field Marshal Tacón, who had similar political views, at the service of the governor, the Count of Villanueva.

7. Eight of the fifteen sugar mills about which information is available were equipped with the Derosne system; two more were under construction with the aforementioned device.

Works Cited

Arango y Parreño, Francisco de. 2005. *Obras*. 2 vols. Havana: Imagen Contemporánea.

———. "Carta al Ministro de Justicia sobre la urgencia de que se establezca la Escuela de Química" (orig. 1829). Francisco Arango y Parreño. *Obras*. Vol. 2. Havana: Imagen Contemporánea, 330–32.

———. 2005. *Discurso sobre la agricultura de la Habana y medios de fomentarla* (orig. 1792). Francisco Arango y Parreño. *Obras.* Vol. 1. Havana: Imagen Contemporánea, 144–226.

———. 2005. "Manifiestos en defensa del informe al superintendente director general de tabacos de la isla de Cuba, en que se pidió la supresión de la factoría." *Obras.* Vol. 2. Havana: Imagen Contemporánea, 96–119.

———. 2005. "Representación al rey sobre la extinción del tráfico de negros y medios de mejorar la suerte de los esclavos coloniales" (orig. 1832). *Obras.* Vol. 2. Havana: Imagen Contemporánea, 334–423.

———. "Respuestas a los reparos." *Obras.* Vol. 1. Havana: Imagen Contemporánea, 199–226,

———. 2005. "Resultan grandes perjuicios de que en Europa se haga la fabricación del refino" (orig. 1794). *Obras.* Vol. 1. Havana: Imagen Contemporánea, 243–54.

———. 2005. "Sobre las noticias comunicadas por el Sr. Síndico D. Francisco de Arango y Parreño a la Junta de Gobierno del Consulado de Agricultura, Industria y Comercio de La Habana, adquiridas en el viaje que por encargo de S.M. ha hecho a Inglaterra, Portugal, Barbada y Jamaica." Francisco Arango y Parreño. *Obras.* Vol. 1. Havana: Imagen Contemporánea, 257–63.

Carrillo y Arango, Anastasio. 1862. *Elogio histórico del excelentísimo señor don Francisco de Arango y Parreño.* Madrid: Impr. Manuel Galiano.

Deerr, Noël. 1949. *The History of Sugar.* Vol. 1. London: Chapman and Hall.

Derry, T. K., and Trevor I. Williams. 1987. *Historia de la tecnología: Desde 1750 hasta 1900* (orig. 1960). Vol. 3(2). *A Short History of Technology: From the Earliest Times to A.D. 1900*). 9th ed. Madrid: Siglo XXI [Veintiuno] Ed.

Egorova, Olga V. 2011a. "A Mystery of One Havana Portrait: The First Steam Machine in Cuba." In *History of Machines for Heritage and Engineering Development,* edited by J. M. Portilla and Marco Ceccarelli. Dordrecht, Netherlands: Springer, 189–213.

———. 2011b. "En pos de las huellas de Betancourt: La primera máquina de vapor en Cuba." *Revista de Obras Públicas* 158/3517: 31–48.

Eltis, David, Stephen D. Behrendt, David Richardson, and Herbert S. Klein, eds. 1999. *The Trans-Atlantic Slave Trade: A Database on CD-ROM.* Cambridge, UK: Cambridge University Press. *http://www.slavevoyages.org.*

Escudero, José Antonio. 2001. *Los orígenes del Consejo de Ministros en España: La Junta Suprema de Estado.* 2 vols. Madrid: Complutense University.

Funes Monzote, Reinaldo. 2004. *De bosque a sabana: Azúcar, deforestación y medio ambiente en Cuba: 1492–1926.* Mexico City: Siglo XXI.

García, Gloria. 2005. "Tradición y modernidad en Arango y Parreño." Introduction to F. de Arango y Parreño, *Obras*. Vol. 1. Havana: Imagen Contemporánea, 1–56.

García de Arboleya, José. 1852. *Manual de la isla de Cuba: Compendio de su historia, geografía, estadística y administración*. Havana, Cuba: Impr. del Gobierno.

González-Ripoll Navarro, Mª Dolores. 2001. "Vínculos y redes de poder entre Madrid y La Habana: Francisco Arango y Parreño (1765–1837), ideólogo y mediador." *Revista de Indias* 61(222): 291–305.

———. 2002. "Dos viajes, una intención: Francisco Arango y Alejandro Olivan en Europa y las Antillas azucareras (1794 y 1829)." *Revista de Indias* 62(224): 85–102.

Higman, B. W. 2001. *Jamaica Surveyed: Plantations Maps and Plans of the Eighteenth and Nineteenth Centuries*. Jamaica: University of the West Indies Press.

Llombart, Vicent. 1992. *Campomanes, economista y político de Carlos III*. Madrid: Alianza.

Mintz, Sidney W. 1996. *Dulzura y poder: El lugar del azúcar en la historia moderna* (orig. 1985). (*Sweetness and Power: The Place of Sugar in Modern History*), translated by L. Moles Fanjul. Mexico City: Siglo XXI Ed.

Moreno Fraginals, Manuel. 1978. *El Ingenio: Complejo económico social cubano del azúcar*. 3 vols. Havana: Ed. de Ciencias Sociales.

Nisbet, Robert. 1981. *Historia de la idea de progreso*. Barcelona: Gedisa.

Pezuela, Jacobo de la. 1863–1866. *Diccionario geográfico, estadístico, histórico de la Isla de Cuba*. 4 vols. Madrid: Impr. Mellado.

Piqueras, José A. 2009. "Los amigos de Arango en la corte de Carlos IV." In *Francisco Arango y la invención de la Cuba azucarera*, edited by Mª Dolores González-Ripoll and Izaskun Álvarez. Salamanca, Spain: University of Salamanca, 151–66.

———. 2010. "La misión de Guárico y el nacimiento del buen esclavista cubano." In *El Caribe hispano de los siglos XIX y XX: Viajeros y testimonios*, edited by Josef Opatrný. Prague: Charles University, 139–56.

———. 2012. *La esclavitud en las Españas: Un lazo transatlántico*. Madrid: Libros de la Catarata.

Saco, José Antonio. 2001. *Memoria sobre caminos en la isla de Cuba*. In *Obras*, edited by E. Torres-Cuevas. Vol. 1. Havana, Cuba: Imagen Contemporánea.

Stewart, John. 1767. *A Description of a Machine or Invention to Work Mills, by the Power of a Fire-Engine, but Particularly Useful and Profitable in Grinding Sugar Canes*. s.l.: s.n.

Tomich, Dale W. 1990. *Slavery in the Circuit of Sugar: Martinique and the World Economy, 1830–1848*. Baltimore, MD: Johns Hopkins University Press, 21–32.

———. 2003. "The Wealth of Empire: Francisco Arango y Parreño, Political Economy, and the Second Slavery in Cuba." *Comparative Studies in Society and History* 45(1): 4–28.

———. 2009. "The Invention of the Cuban Sugarmill: Space, Time and Labor Management, 1820–1860." In *Francisco Arango y la invención de la Cuba azucarera*, edited by Mª Dolores González-Ripoll and Izaskun Álvarez. Salamanca, Spain: University of Salamanca, 133–49.

Antislavery and Nationalism on the Two Sides of the Atlantic

In Search of Forgotten Links between the Nineteenth-Century Americas and Europe*

Enrico Dal Lago

Within the contours of the now-established discipline of Atlantic history, scholars have always treated the movements for the abolition of slavery that arose in different countries and at different times between the 1820s and the 1840s as mostly discrete entities, with little relation to one another, unless they were part of the great Anglo-American cultural sphere. In a recent synthesis in transnational perspective, Daniel Rodgers has claimed that all the great nineteenth-century reform movements in the United States were related to movements happening elsewhere that were just as important as those happening here, if not more so. Despite these very promising premises, however, what Rodgers has really meant is that "[U.S.] Northern antislavery activists turned to England in search of connections, prestige,

*I wish to thank Gearoid O'Tuathaigh and Rafael Marquese for their valuable comments.

funds, and arguments" (D. Rodgers 2008: 149). In other words, as a number of studies have shown, William Lloyd Garrison's inspiration was "William Wilberforce's and Joseph Sturges' England."

There are still very few studies, then, that compare British and American abolitionist movements with equally radical activities opposing slavery that arose in Ireland or France. And yet, abolitionism was genuinely both trans-Atlantic and intercontinental, and the frequent contacts between all the major figures of abolitionism—who mostly participated at the 1840 World's Anti-Slavery Convention in London—testify to that. Even less known or studied is the fact that the international dimension of those who opposed slavery did not confine itself to abolitionist circles but often embraced other progressive causes—not only women's rights, but nationalism intended as a self-justified struggle against national oppression—on both sides of the Atlantic.

For true nineteenth-century progressives—individuals such as American William Lloyd Garrison, English William Henry Ashurst, Irish Daniel O'Connell, and Italian Giuseppe Mazzini—the fight against slavery was part of a much larger struggle that humankind had engaged in on its path to progress, a struggle that was to lead to the eventual victory over all retrogressive institutions throughout the Atlantic world. In the nineteenth century, the ideologies at the heart of antislavery—and particularly its radical variant, abolitionism—and nationalism came to be linked by a strong belief in progress. As a number of important studies—first and foremost those by David Brion Davis—have shown, since the second half of the eighteenth century, slavery had become, in the minds of many intellectuals and, in general, in public opinion, a backward, barbaric institution; as a consequence, emancipation and abolition stood as the very symbols of progress. Significantly, at around the same time, nationalism had also started to be linked to the idea of progress, when the idea of the modern nation—and the modern notion of citizenship rights derived from the Enlightenment—had spread throughout Europe as a consequence of the French Revolution (Davis 1984: xvi–xvii; Davis 1975; Bender 2006: 116–81).

After hailing the birth of Euro-American liberal nationalism during the revolutionary period and then the birth of independent nations in the area of the former

Spanish American Empire, in the first half of the nineteenth century Atlantic progressives stood at the forefront of the second abolitionist wave—the "new abolitionism"—a radical movement that, from the late 1820s onward, demanded "immediate" slave emancipation. Important victories in this sense were then being obtained with the abolition of slavery in several of the "new" Latin American countries—from Chile (1823) to Mexico (1829)—and with the abolition of Brazil's internal slave trade in 1831. In Latin America, the movement for the abolition of slavery had received an initial boost when the "Liberators" Simón Bolívar and José de San Martín had promised freedom to all the slaves who joined them in the struggle against the Spanish Empire. After independence had been achieved, especially those states that had smaller slave populations had proceeded to abolish slavery altogether, whether with or without compensation for slaveholders. As a result, a link between Latin American nationalism and abolitionism then was forged in the minds of many people—a link that would be constantly present, consciously or subconsciously, and appeared also in the ideas that characterized the different Atlantic progressives (Jackson 2005: 211–48).

Although aware of these crucial developments, in the 1820s and 1830s, Atlantic progressives focused specifically on the struggles for the "immediate" abolition of slavery in the British Empire and in the United States, all the while supporting in "thought and action" (Mazzini's famous slogan) the efforts at building liberal nations that were taking place in different parts of Europe. Thinkers and activists such as William Lloyd Garrison, William Henry Ashurst, Daniel O'Connell, and Giuseppe Mazzini—Atlantic progressives whom we may specifically qualify as nineteenth-century abolitionists, nineteenth-century nationalists, or both—believed that the twin struggles against slavery and against national oppression led humankind along an increasingly progressive path. National independence, political self-determination, and freedom from oppression were all linked in a great struggle whose aim was the progress of humankind toward a new, improved era based on the principles of liberty and justice. Put simply, for Atlantic progressives, there could be no real freedom—whether in the form of the abolition of slavery or in the form of national liberation—without equality, and thus, until that point of comprehensive freedom, humankind could not be said to be yet walking on its progressive path (Dal Lago 2012: 123–44).

Atlantic Abolitionism

As Carl Guarneri has noted, "antislavery agitators, like revivalist preachers before them, followed a northern transatlantic circuit, shuttling frequently between Britain and the United States to whip up popular support" (Guarneri 2007: 153). In other words, nineteenth-century American and British radical antislavery advocates, from William Lloyd Garrison to John Sturges, as supporters of the "new abolitionism," were ideal members of a sort of "abolitionist international"—to which both Irish and French antislavery activists belonged as well—whose roots lay deep in the Age of Revolution; specifically, there was a strong link with the transformations brought to the Atlantic world by the spread of the notions of human rights and democratic equality from the United States and France—passing through Haiti. The momentum had waned after reaction had succeeded revolutionary change on both sides of the ocean, and after the Atlantic economy had instilled new life into New World slavery after 1800. However, on one hand, as Christopher Schmidt-Nowara has noted, "the specter of the Haitian revolution haunted plantation belts" with the nightmare scenario of a bloody end to slavery (2008: 103); on the other hand, abolitionists were also quick to regroup and increase their pressure on various national governments for slave emancipation. Thus, we should see the succession of provisions for the abolition of slavery in the first half of the nineteenth century, first in Britain between 1833 and 1838, and then in France in 1848, partly as the crowning achievement of a single, Atlantic, radical abolitionist movement, with different national strands or varieties.

In the 1820s, in the United States, while most white antislavery advocates gathered in the American Colonization Society—founded in 1816—and supported plans for returning slaves to Africa after gradual emancipation had been achieved, African American activists pursued their own radical "new abolitionist" agenda, which had a distinctive Atlantic dimension. Thus, when in 1829 David Walker launched his famous *Appeal to the Colored Citizens of the World*, in which he denounced colonization and incited the slaves to take arms and rebel against their masters, he imagined himself to be speaking to all slaves of African descent in the Americas and beyond. Walker's crucial influence on William Lloyd Garrison's enunciation of "immediate, unconditional, uncompensated emancipation," from the very first issue of his radical antislavery journal *The Liberator* in January 1831—the conventional date of the beginning of the "new abolitionism" in the United States—is now well established in the historiography, and so is Walker's inspiration of Nat Turner and his revolt in Virginia in 1831. Equally crucial, though, was Walker's influence on Garrison's growing understanding of the Atlantic dimensions of the abolitionist struggle. Beginning with the 1832 foundation of the New England Anti-Slavery Society, in the decade of the 1830s, under Garrison's guidance, abolitionism in the United States grew to become a national movement, building at the same time close transatlantic links with supporters from other countries (Garrison 1831; Newman 2002: 1–15).

In 1833, sixty-two representatives of the three main abolitionist groups based in the United States met in Philadelphia and founded the American Anti-Slavery Society, the first national organization whose aim was the immediate emancipation of slaves in the U.S. South. Its "Declaration of Sentiments," written by Garrison, endorsed the Christian attitude of nonviolent resistance and condemned slavery as a violation of the principles stated in the Declaration of Independence and as a sin in the eyes of God. In an Atlantic world characterized by the increasing importance of both abolitionism and nationalism, Garrison and the "Garrisonians"—his supporters in the American Anti-Slavery Society—thought that reform was needed in several spheres; they therefore became involved in other movements for social reform in America, and they actively supported progressive national movements in Europe. The Garrisonians also welcomed women and, with their broader Atlantic view, supported them in a struggle that was fast becoming transnational in its modes and links. Then, in 1840, the "anti-Garrisonians"—opponents of Garrison—left to found the American and Foreign Anti-Slavery Society. The Garrisonians remained in control of the original American Anti-Slavery Society, which, even though diminished in numbers, for the next twenty-five years remained a far more radical and transnational organization, both in its principles and in its links with various Atlantic progressives (Davis 2007: 3–18).

Within the contours of Atlantic abolitionism, there were close links between Britain and the United States in the first half of the nineteenth century. For this reason, it is possible to see clear parallels in the development of antislavery sentiment and achievements in the two countries. In 1823, several antislavery activists, such as Thomas Clarkson, William Wilberforce, and Thomas Fowell Buxton, gathered to form an Anti-Slavery Society; its objectives were primarily to protect slaves from mistreatment, and, similarly to the American Colonization Society to achieve gradual emancipation. In 1830–1831, the London group of the Anti-Slavery Society broke away, embracing the "new abolitionism" and establishing the radical Agency Committee, whose goal, similar to that of the American Anti-Slavery Society in the United States, was to disseminate abolitionist literature and ideas, to encourage the signing of petitions to persuade people to endorse, in the words of Howard Temperley, the "immediate and unconditional emancipation of all the slaves in Britain's overseas possession" (Temperley 1997: 10). Partly as a result of this flurry of activity, partly fearing a massive slave insurrection, and partly influenced by the increasingly popular argument on the moral and economic superiority of free labor over slavery, in 1833 the British Parliament passed the Emancipation Act. The Act freed almost 800,000 slaves in the British colonies by August 1, 1834, but also compensated slaveholders, stating that ex-slaves had to undergo an unpaid "apprenticeship" period, originally of twelve, then six, and finally four years, so that actual emancipation really occurred in 1838.

According to David Brion Davis, "whatever compromises seemed necessary, Britons and many Americans hailed the Emancipation Act as one of the greatest humanitarian achievements in history" (Davis 2006: 238)—"the mighty experiment," as it was called. Yet even after the act was passed, the most radical abolitionist members of the Agency Committee regrouped in 1837 under the leadership of Joseph Sturges in the Central Negro Emancipation Committee, and their pressure on the British Parliament was crucial in reducing and then ending apprenticeship altogether. After winning the battle over "apprenticeship," it was this same group of individuals, still led by Joseph Sturges, that in 1839 founded the British and Foreign Anti-Slavery Society, whose declared aim was to work for the eradication of slavery throughout the world. To this end, in the following years, this society not only collaborated closely with antislavery activists in different countries, but also—in truly cross-continental fashion—organized the World's Anti-Slavery Conventions of 1840 and 1843, two major events in the story of Atlantic abolitionism and transatlantic links between the United States and Europe (Drescher 2002).[1]

In the context of Atlantic abolitionism, Ireland might appear as somewhat peripheral. Yet the nineteenth-century Irish culture of reform—especially as expressed by Daniel O'Connell—provided a crucial link between a well-established Anglo-American tradition of radical antislavery and an incipient tradition of European nationalism, or at the very least of recognition of the rights of oppressed nationalities. In fact, in Ireland the antislavery movement had been active since at least 1824; then, in 1829, Charles Orpen had founded the most important Irish antislavery society—the Dublin Negro's Friend Society—sympathetic to Britain and dominated by Protestants. In fact, even in 1830, Protestants and Quakers were a driving force behind Irish antislavery. However, it is also true, as Nini Rodgers states, that "from 1801 to 1833, from the passing of the Irish Act of Union to the abolition of slavery throughout the British Empire, within the Westminster Parliament, the issues of Catholic emancipation and African slavery were closely linked" (N. Rodgers 2005: 259). In this connection, it is worth noting that in 1823, when Thomas Fowell Buxton founded the Society for the Amelioration and Gradual Abolition of Slavery, O'Connell began the Catholic Association in Ireland.

Largely as a result of O'Connell's efforts and his widespread popular support, in 1829 the British Parliament granted Catholic emancipation by passing an act that allowed Irish Catholics the right to be elected as MPs without being forced to abjure their own confession. Eventually, the wave of reform that had started in the British Atlantic with Catholic emancipation reached its greatest momentum in 1833 with the abolition of slavery in the British Empire. Significantly, O'Connell had been at the very forefront of debates, both within and without Parliament, supporting wholeheartedly slave emancipation, and then, after 1833, calling for an end to the apprenticeship system for ex-slaves. Thus, as a Catholic, O'Connell was instrumental in creating an alternative abolitionist tradition in Ireland—one in which an embryonic form of Irish nationalism in its milder version of struggle for Catholic parliamentary representation was very much tied to the suppression of slavery as part of a general move toward progress through reform. To this end, not only did O'Connell place himself at the center of the transatlantic abolitionist networks, becoming a close friend of William Lloyd Garrison, but he also overcame his own initial diffidence and allied with the Protestant and Quaker abolitionists of the Dublin Negro's Friend Society, which in 1837 had changed its name to the Hibernian Anti-Slavery Society. By 1840, when the World's Anti-Slavery Convention took place in London, Irish abolitionists had all come to recognize that they were working toward the same goal (Riach 1976: 3–25).

From the perspective of Atlantic abolitionism, France provides an altogether different case. In fact, the French abolitionist tradition was as old as the 1788 foundation of the Société des Amis des Noirs. In 1794, the Jacobins had decreed the emancipation of slaves in the French colonies—partly as a response to the Haitian Revolution that had brought slavery to an end in St. Domingue—leading to the foundation of the short-lived Société des Amis des Noirs e des Colonies (1796–1799). In 1802, though, Napoleon had reinstated both the slave trade and slavery in the colonies. Thus—in a pattern that, starting from France, had then expanded to the rest of the Atlantic world in the Age of Revolutions—the abolition of slavery had become clearly linked to the construction of the nation, and specifically of a French democratic nation. Even though this link was forced underground during the Napoleonic and early Restoration period, it provided a lasting model, first for the national revolutions that led to the formation of abolitionist republics in Latin America in the 1810s and 1820s, and then for the national revolutions that would lead to democratic and antislavery governments both in France and in the rest of Europe during the 1830s and 1840s (Blackburn 1988: 161–264).

Starting from the 1820s, in their opposition to slavery, French abolitionists, both Protestant and Catholic, received inspiration and support from Britain, and in 1821 founded the mild, liberal-oriented, Société de la Morale Chrétienne, directed mainly toward ameliorating the lives of slaves, and against the slave trade. After the 1830 revolution, liberal Louis Philippe suppressed the slave trade, and then in France, as in Britain, the abolitionist movement focused its efforts on the emancipation of all the slaves in the colonies. In fact, in 1834, encouraged by British antislavery activists, French abolitionists founded the Société Française pour l'Abolition de l'Esclavage, headed by François Isambert. From the perspective of Atlantic abolitionism, this society was gradualist rather than immediatist. Still, its pressure on the French Parliament led to slave emancipation becoming again a truly national issue. In general, the French abolitionists began to embrace immediatism after 1845, and then more forcefully following 1847. Shortly afterward, in February 1848, a new revolution overthrew the July Monarchy of Louis Philippe and established a national French Republic, in whose government sat immediatist Victor Schoelcher; he did not waste time, and almost immediately decreed emancipation, freeing more than 235,000 slaves in the French colonies in the Caribbean (Pètrè-Grenouilleau 2008: 7–23; Jennings 2000).

The abolition of slavery in the French colonies in 1848, in turn, led the Dutch and Danish governments to take similar measures for slave emancipation in their New World colonies. Thus, 1848 is truly a significant date at the conclusion of an antislavery momentum caused by the rise of "new" abolitionist movements in the second half of the 1820s. In a relatively short time, the movements, located in the main countries that controlled the slavery business that held hundreds of thousands of people in bondage, had succeeded in putting in practice agendas that were mostly immediatist, exerting pressures on their respective national governments for immediate emancipation. Moreover, the abolitionist movements had become part of a wider Atlantic network, whose distant origins were in the Age of Revolutions. Now, through transatlantic contacts and connections—which reached their peak at the time of the World's Anti-Slavery Convention of 1840—these movements were able to spread the "new" immediatist version of abolitionism from the English- to the French-speaking areas of the Atlantic world and beyond.

In the words of Thomas Benjamin, "from the early 1830s to the late 1840s, most of the slave systems of the Caribbean, the center of the New World plantation complex, were destroyed by European reformers and by the slaves themselves" (Benjamin 2009: 641). Equally important was the fact that, in the process of destroying the slave systems, the national governments had acted under the pressure of national antislavery organizations. These organizations, even though they were part of an Atlantic abolitionist movement, acted in the name of overall programs of national reforms, thus linking once more the concept of creating democratic nation-states with abolishing slavery—as had already happened during the Age of Revolutions.

Atlantic Progressives and Their Causes

It is within the context of Atlantic abolitionism that we should situate the "thought and action" of the four Atlantic progressives—first and foremost William Lloyd Garrison, and then William Henry Ashurst, Daniel O'Connell, and Giuseppe Mazzini—to whom we referred at the beginning of this paper. What linked their activities and what led them, in three cases out of four, to become acquainted with one another, was in fact their shared belief in the centrality of the radical fight for the abolition of slavery as an indispensable condition for humankind's march toward progress. Thus, after emancipation had been achieved in the British Empire in 1834, they all either participated in or expressed their support for the international effort of the World's Anti-Slavery Conventions directed toward the abolition of slavery worldwide, and especially in the United States, where William Lloyd Garrison headed an increasingly radical and international abolitionist movement. At the same time, during the 1830s and 1840s, as national revolutions sprang up all over Europe, Atlantic progressives, already aware of the connection between radical antislavery and democratic nationalism, actively supported, in different ways and degrees—the most extreme of which was represented by Giuseppe

Mazzini's activities for the liberation of the Italian nation—the struggles for national self-determination.

Among Atlantic progressives, William Lloyd Garrison was certainly the one who provided the most indispensable link between the different strands and varieties of Atlantic abolitionism and European democratic nationalism. In 1831, in beginning an immediatist tradition in the United States, Garrison tightened the connections between American and British antislavery, creating the preconditions for an essential link between radical abolitionists—most of whom were immediatist—in both countries, as well as in Ireland and, later on, in France. On the other hand, it was Garrison's own increasingly universal vision of the problem of slavery that led him to broaden rapidly his view of immediate emancipation and consider it part of a general reform, first of American society, and then of the world at large, directed toward the elimination of all the obstacles to humankind's march toward progress (Garrison 1831). As early as 1833, in the American Anti-Slavery Society's "Declaration of Sentiments," Garrison showed that the fight for the abolition of slavery in the United States assumed also a universal value, since its ultimate success would have been a "triumph of JUSTICE, LIBERTY, and HUMANITY" (Garrison [1833] 2002: 300). After the 1840 separation from the American and Foreign Anti-Slavery Society, then, on one hand, Garrison tightened his links with Atlantic abolitionism, becoming a central figure in it also, through his participation at the World's Anti-Slavery Convention in London in 1840. On the other hand, Garrison became an increasingly vocal supporter for other equally radical reform movements, which he as a now-mature Atlantic progressive rightly saw as tightly linked to the cause of Atlantic abolitionism: the women's rights movement and democratic nationalism (Blackett 2008: 13–40).

As a result, Garrison became involved with the activities of the most important women's rights activists of his generation—several of whom he had welcomed into the American Anti-Slavery Society—and he also became acquainted with some of the most famous nationalist politicians and activists of the time, Daniel O'Connell and Giuseppe Mazzini. It is significant that Garrison became first acquainted with O'Connell and Mazzini as a result of their support for an absolutely uncompromising position—close to Garrison's own—on the immediate emancipation of the slave population in the United States; it is an important testimony to the way that the network of Atlantic abolitionism gathered activists from different countries and backgrounds fighting for similar ideals. In the course of the 1840s, Garrison continued to wholeheartedly support O'Connell's positions vis-à-vis the Irish question until the latter's death in 1847. Also, Garrison supported Mazzini's nationalist activities in Italy, particularly at the time of the 1849 Roman Republic, when Garrison went as far as to publish regularly in *The Liberator* William Henry Ashurst's reports on Mazzini's achievements in Rome (McDaniel 2013).

It was hardly a coincidence that Garrison's correspondent from Mazzini's Roman Republic for *The Liberator* was William Henry Ashurst, who then used to sign his articles under the pseudonym "Edward Search." Born in London and trained as a lawyer, during the 1830s Ashurst had become a follower of the utopian socialist ideas of Robert Owen, and through the publication of articles in different journals—notably *The Reasoner* and *The Spirit of the Age*—he had become known to British society as a political activist and a radical. It was in *The Reasoner* that Ashurst first used his Edward Search pseudonym, and he continued to use it throughout his life while following and reporting about different radical activities. Ashurst's daughter, Emily Venturi, author of a brief biography of her father as a quintessential Atlantic progressive, quoted him saying that "agitation is for the people that troubling of the water which produces health and vigor" (Venturi 1904: 6). And according to Matthew Lee, Ashurst's involvement in "feminism, anti-slavery, European (and especially Italian) nationalism and republicanism, secularism, and administrative reform paint the picture of a uniquely energetic and vigorous man" (Lee 2004).

After meeting William Lloyd Garrison at the 1840 World's Anti-Slavery Convention, Ashurst began a long-time friendship and collaboration on *The Liberator.* Thus he acted as an indispensable link between Atlantic abolitionism and other forms of radical activity, as well as between Atlantic progressives living on the two sides of the ocean and involved in parallel and connected causes. For the best part of twenty years, Ashurt's house in Muswell Hill in London became a meeting point on Sunday afternoons for an ever-larger group of radical activists,

Garrison and Mazzini among them; they were all nicknamed the "Muswell Hill brigade." Ashurst collaborated with Mazzini especially at the time of the 1849 Roman Republic, when he documented the events and dutifully reported back to Garrison, who regularly published in *The Liberator* his articles on Italy's situation, signed "Edward Search." Significantly, Ashurst died in 1853, while visiting Garrison and his fellow abolitionists in the United States, functioning as a link between Atlantic abolitionism and European radicalism and democratic nationalism up until the end (O'Connor 1998: 71–76).

Like William Henry Ashurst, Daniel O'Connell was trained as a lawyer, but he was also Irish and a Catholic land owner. After the 1801 Act of Union of Britain and Ireland, O'Connell threw himself body and soul into the fight for Catholic emancipation, eventually founding the Catholic Association in 1823. His nature as an Atlantic progressive showed in his political innovations, which became a model for subsequent Atlantic reform movements—particularly his campaign initiatives to mobilize the Irish people on an unprecedented mass scale. Between 1824 and 1828, through these mass campaigns, O'Connell put pressure on public opinion and eventually gained a parliamentary appointment and status as a European radical reformer and advocate of national rights. O'Connell's status, then, achieved Atlantic resonance with the British Parliament's 1829 passing of the Catholic Relief Emancipation Bill. Once in Parliament, throughout the 1830s and 1840s, O'Connell continued to fight for the improvement of conditions of the Irish Catholic population, notably through his long-term campaign for the repeal of the Act of Union—thus proving until the end to be a progressive reformer with the interests of the Irish nation at heart, but not a revolutionary nationalist like the members of the Young Ireland movement, who were active between 1842 and 1848 (Conzemius 1980).

What made O'Connell an Atlantic progressive was that, much like William Henry Ashurst, he provided an indispensable link between different causes that Atlantic progressives were pursuing on both sides of the ocean. In fact, O'Connell himself—nicknamed "The Liberator," like Bolívar and also Garrison's abolitionist paper—provided a model for Atlantic progressives to imitate. His involvement in progressive causes directed toward the amelioration of humankind's conditions—

explicitly, therefore, the conditions of both Irish Catholics and of American slaves—had resonance throughout the 1830s and 1840s, until his death in 1847. During this period O'Connell was a major figure in Atlantic abolitionism, and eventually he represented Ireland and the Hibernian Anti-Slavery Society at the World's Anti-Slavery Convention in London in 1840. Thus, ultimately O'Connell provided Atlantic progressives such as Garrison and Ashurst, whom he also knew, with a link not only between two different types of progressive causes in the Atlantic world—European (and specifically Irish) nationalism and Anglo-American abolitionism—but also between radical reform and the democratic means to achieve it (Kinealy 2010).

Giuseppe Mazzini had many features in common with Garrison, Ashurst, and O'Connell. Although the nature of Mazzini's Atlantic progressivism showed through his involvement in a variety of causes, Mazzini came to be identified very soon with the cause of Italian and European democratic nationalism. In 1831, from his exile in Marseille, Mazzini founded Young Italy and began publishing his paper *La Giovine Italia*, proclaiming publicly his commitment to the creation of an Italian "republic, one, indivisible" and to the "abolition of every aristocracy and privilege" (Mazzini 1966, 1: 325). Mazzini thus created a new tradition of democratic nationalism—one that was also to provide a successful model in Europe and beyond. When in 1834 he founded Young Europe, Mazzini acted as an intellectual and agitator whose grandiose vision for the future was to coordinate all democratic movements in Europe to create a continent of nations free from despotic regimes. Despite the repeated failures of his revolutionary programs, in his years of exile, mostly spent in London, Mazzini found himself surrounded by European and American activists, who admired him for both the breadth of his vision and his absolute ethical commitment (Sarti 2008: 275–98; Dal Lago 2013).

In London, Mazzini met Ashurst in 1844 and Garrison in 1846; he became life-long friends with them both. By the 1840s, Mazzini was well acquainted with the world of British and American reform and he had become a champion of radical causes; he was particularly well known among the main proponents of the Chartist movement, and their working-class radicalism influenced him deeply.

It was through British radical circles that Mazzini came in contact with Atlantic abolitionism, and he embraced it wholeheartedly. Thus, while he continued to work for the liberation of Italy and other oppressed nationalities in Europe, Mazzini also spoke out against slavery in radical abolitionist terms, comparing America's "black slaves" with Europe's "white slaves."Even more than O'Connell, then, he provided an effective link between Atlantic abolitionism and European nationalism. Ultimately, both American abolitionists and British reformers—and first and foremost Garrison and Ashurst—showed that they had understood the connection when they gave their unwavering support to Mazzini's failed attempt to establish the embryo of an Italian democratic republic in Rome in 1849 (Duggan 2008: 187–209).[2]

Each in his own way, Garrison, Ashurst, O'Connell, and Mazzini demonstrate the features that characterized mid-nineteenth-century Atlantic progressives. The basic feature they shared was their commitment, to varying degrees, to a number of different causes intended to ameliorate conditions for large sections of humankind. All were involved in movements that addressed in the most radical ways the most pressing problems related to inequality of race, gender, class, and national oppression: antislavery, women's rights, abolition of privileges, and democratic nationalism. However, we can also say that their involvement functioned at two different levels. On one hand, it was strictly related to the particular problems faced by the country—or "imagined" country—they belonged to, and thus it focused on the one movement, among all the movements, that addressed the most pressing national problem: abolitionism in the United States, abolitionism and social reform in Britain, Catholic emancipation in Ireland, and nationalism in Italy. On the other hand, the Atlantic progressives' international dimension, which resulted from the existence of established networks within Atlantic abolitionism and European nationalism, allowed them to see the specific problems of their nations as part of a broader set of problems that the entirety of humankind faced. This was ultimately the reason they collaborated in progressive causes: the fact that they all saw those causes as connected in a worldwide effort to uplift humankind to bring it along its rightful progressive path.

Atlantic Abolitionism and European Nationalism

The strength of the connections among the different abolitionist movements was tested at the World's Anti-Slavery Convention in London in 1840. There for the first time delegates and representatives of the abolitionist movements of Britain, the United States, and France gathered to discuss an agenda whose first objective was the abolition of slavery in the entire world. However, and despite different problems, the World's Anti-Slavery Convention ended up being much more than simply a celebration of Atlantic abolitionism; the issue of women's rights had an important part in it, and the presence of reformers involved in many different progressive causes other than abolitionism broadened its scope and resonance. Three of the four Atlantic progressives we have analyzed—all of them world-renowned public figures—participated in the convention, and the fourth supported it. This fact demonstrates the strong link between democratic nationalism, Atlantic abolitionism, and other reform movements. And if 1840 was the peak of transatlantic activity and ardor for Atlantic abolitionism, 1848 was doubtless the peak of continental embrace of European nationalism, since in 1848 nationalist movements sprang up almost everywhere in Europe, and most were democratic and aimed at establishing republican nation-states. These two events in these different years should be seen as parts of a common story, with links represented by the Atlantic progressives.

Realizing the importance of showing the world the strength of the connections of a united front of Atlantic abolitionism, in 1839 Quaker Joseph Sturges, head of the British and Foreign Anti-Slavery Society, had issued a general call for delegates for a World's Anti-Slavery Convention to be held in London the following year. In the words of Douglas Maynard, this "represented an attempt to strengthen and enlarge the crusade against slavery by drawing together into one combined effort the abolitionist forces of the mid-nineteenth century" (Maynard 1960: 452). Though the proceedings list more than 500 delegates, the actual attendance was 409. Understandably, the majority of the delegates—about 80 percent—were British abolitionists; 50 delegates were from Scotland, Ireland, and the British Caribbean, 40 from the United States, 4 from France, and 1 each from Haiti, Spain, and

Switzerland. The disproportionate number of British participants, even compared to the American delegation, has led some scholars to question the world significance and resonance of the convention, but the truth is that, from the perspective of Atlantic abolitionism, regardless of the actual numbers, the leading activists were all present, and they deliberated together for the first time, making decisions that would affect the course of the struggle against slavery worldwide.

The convention lasted thirteen days—from June 12 to 25, 1840—and, in general, saw reports presented about slavery in different areas of the world. Discussions were held over the best strategies to fight slavery. It was decided that the strategy should focus on increased use of the press and the publication of pamphlets, together with the presentation of antislavery resolutions to the governments of countries in Europe and the Americas that supported or allowed slavery. From the first day, the issue of the participation of women catalyzed the group's attention, especially because of the number of female delegates appointed from the United States—among them Lucretia Mott, a leading female abolitionist from Pennsylvania and a staunch advocate of women's rights in America. In the end, however, women were not allowed to take an active part, but only to assist from the balcony of the hall where the convention was held, but the controversy did much to stir public opinion regarding the link between the fight against slavery and the struggle for women's rights. The controversy was heightened by the decision of William Lloyd Garrison and his delegation to join the women on the balcony as a sign of protest (Kennon 1984: 244–66).

The World's Anti-Slavery Convention signaled the peak of Atlantic abolitionism. Though the convention had enormous repercussions on public opinion, and its success led to a second convention in London in 1843, the main issue that the convention addressed—slavery in the United States—continued to exist, with varying fortunes, for the following two decades. Although Atlantic abolitionism and collaboration and links were less effective during the 1850s and 1860s, the internal situation of the United States changed dramatically, leading to the centrality of slavery in the political conflict between northern and southern states. Garrisonian nonresistant abolitionism was left aside, while radical abolitionists such as John Brown engaged in direct, violent action against slaveholders. In the 1840s and 1850s, a series of moderate antislavery coalitions came to increasingly express the political views of a majority of voters in the North. The last of these coalitions—the Republican Party—saw the rise to prominence of Abraham Lincoln and then his election to the presidency of the United States, an event that led to the Civil War, and eventually, to the Emancipation Proclamation of January 1, 1863, and thus the end of American slavery altogether (Stewart 1996: 151–80).

If the World's Anti-Slavery Convention had signaled the high tide of Atlantic abolitionism in 1840, it was the European-wide Revolution of 1848—the "Springtime of the People"—that signaled the high tide of European nationalism. Even though scholars have rarely connected the two movements, the truth is that the recognition of oppressed nationalities, and the democratic demands that national revolutionaries voiced in different countries in Europe in 1848–1849, were very much in line with what Atlantic progressives involved in radical antislavery activities thought as the indispensable requirements for human progress. Thus, according to Christopher A. Bayly, while "political and nationalist demands . . . were at the forefront of the intentions of the educated participants . . . the leaders of 1848 demanded suffrage reform and self-determination," and, therefore, "the language of the rights of man and the invocation of the revolutionary tradition" were very much at the center of political action (Bayly 2004: 158). This language had its distant roots in the principles set out during the Age of Revolutions on both sides of the Atlantic, even though, in the European case, the reference to the French Revolution and its legacy was much more direct.

At the same time, there is little doubt that the actual language the European revolutionaries used to voice their demands for national self-determination and suffrage reform was inherited directly from the struggle against slavery and from Atlantic abolitionism. The expressions that characterized the discourses on national freedom were borrowed from the speeches and pamphlets that talked about human freedom. For Atlantic progressives such as Garrison, Ashurst, O'Connell, and Mazzini, the link between slavery's abolition and national self-determination was almost self-evident. For this reason, they were actively involved in different progressive causes, and especially in the radical antislavery cause, through their participation in Atlantic abolitionism, while also supporting also European democratic nationalism. Thus, when the 1848 European Revolutions began (without O'Connell, who had died in 1847 after seeing Ireland strangled by the Great Famine and England taken over by the Chartist movement), Garrison and Ashurst enthusiastically sustained Europe's national movements from the columns of their papers and in their speeches, and Mazzini became a protagonist in the nationalist struggles in the continent. In rapid succession, between January and October 1848, movements for national self-determination and suffrage reform broke out in Sicily, Naples, Paris, Frankfurt, Berlin, Vienna, Prague, Budapest, Venice, and Rome, enveloping the entire continent in a massive revolutionary wave. And to be sure, the link between national self-determination, democratic government, and the abolition of slavery became even clearer. It was sealed once and for all when the new democratic government that established the French Republic in February 1848 decreed the emancipation of all the slaves in the French colonies (Roberts 2009).

The struggle for national self-determination in Italy, where Mazzini hoped to establish a democratic republic, prompted particularly sympathetic reactions from all the Atlantic progressives. Mazzini himself was actively involved in the revolution that led to the formation of the Roman Republic, and he guided the its government for a few months between March and July 1849, leading it, in the process, to issue a democratic constitution that reversed centuries of papal abuse, abolished the Inquisition and ecclesiastical privilege, and protected freedom of thought and religion. Even though the Roman Republic ended tragically, Mazzini earned the admiration of both his fellow European revolutionaries and the American radicals; Garrison himself did not miss any opportunity to magnify Mazzini's achievements, publishing the carefully documented articles written by William Henry Ashurst. In truth, though, after 1849 Mazzini became more and more isolated, as fewer and fewer Italian patriots were convinced of the possibility—and some even of the necessity—of building a democratic republic. Thus, throughout the 1850s and 1860s, a moderate solution to the Italian problem—one with the House of Savoy at the head of a unified and free Italian monarchy—became increasingly popular; and eventually it became a reality when Victor Emmanuel II proclaimed the Kingdom of Italy in March 1861, while Mazzini, holding to his republican convictions, again went into exile (Riall 2009).

The American Civil War concluded with the emancipation of all the slaves in the southern United States; Italy had become a free nation only four years earlier. In 1865, only the youngest two of the four Atlantic progressives we have treated, Garrison and Mazzini, were still alive. Garrison obtained his ultimate victory with slave emancipation in the United States, but Mazzini saw his dream of a democratic republic in Italy—and beyond that of a communion of democratic republics in Europe—pushed aside by the emergence of an Italian monarchy. Still, the formation of a liberal Italian nation, almost contemporary with the reunification of a wholly free United States, concluded symbolically a long era of democratic struggles that had started with the formation of the "new" abolitionist movements in the late 1820s and early 1830s. By the 1860s, slave emancipation and national self-determination had become part of a distinctively Western and Atlantic tradition of freedom, though in many ways a less radical tradition than the one Atlantic progressives had worked to create and sustain a few decades earlier—first through the network of Atlantic abolitionism and then through support for European democratic nationalism.

Conclusion

The "entangled histories" of the lives of Atlantic progressives show how much it is possible to gain from the analysis of American, British, and French abolitionism, and Italian and European nationalism in a broader, comparative perspective. The Atlantic progressives' networks built on established connections that dated to the Age of Revolutions, and their fundamental beliefs had been shaped by a commitment to the ideals expressed first in the American and French Revolutions. But from the 1820s onward, Atlantic progressives gathered around a "new" view of the struggle against slavery, and by supporting an immediatist, radical version of abolitionism, they discovered that radical activists—not just abolitionists, but also democratic nationalists—shared some of their most profound beliefs in both the United States and Europe. Atlantic progressives such as William Lloyd Garrison were at the forefront of radical activities aiming to abolish slavery in the United States, while Atlantic progressives such as William Henry Ashurst were involved in a variety of reform movements—from abolitionism to women's rights—in Britain. At the same time, Atlantic progressives such as Daniel O'Connell were at the forefront of movements aiming to ameliorate the conditions of the Catholic Irish population through parliamentary reform, and Giuseppe Mazzini fought a democratic nationalist battle to create an Italian republic.

What united all these efforts was the common unwavering belief in progress, and in the ideal that all the causes that led to humankind's gains in terms of human rights were self-justified struggles, for they allowed more people to share in the benefits that progress inevitably brought. It was a highly teleological view, but also one that succeeded in creating the preconditions for the creation of a large international and transatlantic movement for freedom, which reached its peak in the 1840s, first with the World's Anti-Slavery Convention in London in 1840, and then with the European revolutionary movements of 1848–1849. In both cases, the networks created by Atlantic progressives showed their strength either through the direct participation or through their firm support for momentous events in the name of common ideals. Only by looking at these premises it is possible to understand how, then, in the 1860s, slave emancipation in the United States and the creation of a liberal Italian nation in Europe were events that had a truly Atlantic dimension.

Notes

1. It should be noticed that the British and Foreign Anti-Slavery Society had little success in fighting the Atlantic slave trade—much of which was illegal. This was especially true in Brazil and Cuba, where British companies and investments played a crucial role in sustaining slavery.

2. It is worth noticing, though, that Mazzini did not support O'Connell's battle for the repeal of the 1801 Act of Union between Britain and Ireland.

Works Cited

Bayly, Christopher A. 2004. *The Birth of the Modern World, 1780–1914: Global Connections and Comparisons*. Oxford, UK: Blackwell.

Bender, Thomas. 2006. *A Nation among Nations: America's Place in World History*. New York: Hill and Wang.

Benjamin, Thomas. 2009. *The Atlantic World: Europeans, Africans, Indians and their Shared History, 1400–1900*. New York: Cambridge University Press.

Blackburn, Robin. 1988. *The Overthrow of Colonial Slavery, 1776–1848*. London: Verso.

Blackett, Richard J. M. 2008. "'And There Shall Be No More Sea': William Lloyd Garrison and the Transatlantic Abolitionist Movement." In *William Lloyd Garrison at Two Hundred*, edited by James B. Stewart. New Haven, CT: Yale University Press, 13–40.

Conzemius, Victor. 1980. "The Place of Daniel O'Connell in the Liberal Catholic Movement of the Nineteenth Century." In *The World of Daniel O'Connell*, edited by Donal McCartney. Dublin: Mercier Press.

Dal Lago, Enrico. 2012. *American Slavery, Atlantic Slavery, and Beyond: The U.S. "Peculiar Institution" in International Perspective*. Boulder, CO: Paradigm Publishers.

———. 2013. *William Lloyd Garrison and Giuseppe Mazzini: Abolition, Democracy, and Radical Reform*. Baton Rouge: Louisiana State University Press.

Davis, David Brion. 1975. *The Problem of Slavery in the Age of Revolution, 1770–1823*. Ithaca, NY: Cornell University Press.

———. 1984. *Slavery and Human Progress*. New York: Oxford University Press.

———. 2006. *Inhuman Bondage: The Rise and Fall of Slavery in the New World*. New York: Oxford University Press.

———. 2007. "Declaring Equality: Sisterhood and Slavery." In *Women's Rights and Transatlantic Slavery in the Era of Emancipation*, edited by Kathryn Kish Sklar and James B. Stewart. New Haven, CT: Yale University Press), 3–18.

Drescher, Seymour. 2002. *The Mighty Experiment: Free Labor versus Slavery in British Emancipation* (New York: Oxford University Press.

Duggan, Christopher. 2008. "Giuseppe Mazzini in Britain and in Italy: Divergent Legacies, 1837–1915." In *Giuseppe Mazzini and the Globalisation of Democratic Nationalism*, edited by C. A. Bayly and Eugenio Biagini. Oxford, UK: Oxford University Press, 187–209.

Garrison, William Lloyd. 1831. "Editorial," *The Liberator*, January 1.

———. 1831. "To the Public," *The Liberator*, January 1.

———. 2002. "The American Antislavery Society's Declaration of Sentiments" (orig. 1833). In *Slavery and Emancipation*, edited by Rick Halpern and Enrico Dal Lago. Oxford, UK: Blackwell.

Guarneri, Carl. 2007. *America in the World: United States History in Global Context*. Boston: McGraw-Hill.

Jackson, Maurice. 2005. "The Rise of Abolition." In *The Atlantic World, 1450–2000*, edited by Toyin Fayola and Kevin Roberts. Bloomington: Indiana University Press, 211–48.

Jennings, Lawrence C. 2000. *French Anti-Slavery: The Movement for the Abolition of Slavery in France, 1802–1848*. New York: Cambridge University Press.

Kennon, Donald R. 1984. "An Apple of Discord: The Woman Question at the World's Anti-Slavery Convention." *Slavery & Abolition* 5: 244–66.

Kinealy, Christine. 2010. *Daniel O'Connell and the Anti-Slavery Movement: "The Saddest People the Sun Sees."* London: Pickering & Chatto.

Lee, Matthew. 2004. "Ashurst, William Henry." In *Oxford Dictionary of National Biography*, edited by H. C. G. Matthew, B. Harrison, and L. Goldman. Oxford: Oxford University Press. www.oxforddnb.com.

Maynard, Douglas H. 1960. "The World's Anti-Slavery Convention of 1840." *Mississippi Valley Historical Review* 47: 452–71.

Mazzini, Giuseppe. 1966. "Istruzione generale della Giovine Italia." In *Scrittori politici dell'Ottocento*, 1: *Giuseppe Mazzini e i democratici*, edited by Franco Della Peruta. Milan: Ricciardi, 325–30.

McDaniel, W. Caleb. 2013. *The Problem of Democracy in the Age of Slavery: Garrisonian Abolitionists and Transatlantic Reform*. Baton Rouge: Louisiana State University Press.

Newman, Richard. 2002. *The Transformation of Abolitionism: Fighting Slavery in the Early Republic*. Chapel Hill: University of North Carolina Press.

O'Connor, Maura. 1998. *The Romance of Italy and the English Political Imagination*. New York: St. Martin's Press.

Pètrè-Grenouilleau, Olivier. 2008. "Abolitionnisme et democratisation." In *Abolir l'esclavage: Un reformisme à l'èpreuve: France, Portugal, Suisse, XVIIIe–XIXe siècles*, edited by Olivier Pètrè-Grenouilleau. Paris: Presses Universitaires de Rennes.

Riach, Douglas C. 1976. "Daniel O'Connell and American Anti-Slavery." *Irish Historical Studies* 20: 3–25.

Riall, Lucy. 2009. *Risorgimento: The History of Italy from Napoleon to Nation-State*. New York: Palgrave Macmillan.

Roberts, Timothy M. 2009. *Distant Revolutions: 1848 and the Challenge to American Exceptionalism*. Charlottesville: University of Virginia Press.

Rodgers, Daniel T. 2008. "Worlds of Reform." In *America on the World Stage: A Global Approach to U.S. History*, edited by Gary W. Reichard and Ted Dickson. Urbana: University of Illinois Press, 147–57.

Rodgers, Nini. 2005. *Ireland, Slavery, and Anti-Slavery, 1612–1865*. New York: Palgrave.

Sarti, Roland. 2008. "Giuseppe Mazzini and Young Europe." In *Giuseppe Mazzini and the Globalisation of Democratic Nationalism, 1830–1920*, edited by C. A. Bayly and Eugenio Biagini. Oxford, UK: Oxford University Press, 275–98.

Schmidt-Nowara, Christopher. 2008. "Empires against Emancipation: Spain, Brazil, and the Abolition of Slavery." *Review* 31(2): 101–19.

Stewart, James B. 1996. *Holy Warriors: The Abolitionists and American Slavery*. New York: Hill and Wang, 151–80.

Temperley, Howard R. 1997. "Abolition and Antislavery Movements: Great Britain." In *Macmillan Encyclopedia of World Slavery*, edited by Paul Finkelman and Joseph Miller. New York: Simon & Schuster Macmillan.

Venturi, Emily Ashurst. 1904. "W. H. Ashurst: Brief Record of his Life." In *Mr. Morris' 80th Birthday Celebration: Report of Proceedings at Banquet, Letters of Regret, &c., with a Brief Record of the Life of William Henry Ashurst*. London: Hepburn & Sons.

African Labor in Guyana and the Expansion of the Second Slavery

Wazir Mohamed

Historical accounts that consider why the sugar industry of British Guiana did not expand at the same rate as that of Cuba are derived from Eric Williams's (1945: 361) explanation that British Guiana "passed too late into the possession of the British Crown." British Guiana became a colony of Great Britain in 1803, a mere four years before the slave trade was abolished in the British Empire. This robbed the colony of its necessary complement of slave labor, and accounts for the problems it encountered in the first half of the nineteenth century as it completed the transition from a multicrop (coffee, sugar, and cotton) colony to a monocrop sugar colony between 1803 and 1850 (Williams 1945: 360–65). However, the overriding factor governing this transition may have been the changes in the world economy and the need to produce competitive products. The reorganization of the economy surrounding sugar production was related to the absence of slave labor, which became even more scarce after the abolition of the slave trade (1807) and the formal emancipation of slaves (1838). Most historical accounts of this period center their analysis on the labor shortage theory. This emphasis shapes the discussion of Guiana's lack of development around the relative absence of available labor to match its inherent capacity, based on available land (Williams 1945; Adamson 1972; Mandle 1973). This theory does not account for the reasons that, despite the labor shortage, Guiana emerged as one of the new sugar colonies, albeit a minor producer, while its counterparts in the Anglophone Caribbean, with the exception of Trinidad and Tobago, experienced decline in their sugar plantation works. In Guiana, the decline of slave labor over the period 1807–1838 was matched by ever-increasing production of sugar.[1]

The point of departure for analysis of Guiana's sugar industry is the counterpoint between the decrease in the number of slaves during the period 1807–1838 and the increases in sugar production and the output of slave labor. Hence, while the number of available slaves declined from an average of 100,000 in 1812 to 82,284 by 1838 (Farley 1956: 62), sugar production increased from the low of 1,410 tons in 1804 to 16,521 tons in 1815, 62,272 tons in 1827, and 54,488 in 1833, the beginning year of the period of slave emancipation in the British colonies (Deerr 1949, 1: 193–204). Some weight must be accorded to the labor shortage theory, but this theory does not fully account for the factors that led to the phenomenal increases in sugar production as the availability of labor declined. Further, the labor shortage theory does not account for why Guyana, a former slave colony in the shadow of abolition and emancipation, rose as a sugar producer during the expansion of the second slavery in Cuba, Brazil, and the United States. Finally, it does not account for British Guiana's distinct social and economic history, despite its common political history with the other colonies of the British West Indies. Even though British Guiana suffered from the labor shortage, which at the time should have been potentially more devastating to it than to its Anglophone counterparts, except the island of Trinidad and Tobago, its sugar economy did not wither and decline. The Guiana story is more complicated than the labor shortage theory admits and cannot be fully understood only from the perspective of the shortage of labor.

Arguments related to the scale of British Guiana's sugar works, and its competitive capacity with Cuba, have so far been related to the volume of sugar produced. Although volume has importance in historical social analysis, it should not take the place of other regional comparisons. It also should not take the place of local circumstances and opportunities that gave available capital some competitive edge over labor. As Williams (1945) rightly establishes, British Guiana's labor problem compounded its inability to become as developed as Cuba. However, as he admits, the labor shortage presented problems, but it did not hinder or prevent the expansion into sugar. Rather, it limited the extent and scale of expansion. This is an important point of departure. British Guiana thus presents the historical observer with the twin problem of association and dissociation with the political, economic, and social history of its Caribbean counterparts. Because it is a former British colony, historians have tended to lump British Guiana with countries with similar economic and historical outcomes, such as Jamaica, Barbados, and the countries of the Anglophone Caribbean.[2] The foundation for this historical structuring can be found in the works of Lowell Ragatz, especially in *The Fall of the Planter Class in the British West Indies* (1928), and also in the works of Eric Williams, especially in the article "The Historical Background of British Guiana's Problems" (1945).

This approach does not account for the global and regional impact of the second slavery on the condition of labor in British Guiana. Sugar's expansion occurred despite the labor supply issue. This was due to the fusion of global factors (the push for regional specialization in the production of commodities—the new commodity frontier) with such local factors as the environment and ecology (Mohamed 2008: 87–154). In the new global context of regional specialization in commodity production driven primarily by the second slavery, Guiana transitioned from multicrop commercial agriculture to the monocrop sugar industry. Of the three products in its arsenal in 1803, ecologically and environmentally determinant conditions favored the transition to sugar.[3] The harsh physical environment provided the spatial context for sugar to thrive and develop, not only because of soil fertility and the availability of flat land, but more importantly, because it afforded the planter class the opportunity for physical dominance over labor (I have developed this point more thoroughly in Mohamed 2008: 93–107).[4] Against this background, plantation owners, trapped between the lack of renewed labor supplies and the need to eke out returns on their investment in land and slaves, engaged in the protracted consolidation of land and labor. Coffee and cotton plantations were either abandoned or converted into sugar works. All available labor (slaves) was concentrated in the consolidated sugar plantations that emerged. Of significance was the way in which global factors such as the increased demand for sugar fuelled the second slavery, which in turn affected the reorganization of land locally to address the problem of the lack of labor supply. The most remarkable aspect of this history was the manner in which sugar commanded and controlled life and habitation, and hence the total control the planter class developed over slaves in the era of antislavery, abolition, and the clamor for emancipation within the British Empire.

It should be noted that the second slavery is a factor not considered as shaping the everyday living conditions of labor in nineteenth-century British Guiana. I do not intend to spend much time discussing the parameters of the second slavery, because this has been adequately discussed in other places, especially, and forcefully, by Dale Tomich (1994: 56–74). Rather, my concentration is on the relevance of the second slavery as an important factor that helped to shape the conditions of labor—more precisely, the renewed regimentation and oppression of slave labor—that was carried out with impunity during the period of transition to the monocrop sugar economy. Above all, I am concerned with how the second slavery acted as the backdrop of this transition, and how the planter class managed to get more work out of the declining labor force.

Local in the Global: Second Slavery in Context

The conditions of life of African slave labor in Cuba and in other places employing slave labor in the sugar production process had a direct bearing on the conditions of life of African slaves on the Guianese sugar plantations. The second slavery was not just an external stimulus, it was the global, external influence that acted as the corollary to the imposition of the new draconian regimes of labor regimentation in British Guiana after 1807.[5] The second slavery served as the standard for labor productivity that influenced the imposition of new labor regimes between 1807 and 1838, the slave period. These regimes, as I explained in an earlier work (Mohamed 2008), were precipitated and supported through postemancipation land and immigration acts, both of which served as mechanisms limiting labor's mobility in the era of liberal freedom. Hence, although it may be true that all history is local, the history of such local spaces is constructed by the relations between labor and capital required for engagement in whichever political economic network each local space engages. Having taken the path to produce sugar, the only option open for Guiana was to contend and compete with the second slavery, or the spaces engaged in sugar production that employed the use of slave labor. For this reason, the second slavery played a very significant role in shaping the relations between labor and capital that developed during the course of the nineteenth century. Slavery in Cuba, the dominant sugar producer of the nineteenth century, through the development of free trade in sugar, had a direct impact on the conditions and outcome for the laboring population of Guiana.[6] As documented by several scholars, including Alan Adamson (1972) and Emilia Viotti da Costa (1994), as the sugar industry was being formed between 1800 and 1838, and as it grew and developed after 1838, distinct spatial expressions of inequality between the laboring population and the owners of capital formed in the colony. Thus, though Guiana was never able to match the might of the Cuban *ingenio*, the fact that sugar became the motor of its economic, political, social, and cultural future was directly related to overexploitation of slave labor. Guiana was not a blank slate upon which history was being constructed (Viotti da Costa, 1994: 43); its economic, political, and social history after 1800 was complicated by the implications of global change, which gave rise to antislavery in the British Empire, the death of mercantilist trade, the beginnings of free trade, and the extension of slavery outside the bounds of Britain's political empire.

Guiana is a classic anomaly. In the period of abolition it was being primed for economic takeoff. Colonial capital investments in the colony were basically caught completely unprepared. At the time of abolition and the global economic ferment, Guiana was in the midst of becoming an investment colony for British capital fleeing from the worn out and declining older British colonies of the Caribbean (Williams 1945: 363–69; Farley 1956: 43). It possessed an abundant natural endowment of flat, fertile, arable land capable of producing sugar competitively, but it lacked a resident labor supply, and was incapable of attracting and recruiting fresh labor.[7] Inability to recruit the required amount of slave labor trapped British capital in the colony. As Rawle E. G. Farley (1956: 61) emphasizes, "investment, even allowing for exaggeration, had run far ahead of labor supply." The overextension of British capital in land and holdings that occurred between 1798 and 1805 was astounding. While the total acreage under cultivation in Demerara in 1798 was 65,279 acres, a further 1,693,194 acres (Farley 1956: 61) was acquired in the same year by British investors. The major roadblocks for investors were the political control exercised by the Dutch until 1803, and the slow pace at which the Dutch West India Company dealt with economic expansion and the supply of slave labor. The differences between Dutch and British plantation culture added further complications for the planter class as they attempted to address the challenges of the transition to sugar in the era of abolition.

This problem is best understood through attention to the transition from Dutch to British colonialism, and the transformation of plantation life as plantations shifted from cotton and coffee to sugar. This culture is best described in the work of Henry Bolingbroke, in which he explained that the Dutch dealt with plantation life differently than the British (1941: 23, 207). The Dutch, who were in control of the colony for almost 200 years, were leisurely in their pursuit of profit, while the British were more entrepreneurial. The Dutch were "old school" colonists who "seemed to aspire to a competency not to a fortune." Bolingbroke observed these differences in approach as the changeover was taking place from Dutch to British rule in the interregnum period of 1796–1802. Having witnessed this changeover firsthand, he explained that the British planters introduced "as much cultivation in one year as a Hollander would accomplish in four . . . the one dashes off and prepares a hundred acres while the other is content with twenty-five." In Bolingbroke's view, the lack of entrepreneurial urgency on the part of the Dutch placed Guiana at a disadvantage in the period of transition to British rule. Furthermore, the difference in culture and approach to plantation life and to expansion underscored why the British inherited a major disparity between available labor and the colony's need. As the British wrestled with the construction of the new sugar economy in Guiana, their dilemma was not only inherited culture, but also the disparity between land and labor.

Having been prevented by the abolition act from importing the required quantities of slave labor, and faced with increased opposition from the planter class in the older Caribbean colonies, British Guiana was forced to reorganize to remain competitive. British capital, already overextended in land and holdings in Guiana, was thus caught in a "pincer movement" of new market forces that produced the free trade era and global competitiveness in commodity production. In the new context of global competitiveness, to maximize the productivity and profitability of the colony, coffee and cotton production gave way to sugar. Market forces propelled British Guiana into the new commodity frontier.

By 1850 Guiana was in an unenviable position, midway between the past, represented by the decline of sugar in the old British colonies of the Caribbean, and the future, represented by Cuba. Significant here is the manner in which the shift in relations of control and power within the world economy was manifested at the local level in the way land and labor were reorganized. The level of labor and land reorganization followed the history of sugar as it evolved in Guiana after the British takeover. Sugar monopolized specific land sets (areas), and as this took place, labor became regimented and concentrated within the specified land sets (consolidated plantations). Transformation of the culture of sugar production and manufacture from that point influenced a similar kind of transformation in the organization of labor. As land was consolidated into larger holdings and concentrated in fewer and fewer hands, the available labor was made to fit the requirement for the expansion of sugar.

Hence, during the course of the nineteenth century, as land was consolidated, labor was regimented. This resulted in phenomenal increases in production per slave. With a slave population averaging 75,000 in 1804, production was 1,410 metric tons; this was equivalent to average sugar production output per slave of 41 pounds per year. On the other hand, with an average slave population of 100,000 in 1815, production was 16,521 metric tons; this was equivalent to average annual sugar production output per slave of 330 pounds. By 1838, the year of emancipation, slave output had risen to 1,282 pounds per slave per annum. If these figures are compared with Cuban production during the similar period, we find that the average production per Cuban slave in 1815 was approximately 501 pounds and this rose to approximately 903 pounds in 1841, and 4,361 pounds by 1868.[8] The most dramatic aspect of this comparison is the rise in the slave output in Guiana between 1804, 1815, and 1838, when there were no striking increases in the slave population. The fact is the slave population had begun a steady decline from around the year 1813, and by the time emancipation came in 1838, it had declined to 82,284. Also relevant in this discussion is the wide variance between Cuban per capita slave production of 501 pounds in 1815 and that of Guianese slaves in the same year. This disparity in per capita output between Cuban and Guianese slaves in 1815 may have to do with the fact that a good number of slaves in Guiana were still engaged in coffee and cotton production. One conclusion we can draw from a comparison of the per capita output per slave of 1,282 pounds at the end of slavery in Guiana with per capita production per slave of 903 pounds in Cuba in 1841 is that exploitative methods in the former matured during the period 1807–1838. In the same vein, in the period 1839–1848, when the exploitative methods of slavery could not be applied, per capita output of exslaves declined. On the other hand, in the period 1849–1887, when the planter class found its footing and was successful in supplementing African labor with indentured labor, following the period of uncertainty during the first ten years of emancipation, per capita production of sugar increased phenomenally. Based on estimates from the figures available, rough as they may be, per capita production by the mid-1880s hovered above 2,800 pounds per sugar worker (indentured and African).[9]

Guianese and British Caribbean historians have yet to make the connection between the second slavery and the overexploitation of slave labor in the period 1807–1838, and similarly between the sustained suppression and marginalization of "free" (former slaves) and indentured labor after 1838 (Viotti da Costa 1994).[10] Suppression, overexploitation, and marginalization of the African workforce took place against the backdrop of the massive expansion of the world sugar economy after 1815. The commonality of the product is the major point of departure here.

Social, labor, and production relations in the different zones were organized around world market competition for cheaper sugar. Cheaper production in places such as Cuba was driven by the expansion of the sugar frontier, fuelled by increasing supplies of new slaves and technology. This expansion had to be matched through increases in the productivity of labor in the places that lacked the ability to increase their labor supply. This distinction is important to understand why there was a dramatic shift in the conditions of life of the slave population in British Guiana in the early part of the nineteenth century. Sugar could not become "king" (as it was nicknamed at the time in the colony) without the imposition and employment of elaborate labor control methods, which, enforced through legal and extralegal means, guaranteed that the output of labor (slave and free) in British Guiana was made competitive with the output of slave labor in the other sugar-producing areas of the Americas. Isolating the impact of slave labor used in the production of one commodity in the non-British colonies on slave labor on the production of a similar commodity in Guiana permits us to understand how social processes at each local level are created as a response to global market pressure. In many ways, scholars, above all Eric Williams (1945) and Alan Adamson (1972), open the debate on the circumstance of the colony's romance with sugar, but they do not meaningfully explain the undulating local narrative of sugar as a response to the global economy.

Whereas the Cuban sugar frontier expanded because the infusion of new slaves and technology, in Guiana production and slave productivity were maximized through technological infusion and consolidation of productive space combined with new and innovative labor control methods. The infusion of technology in the sugar industry of Guiana did not destroy outdated forms of labor organization, as it did in England; it was used as a means to further new forms of exploitation of slave and "free" labor. It was accompanied by new forms of social organization of the plantation, which deepened the preexisting rift between capital and labor. Expansions in the capabilities of the plantation were used as a precursor to renew, recast, and expand the control previously devised by capital over labor. The importation and installation of new technologies modernized the sugar production processes and pushed labor to the limits of endurance. As we have seen elsewhere, especially in other areas of expansion of commodity frontiers, new industrial technologies, which had become useful in the maximization of industrial production and worker productivity in England, were transferred to slave plantations to achieve the same end. It was in this context that the steam engine found its way to British Guiana, where it was in use from as early as 1805. The use of steam and the vacuum pan (introduced in the 1830s) maximized factory production processes, which made possible more efficient factories, requiring more sugar cane and thus more from labor (Stoll 2011: 140–44). Guiana, unlike Jamaica or Barbados, presented the possibility of technological adaptations, which enhanced processing capabilities and rapidly drove the consolidation of smaller operations into larger sugar works between 1834 and 1880. Technology aided expansion by consolidating land and labor and reducing the number of plantations. While cost was pushed downward through expansion of the sugar frontier in Cuba, which was driven by technology and infusion of slave labor, in Guiana cost was driven downward through technological adaptation, consolidation of land and holdings, and regimentation of labor. Guiana's competitive relationship within the global sugar economy depended on maximization of labor. The Guiana story represents a departure from the conventional narrative: without labor control methods—rather, without extremely exploitative approaches to the management of labor—it could not have remained competitive.

New methods of labor control evolved as the colonial class in the colony reorganized the plantation system to meet the standards for competition within the new global division of labor. To protect the interest of British capital, the local planter class and the planter-controlled state paid lip service to the legal statutes and stipulations dealing with rights and privileges of slaves, exslaves, and indentured laborers, but in many instances they treated them with utter disregard. In an era when slavery was downplayed in the British colonies, and when freedom for slaves and free trade were high on the agenda in the corridors of Whitehall, colonial capital, represented by the planter class, reinterpreted and reshaped the meanings of the slave and labor codes at the local level. Over the course of the nineteenth century, renewed exploitation of slave and "free" labor in British Guiana took place in contradiction to the liberal elites at home. On the one hand, these elites championed the values of antislavery and free trade, and on the other hand, they sought to give protection and cover to the convoluted lives of the planter class who were invested in the colony. The planter, the slave, the free, and the indentured laborer of British Guiana were all caught between the liberal values of freedom and the law of capital to produce increasing returns on investment. The many-sided debates taking place both in England and in the colony were overshadowed by the need to protect the "best interest" of the planter class. The result of this conflict was new forms of draconian exploitation of slaves, former slaves, and new laborers in British Guiana. The advances in the colony from a multicrop to a monocrop economy were thus tied to new forms of exploitation designed to extract more from the output of labor.

Methods of Labor Control: 1807–1838

Against the backdrop of global competition in the sugar market, whose cost and price was driven by the second slavery, the character of slave life and slave experience changed dramatically. This changed attitude toward labor and increased exploitation is captured in the following passage from Viotti da Costa: "From the time Demerara was integrated into the British Empire, the slaves' conditions of living and perceptions had been changing in significant ways—and would change even more as emancipation approached. Massive capital investment transformed the landscape and altered both the nature of plantation life and the slave experience" (1994: 39). Viotti da Costa's seminal work captures in vivid detail the dramatic and draconian changes that occurred in the slaves' living conditions and experience. Although the colony had inherited a slave labor force of less than 100,000 (Viotti da Costa 1994) at the time of abolition, and its land capacity required that it should have had in excess of 1,000,000 (Williams 1945), sugar production did not decline. The reorganized and reshaped plantation system, characterized by the movement from cotton and coffee to sugar, did not just reflect the global shift to regional specialization in the production of commodities, it was associated with the shortage of labor in the colony.[11] The reorganization of plantations, product cycles, and crops was accompanied by the parallel process of reorganization, consolidation, and regimentation of the small labor force to meet the demand for increased productivity of labor. In other words, the cost of the labor input was cheapened. As plantations were consolidated and as sugar factories grew, so did the demand on labor. And as the demand on the labor time grew, so did exploitation and exploitative tendencies. In Guiana, exploitation of slaves exploded.

During the nineteenth century, these exploitative tendencies, which I will discuss later, were fostered under the cover of the long struggle between the British elite, liberals, abolitionists, and "progressives," who by and large argued for abolition of slavery and for free trade, and the planter class in the colony, who argued against free trade and for the continuation of slavery or forms of slavery. (This is by no means an attempt on my part to deny the dynamic nature and the ups and downs of the ongoing struggle between the colonial elites in the mother country and the plantation elites, resident and nonresident, of the colony. I make this sweeping generalization to avoid a full discussion of the complexity of the points of similarity and areas of difference between elites on different sides of the Atlantic, whose common interest was profit from investment.) The larger point here is that in the era of the rise of liberal ideas, capitalist elites at both ends of the spectrum, operating under the cover of abolition and free trade, were able to extract more input from labor. Under the shadow of the abolition and free trade debate, and amid the changes brought about by the ferment as British capital pivoted away from mercantilism, old distinctions between labor and colonial capital were recast to meet the challenge of the new global reality of the rise of new producing areas to meet the challenge of the industrial age for ever-expanding supplies of commodities for manufacture and processing. Labor—African slaves and, later, exslaves and indentured servants in Guiana—was caught between liberal freedoms and colonial capital's need to meet the demands of the global market.

History does not deny that labor (slaves, exslaves, and indentured servants) made their mark on the history of Guiana. But history is not only written from within; it is also influenced by outside forces, and by circumstances. During the nineteenth century, the struggle for basic rights by the laboring population was circumscribed by dint of circumstances. Liberal ideas and the freedoms and basic rights inherent therein were overshadowed and constrained by the colony's competitive space in the global sugar industry, whose engine of growth was driven by the power of the second slavery.

The expansion of slavery in the new sugar colonies in combination with technology not only drove up volume of production, it cheapened the cost of the labor input for the global commodities sugar, coffee, and cotton, which were tied to and which drove the pace of expansion of the industrial revolution. One signally important result of this combination was the impact on the productivity of slave labor. Maximization and incremental increases in the productivity of slave labor inevitably drove down the cost of the labor input in the production process and hence the price of sugar (Tomich 1991: 302). In the climate of a world sugar economy dominated by an ever-decreasing cost of labor, two courses were open to colonial capital in British Guiana: capitulate and abandon the colony through granting liberal freedoms to labor, or maintain and expand the ability to compete by matching the growing denials and erosion of freedoms for labor in the new slave-producing colonies. Colonial capital in Guiana chose the latter, which resulted in the constant erosion of the rights of labor during the course of nineteenth century. To understand the link between the second slavery and the constant erosion of rights of labor, exploitative relations that developed in three time periods must be analyzed: the period that followed the first abolition of the slave trade (1807–1834), the period of emancipation (1834–1848), and the period of indenture and the stagnation of emancipation (1849–1884).

In the first period, from 1807 to 1834, between the act of abolition of the slave trade to the British Colonies and the beginning of the emancipation process, the conditions of slavery were the harshest in the history of the slave population of the colony. At no point during this period did the number of available slaves exceed 100,000, far from the estimated requirement of 3.4 million slaves, especially if all the land grants over the period in two counties, Demerara and Essequibo, were to be fully cultivated. In the climate produced by abolition, demand for labor greatly exceeded supply. As a result, the dwindling slave population was made to work harder and under more exacting conditions. To put it mildly, this was a period of intense distress for the slave population, who were required to work longer hours in an ever-more-regimented fashion. This not only created hardships due to lack of sleep and rest, but it curtailed their ability to organize, plant, and care for their provision grounds as the law required. The Colonial Office and officials in the colony were complicit, as the sugar-planting class turned a blind eye to the necessity for slaves to have such spaces as were provided by statute, and afforded without contest to slaves in the other Caribbean island colonies.

Restrictions on their personal time left the slaves with little or no time to plant and tend to their provision grounds or to other personal issues, such as going to church and market (Viotti da Costa 1994: 40). The evidence suggests that the planter class was allowed to flout the laws, while the colonial office and colonial officials either sat idly by, or on occasions issued proclamations that were not enforced. As the *Royal Gazette* (September 18, 1813, and October 18, 1821) pointed out, despite several calls and proclamations from the colonial office and the resident governor, Murray, and the threat of prosecution to ensure that planters complied with the law that required one acre to be set aside for provision ground cultivation for every five slaves, there was no improvement (Viotti da Costa 1994: 54–55). That the colonial office and the planter class were complicit in breaking the law with regard to provision grounds is further confirmed by the testimony before a committee of the House of Commons in England in 1832. According to the testimony of Reverend Wilshire Staunton Austin, provisions grounds were scarce in Demerara compared to other British colonies (Viotti da Costa 1994: 55). The tacit elimination of the provision-ground culture, which had become the hallmark of the slaves' struggle for some degree of independence, represented the most heinous disregard for the rights of slaves. It also reflected the extent to which the planter class was prepared to flout the law to create a competitive edge for itself in the reconfigured global sugar economy. The virtual disappearance of the provision grounds meant that the slave population had become yet more dependent on their masters. It robbed them of food security as well as their ability to construct an independent life within the bounds of the plantation economy.

If regimentation and restriction of their free time were not oppressive enough, new restrictions were also placed on the slaves' ability to purchase their freedom. The slave population could not purchase freedom as their counterparts did in the older colonies of the West Indies. In 1815, the Colonial Office imposed harsher restrictions on the ability of slaves in Guiana to purchase their own freedom or that of their relatives and friends (Viotti da Costa, 1994: 56). These new laws ended previous acts (1793 and 1804) that outlined the path to orderly manumission.[12] When these acts were enforced after 1815, they were effective weapons that curbed the possibility of an additional hemorrhage of slaves. Every avenue, every loophole that afforded opportunities for slaves to escape the dreariness of slavery was being shut off.

This process of restriction also entailed closing off opportunities for the growth of runaway slave communities, which had been prevalent in the old colonies of the West Indies, in Haiti, in Brazil, in Suriname, and in some of the other French and Dutch colonies. Faced with a scarcity of labor, the planter class did not tolerate the growth of communal competition. As a result, every attempt by slaves to establish runaway communities was smashed.[13] In British Guiana, runaway slave communities were constantly hunted and hounded (Thompson 1987: 129–52). There are no records that any of these communities survived the slave period. They were completely rooted out before emancipation (Thompson 1987: 141–46). Though Guiana was endowed with plentiful unempoldered land, runaway slave communities could not survive the onslaught of the colonial overlords.

Faced with such conditions, the slave population in Guiana continued to search for possibilities for escape and revolt. It was against the backdrop of these conditions that the slaves rebelled in 1823 (Viotti da Costa 1994). The well-documented insurrection by slaves in Demerara, while influenced by the desire for freedom, was given added fuel by the new methodologies of labor control and regimentation. The legendary significance of this revolt stands out in the well-researched published manuscripts dealing with slave resistance in the New World. But what concerns us is not so much the account of this revolt, but the fact that, despite the revolt, the conditions of African labor did not improve in any significant way. More than 180 years later, the descendants of the African population that engaged in the insurrection still found themselves at the bottom of the social ladder in modern Guyana. Although this revolt is one of the best documented, it was not the first or the last attempt by the African population to engage in active struggle with the planter-dominated colonial state to define new spaces of freedom.

Post Emancipation: Sugar's Dominance

The most momentous of these struggles were the trade-union-like struggles between the freed slaves and the planter class between 1838 and 1848, and the struggles for local self-governing villages after 1850. Despite the 1823 revolt and the struggles that ensued after emancipation, the sugar-dominated planter economy was able to maintain its control over labor. This dominance can be measured in terms of the ever-declining possibility for major portions of the African population to get jobs in the sugar industry between 1848 and 1884. During this period, indentured immigration increased; wages not only stagnated, they were reduced to the level they were at the beginning of the "apprenticeship" period, 1834–1838. This was also the period of stagnation and decline of the "free village movement," which the freed slaves had fought to establish and organize in the first ten years of emancipation, 1838–1848. Emancipation exacerbated the labor problem and opened the space for the class struggle that ensued during the ten-year period from 1838 to 1848.[14]

In such a volatile climate, sugar production declined sharply, as the exslaves attempted to create spaces of freedom by establishing independent villages, from which they bargained for better wages and conditions of work. In this short ten-year period, the planter class suffered a temporary setback. They were not able to maintain the absolute control they had under the condition of slavery, and were unable to organize the regimentation of labor within the specified plantation space. Under slavery, labor's sphere of operation was limited. The ecological, economic, and political conditions limited its freedom within the framework of the planters' economic and political vision for the colony. Although Guiana had abundant available land, labor could not move away from the plantations to become a runaway peasantry, as they did in other colonies. This absolute level of control was altered after emancipation, when the exslaves were notionally "free" to choose employers. The postemancipation period was marked by the unprecedented growth of independent villages and what amounted to trade union activity and organization among the exslave workforce. Through these processes they were able to alter, albeit temporarily, the control over their labor power and over their everyday existence, which planters had established during slavery. The villages offered them independent residential life, but not independent economic life.[15]

Because sugar and its interests in the colony controlled law making, which covered the price, terms, and location of villages and individual and collective holdings, the exslaves' quest for an independent economic life was thwarted. Within this nexus, by 1848 the sugar barons had succeeded in limiting the mobility of the exslaves and their quest to create a counterhegemony to sugar's dominance. Although they could not turn back the village movement, they successfully created and implemented policies, such as the land acts of 1839, 1851, and 1856, that limited the advance of the villages as independent economies (Adamson 1970; Mohamed 2008: 154–213). They also used the strategic importance of sugar for the colony to alter the labor market. They bypassed the terms of the abolition and emancipation acts and imported indentured labor. Sugar's rapid advance after 1848 was related to the defeat of labor and the growth of the planter-controlled and -directed labor market. Sugar's defeat of labor was facilitated through both land and immigration acts. Through land acts, the planter class contained the hemorrhage of labor away from the plantation zone. Although these acts could not force the African population to give continuous labor to the plantations, they demarcated how, where, and under what circumstances villages could be established, and the extent to which their lands could be collectivized (Adamson 1972: 64–67; Mohamed 2008: 255–96). An examination of the land market brings into sharp focus the fact that almost every piece or block of land purchased by the exslaves between 1839 and 1848 (the period of the growth of the village movement) was done on lands contiguous to existing and functioning plantations. The fact that the planter class was able to limit habitation of the African population to locations on or near plantations was an important factor in the construction of this group of laborers into a "reserve army of labor," to use Marxist terminology, (see Mohamed 2008: 254). The land acts contained the movement of African labor and kept it in proximity to functioning plantations.

The other component of this process was indentured immigration, which was implemented in Guiana with the added ingredient of the indentured contract. The indentured contract and the land laws must be understood as conjoined processes. They came at the particular juncture of the mid- to late 1840s when the global process toward free trade in sugar had matured. The adaptation and implementation of these twin processes occurred against the backdrop of world market conditions that led the British government to discontinue the longstanding preferential access to the British market that colonial producers had within the Empire. The imposition of free trade in sugar after 1846 brought in its wake indentured immigrant contract labor. Through this imposition, the planter class succeeded in suppressing the wages and economic standing of Africans in the colony. The presence of this new group of laborers served as a buffer between the planter class and exslaves and drastically altered the latter's capacity to organize and engage in collective trade union action. The presence of indentured laborers in large numbers also limited the capacity and ability of exslaves to organize as a peasantry, as their counterparts in the old Caribbean had begun to do during the same period. What Guyana witnessed was the local effect of the transition within the world economy from mercantilism to free-trade capitalism. This transition gave rise to the presence of both slave- and free-produced sugar in the world market.

Under the cover of free trade, the sugar barons used the land and immigration to reorganize and reestablish control over labor, which they had lost in the period of implementation of the abolition and emancipation acts. Under the aegis of these acts, labor was brought to and kept on its knees between 1850 and 1884. Decent wages and conditions fought for and won by the freed slaves in the early 1840s were rolled back to the levels they had been at the beginning of the apprenticeship period.[16] The land and immigration acts established after 1846 have to be understood as integrated parts of the whole mechanism used by sugar to control labor after 1850. Scholars often isolate these moving parts and treat them as separate processes. They are not separate. For the land acts to work as limiting instruments to thwart the demands of labor, immigration, or new labor, had to be present. In much the same way, indentured immigration and the establishment of penal contracts after 1848 cannot be analyzed without reference to the land acts.

Conclusion

Planter dominance over the exslaves was achieved only after the indentured contract was thrown into the mix. One of the primary forms of labor control, the indentured contract was instituted to supplement the labor of the exslaves, to reduce the cost of their labor, and to cushion the sugar industry from the dramatic effects of the equalization of sugar duties after 1846. Thus, as a form of labor control, the indentured contract was associated with the demands of competition consequent to the equalization of sugar duties. The evolution of the penal approach to labor had everything to do with competition from slave-produced sugar. It was competition from slave-produced sugar that eventually opened the floodgates for this "new form of slavery" (Tinker 1993). Things were connected.

The success of this strategy of labor control can be measured by two factors: the ways in which indentured labor supplemented the plantations' need for the labor of exslaves, and the extent to which it reduced the cost of producing sugar. The indentured contract was a guarantee against high wages.[17] It was also a guarantee of a resident labor force, which precluded exslaves from employment unless there was a shortage on a particular plantation or in circumstances where the indentured laborer lacked the requisite skill to perform a particular task. In this climate, the desire of exslaves to work was squeezed between the planter class and the indentured laborers. Wages offered and received depended in large measure on whether an estate had a good-enough indentured gang to do the work that the Africans were capable of doing. This was the daily experience of the exslaves after the sugar strike of 1848 and until they stopped searching for estate employment and began to move to the gold fields and to other endeavors in the 1880s. As Walter Rodney (1981a: 31–45) reports, wage rates for the African (exslave) sugar workers were stagnant after 1848. Rodney concludes that wage rates in large measure were determined by the extent to which the bound (indentured) labor force was up to each task, "so long as each estate had its indentured gang . . . it was fortified to deal with the independent task-gangs" (Rodney 1981a: 44). In the final analysis, the indentured contract allowed the planter class to establish a degree of interdependency between indentured workers and exslaves, both of whom were caught in an unequal competition for the stagnant wage rates (Rodney 1981a: 43–44). This interdependent race to the bottom was tied to the global sugar economy driven by slave labor, within which the indentured contract, as instituted, altered the market condition for free labor.

Against this background, the strides made by sugar between 1850 and 1884, a period when production shot up from 32,692 tons to 121,840 tons (Deerr 1949), were achieved because of the firm control the planter class exercised over the overall economy. Domination was possible because of sugar's triumph over the total economy. Indentured immigration, specifically the terms of the indentured contract, which Hugh Tinker describes as a "new form of slavery" (Tinker 1993), was the final element in the advance of sugar's quest for dominance over labor. This draconian system, which existed in the margins of European capitalism and was employed in the British sugar colonies in the nineteenth century, was solely responsible for the marginalization of Africans in Guyana. It seeped into the fabric of colonial life under the umbrella of "the impending labor shortage," which was anticipated to follow immediately after emancipation, with the expectation that exslaves would abandon the plantations. This system of labor control, which was finally abolished in Guyana in the second decade of the twentieth century, was allowed to operate and prosper under the watchful eye and gaze of the humanitarians, reformers, and abolitionists—who by and large did not disfavor it until after the 1870s, at which point the clamor for reform and a possible end to the system was joined. Until that point, the men of virtue who had valiantly campaigned for an end to slavery turned a blind eye to this travesty (Tinker 1993: 236–366).

Although indenture brought relief to the labor supply problem endemic to Guiana, its implementation was detrimental to the growth of a free-labor market. The labor shortage was solved by curtailing the free expression of independent economic action of exslaves. The actions of the colonial state and the planter class in Guiana called into question the lofty principles of supply and demand adumbrated by Adam Smith in the *Wealth of Nations* and exposed the limits of British liberalist thought. In the final analysis, the actions of the colonial state and the planter class demonstrated the class and racial disparity between European thought and European action. It exposed the widely accepted notion that the market regulated the relations between capital and labor under conditions of freedom and equality. In Guiana, it was only the demand for labor that mattered. Although a labor market existed, its existence was artificially maintained, and it was uniquely based on plantation demand.

Notes

1. Noël Deerr (1949) shows that sugar production in the era of decreasing labor increased from the low of 1,410 tons in 1804 to 54,488 tons in 1833.

2. In this chapter, I use Guiana, Guyana, and British Guiana interchangeably. Whenever these terms are used in this chapter, they invariably refer to the same colony and country. Guyana, formerly Dutch, was held by the British as a British colony between 1802 and 1966.

3. Guiana lost its competitive advantage in the production and export of cotton and coffee to the United States and Brazil as the expansion of these industries in those countries was fuelled extensively by slave labor in the early nineteenth century.

4. Walter Rodney (1981a: 1–19), Adamson (1972: 15–33), and Clementi (1937) lay out the ecological issues that presented problems for labor's autonomy.

5. Because British Guiana was a British colony, slaves in British Guiana were emancipated on August 1, 1838.

6. The viability of preferential access to the British market by Guianese and British Caribbean sugar gradually eroded between 1823 and 1847, and finally ended in 1874, when all tariffs were removed; see Beachey 1957: 44–4x.

7. Guiana had passed too late into the hands of the British Empire for them to do anything about the labor problem created in the Dutch period. The Dutch, who had been in continuous, though not unchallenged, occupation of Guiana until 1796, had failed to accede to the demands of planter interests for the supply of slave labor to keep up with capital and land.

8. The figures used in this comparison are taken from Tomich (1991: 304), Farley (1956: 62–66), and Deerr (1949). To arrive at the approximate averages, I assumed that a metric ton is equivalent or was at that time equivalent to 2200 pounds.

9. These estimates are based on tables of the number of indentured laborers available for work and the production totals; see Nath (1950) and Deerr (1949).

10. Emilia Viotti da Costa is among several historians who have outlined the extent to which slave conditions were the harshest in British Guiana compared to other areas of the British Caribbean in the period immediately following the abolition of the slave trade.

11. Between 1813 and 1853 almost all the coffee and cotton plantations in the colony were abandoned, sold, or absorbed into sugar production as part of a larger consolidation of plantations. In 1838–1853, of the 38 sugar estates abandoned, all except three had production returns of more than 150 hogsheads of sugar and none had surpassed the 200-hogshead mark. These were plantations that were less endowed with capital and technology; see Adamson (1972: 160–61). After 1850, there was a phenomenal increase in mergers and consolidations of sugar estates. This is reflected in the vast reduction of estates between 1850 and 1870, from 404 to 135; see Beachey (1957: 118).

12. The *Royal Gazette*, March 11 and 14, April 10, and July 8, 1815. C.O. 111/76, 111/99, 111/123).

13. Runaway and maroon communities were smashed by the colonial police with help from the Amerindians. These communities were located mostly in the Mahaica and Mahaicony regions of Demerara. Maroon communities were also established by runaway slaves in Berbice and Essequibo. Reports on these communities and the encounters with the colonial authorities are recorded in many scholarly reports: see Viotti da Costa (1994: 80–81) and Alvin O. Thompson (1987: 129–52); see also the accounts given by Farley (1956: 178–84).

14. See James Rose (1989, 1990), where he discusses and analyzes the sugar strikes of 1842 and 1848.

15. See Hall (1978: 7–24) and Rodney (1981b: 643–66). Douglas Hall and Walter Rodney in separate pieces discuss the previously held view that the exslaves had abandoned the plantations en masse; they outlined that this was not the case.

16. The penal long-term indentured contract was not connected simply with the "labor shortage," but with the need for a pliant labor force to reduce wages and alter the working conditions that were negotiated between estates and the Creole African workforce.

17. Within three years after the first dose of the penal contract was instituted, the wage bill for the production of one hogshead of sugar was reduced by almost £3 British. In 1841 the wages to produce one hogshead of sugar were £14.8; in 1847 they had been reduced to £11.13, and in 1851 to £8.16 (see Moore 1970: 159).

Works Cited

Adamson, Alan. 1970. "Monoculture and Village Decay in British Guiana, 1854–1872." *Journal of Social History* 111 (4): 386–405.

Adamson, Alan. 1972. *Sugar without Slaves.* New Haven, CT: Yale University Press.

Beachey, R. W. 1957. *The British West Indies Sugar Industry in the Late 19th Century.* Westport, CT: Greenwood Press.

Bolingbroke, Henry. 1941. *A Voyage to the Demerary.* Orig. publ. 1807. Georgetown, Guyana: Daily Chronicle.

Clementi, Cecil. 1937. *A Constitutional History of British Guiana.* London: St. Martin's Press.

Deerr, Noël. 1949. *The History of Sugar.* London: Chapman and Hall.

Farley, Rawle Egbert Griffith. 1956. "Aspects of the Economic History of British Guiana 1781–1852." Unpublished PhD diss., University of London.

Hall, Douglas. 1978. "The Flight from the Estates Reconsidered: The British West Indies, 1838–42." *Journal of Caribbean History* 10 & 11: 7–24.

Mandle, Jay R. 1973. *The Plantation Economy.* Philadelphia: Temple University Press.

Mohamed, Wazir. 2008. "Frustrated Peasants, Marginalized Workers: Free African Villages in Guyana, 1838–1885." Unpublished PhD diss., Binghamton University, Binghamton, NY.

Moore, Robert. 1970. "East Indians & Negroes in British Guiana 1838–1900." Unpublished PhD diss., University of Sussex, England.

Nath, Dwarka. 1950. *A History of Indians in Guyana.* London: Butler & Tanner.

Ragatz, Lowell Joseph. 1928. *The Fall of the Planter Class in the British Caribbean*. New York: Century Co.

Ramsahoye, Fenton H. W. 1966. *The Development of Land Law in British Guiana*. New York: Oceana.

Richardson, Bonham C. 1997. *Economy and Environment in the Caribbean: Barbados and the Windwards in the Late 1800s*. Kingston, Jamaica: The University of the West Indies Press.

Rodney, Walter. 1979. *Guyanese Sugar Plantations in the Late Nineteenth Century: A Contemporary Description from the Argosy*. Georgetown, Guyana: Release Publishers.

———. 1981a. *A History of the Guyanese Working People, 1881–1905*. Baltimore, MD: Johns Hopkins University Press.

———. 1981b. "Plantation Society in Guyana." *Review* IV (4): 643–66.

Rose, James. 1981. "The Plight of the British Guianese Creoles 1835–1873: A Study in Antagonistic Class Relations." Unpublished MA thesis, University of Guyana, Turkeyen.

———. 1989. "The Strike of 1842." *History Gazette* No. 13.

———. 1990. "The Strike of 1848." *History Gazette* No. 23.

———. 1998. "The Strikes of 1842 and 1848." In *Themes in African-Guyanese History*, edited by Winston McGowan, James Rose, and David Granger. Georgetown, Guyana: Free Press, 158–98.

Ruhomon, Peter. 1988. *Centenary History of the East Indians in British Guiana, 1838–1938*. Georgetown, Guyana: Guyana National Printers.

Saunders, Kay. 1984. *Indentured Labor in the British Empire 1834–1920*. London: Croom Helm.

Stoll, Allyson Ann Marie. 2011. "Not for 'Want of Go-Aheadism' in Field and Factory: The Technological Trajectory of the Guyana (British Guiana) Sugar Industry from 1800 to the 1930s." Unpublished PhD diss., Cornell University, Ithaca, NY.

Thompson, Alvin O. 1987. *Colonialism & Underdevelopment in Guyana 1580–1803*. Bridgetown, Barbados: Carib Research & Publications.

———. 2002. *Unprofitable Servants: Crown Slaves in Berbice, Guyana 1803–1831*. Kingston, Jamaica: University of the West Indies Press.

———. 2006. *Flight to Freedom: African Runaways and Maroons in the Americas*. Kingston, Jamaica: University of the West Indies Press.

Tinker, Hugh. 1993. *A New System of Slavery: The Export of Indian Labor Overseas 1830–1920*. London: Hansib Publishing.

Tomich, Dale W. 1990. *Slavery in the Circuit of Sugar: Martinique and the World Economy, 1830–1848*. Baltimore, MD: John Hopkins University Press.

———. 1991. "World Slavery and Caribbean Capitalism: The Cuban Sugar Industry, 1760–1868." *Theory and Society* 20 (3): 297–319.

———. 2004. *Through the Prism of Slavery: Labor, Capital, and World Economy*. Lanham, MD: Rowman & Littlefield.

Viotti da Costa, Emilia. 1994. *Crowns of Glory, Tears of Blood: The Demerara Slave Rebellion of 1823*. New York: Oxford University Press.

Williams, Eric. 1942. "The British West Indian Slave Trade after its Abolition in 1807." *Journal of Negro History* 27(2): 175–91.

———. 1945. "The Historical Background of British Guiana's Problems." *Journal of Negro History* 30: 357–81.

———. 1964. *Capitalism and Slavery*. London: Andre Deutsch.

Young, Allan. 1958. *The Approaches to Local Self-Government in British Guiana*. London: Longmans, Green & Co.

On the Blurred Boundaries of Freedom

Liberated Africans in Cuba, 1817–1870*

Inés Roldán de Montaud

The Origins of Liberated Africans in Cuba

In 1807, Britain outlawed the slave trade and set about abolishing it worldwide. On September 23, 1817, the British government persuaded Spain to sign a treaty forbidding its subjects from slaving on the African coast, north of the equator, from 1820 onward. This treaty authorized the contracting parties' warships to search merchant ships from both countries suspected of carrying illegally traded slaves abroad. The Mixed Commissions for the suppression of the transatlantic slave trade, set up in Havana and Sierra Leone, were to determine the legality of these captures. In the event of a guilty verdict, the slaves found on board would receive a certificate of emancipation and would be handed over to the government on whose territory the

*This work has been done as part of research project HAR2009-07103, Diccionario biográfico español de ministros de Ultramar, for the Spanish Ministry of Science and Innovation. Translation of "En los borrosos confines de la libertad: El caso de los negros emancipados en Cuba, 1817–1870"; translated by Dale Tomich.

ruling Commission was based. The so-called liberated Africans, or *negros emancipados* as they were named in Cuba and Puerto Rico, would then be employed as free workers or servants (Article XIII).[1] The Royal Charter of December 19, 1817, brought the treaty into force, banning Spanish subjects from trafficking on the coasts of Africa and stipulating that all black persons acquired on that coast should be declared free at the first point of call in the dominions of the vessel transporting them. These two texts provided the legal origin of Cuban liberated Africans.

The chance occurrence of being captured by warships or discovered by the island's authorities turned these future slaves into free people. The group of people thus created by international agreement did not fit into plantation society. According to the law, they were not slaves, but in fact they could have no other status, because nothing else was possible under the rigid slave society structure on which the Spanish colony's economic organization was based. In effect, preservation of the social order demanded that slaves and those who came from slavery, and by extension, from Africa, be retained in their subordinate role. It was therefore no easy matter for slaves to access the civil condition of free persons, and the growing group of free blacks and mulattos was observed with ever more concern as its population increased in proportion to the number of whites (Martínez-Alier 1979: 19; Klein 1986: 140).

The integration into Cuban society of just over 26,000 slaves who were declared emancipated between 1820 and 1866 as free persons of color proved impossible. It is estimated that between 1817 and 1873, some 340,000 slaves were introduced into Cuba, so that the liberated Africans accounted for barely 7.6 percent among them. Given their relative numerical insignificance, the presence of this group of *emancipados* posed more problems than might be imagined, precisely for the danger they were considered to represent for the social order. Their mere existence questioned the very legitimacy of slavery (Aimes 1967: 237).

Although there are excellent studies on Caribbean slave societies, this group of people—described by Spanish historian Jacobo de la Pezuela in 1864 as a "new coloured class that were neither serfs nor could yet cease to be so" (Pezuela 1863, 2: 293; trans. by I. M.), and more recently by David Murray as "a new class of slaves" (1980)—has rarely warranted the attention of researchers (Bethell 1966: 79–93; Franco 1980: 342–60; Roldán de Montaud 1982: 559–641, 2011: 159–92; Martínez-Fernández 1995: 205–25, 1998: 41–64). In this chapter, we consider the circumstances that led to the formation of this group and the conditions in which they led their lives in a slave society, which initially reacted by adopting a series of expulsion projects, and subsequently by completely assimilating them into the slave population. All of this demonstrates once again that the path to freedom was an extremely difficult one for black slaves to follow in Cuba's slave society.

The progress of this small group of slaves can be contrasted with that of similar groups in many other places where Britain forced countries to sign treaties against the slave trade, although the Brazilian case, where they were known as *Africanos livres*, is particularly interesting because of its close similarities with the Cuban situation (Conrad 1973: 50–70; Gallotti Mamigonian 2005: 389–417, 2009a: 236–63, 2009b: 41–66). There were also liberated Africans in places as distant as the British West Indies,[2] Sierra Leone, the United States, Cape Town, Mauritius, and on the Indian subcontinent, among others (Schuler 2001: 133–60; James 1991; Carter 2003).[3] To refer to this new social category, recent historiography has coined the expression "recaptive Africans," on the grounds that it best reflects the situation of these individuals, who very rarely came to enjoy freedom after being released from the slave ships. Everywhere, they faced a similar fate and were turned into forced laborers, or apprenticed or indentured laborers, or they were simply reduced to slavery. It is estimated that since 1807, the British removed from illegal traffic about 160,000 human beings (Schuler 1980: 134). The group of Cuban *emancipados* forms part of this group.

Although this study, which is based primarily on sources from Spanish archives, tackles a large proportion of the problems experienced by this group of liberated Africans, many aspects remain unexplained, essentially those related to their everyday lives and to their own perceptions of their status and situation, their relations with free persons of color, and their fight for the freedom that had legally been recognized for them—a struggle on which many embarked with the support of British diplomats in Cuba.

In December 1824, the Mixed Commission of Havana declared the emancipation of the 147 blacks brought by the *Relámpago* expedition and handed them over, with their corresponding certificate, to Captain General Dionisio Vives (table 6.1). They were transferred to a farmhouse on the outskirts of Regla, where runaway slaves were kept, and then distributed among some of the neighbors and public institutions of Havana, on terms prepared by British commissioner J. T. Kilbee and accepted by Vives.[4]

The possibility that they would soon swell the ranks of the free persons of color, which then totalled about 100,000, and that their situation might have a negative effect on the 290,000 existing slaves, aroused considerable fear among the authorities. The first reaction to the existence of these free *bozales* was to expel them. In General Vives's view, they should be returned to their place of origin at the expense of those who had brought them to Cuba (Murray 1980: 275–76).[5] The superintendent-general proposed that they be ceded to the British government for transfer to Jamaica. The municipal council of Havana suggested a reform of the treaty so that in the future captured ships would be tried in Sierra Leone.[6]

With the ruling against the *Águila* in June 1832, with 601 *bozales* on board, the number of black *emancipados* rose to 3,000. The authorities' increasing concerns led them to speed up negotiations with Britain, which agreed to receive in Trinidad the black people emancipated in the last two years and any who would be liberated in the future.[7] In May, the 196 *bozales* on the *Negrita* embarked for Jamaica, and were followed by those on the *Joaquina*, *Manuelita*, and *Rosa* the year after. In all, they made up 987 of the 5,245 slaves emancipated to that date.[8]

The handing over of liberated Africans to the British authorities did not last long, grinding to a halt in 1835, when Miguel Tacón occupied the Captaincy General. This marked the start of the distribution of *emancipados*—who were exchanged for large sums of money, making corrupt public employees rich and providing resources that would pay for diverse public works—a task that Tacón set about with enthusiasm (Roldán de Montaud 1982: 574–77.

When Queen Regent Maria Christina encountered difficulties defending her daughter's right to the Spanish throne, she sought a rapprochement with the Brit-

Table 6.1. Liberated Africans in Cuba, 1824–1866

Year	Expedition	No.	Year	Expedition	No.	Year	Expedition	No.
1824	Relámpago	150	1842	Aurelia Feliz	158	1857	Jaruco	91
1826	Cayo Verde	61		Demayajabos	84		Morro	85
	Campeador	229		San Marcos	47		Páez	356
	Fingal	58		Macambo	152		Primer Neptuno	534
	Orestes	212		Yumuría	90		Leckington	497
	Mágico	176		Caleta de Barca	15		Santa Susana	29
1828	Gerges	395		Punta de Maya	10		Sagua Pelada	3
	Firme	484	1843	Puerto Escondido	85		Guadalquizal	1
	Intrépido	135	1846	Cabañas	10	1858	Lanzanillo	497
1829	Josefa	206	1847	Trinidad	134		Guantánamo	361
	Voladora	331	1849	Cabañas	85		Punta de Guano	190
	Midas	281		Santa Clara	172		Venadito	615
	Gallito	135	1851	Cárdenas	402	1859	Blasco de Garay	438
1830	Emilio	188	1852	Granadilla	25	1860	Gibacoa	47
	Santiago	105	1853	Cárdenas y Matanzas	275		Luisa	142
1832	Águila	601		Remedios	52		Cayo Cádiz	562
	Indagadora	134		Sagua la Grande	16		Segundo Neptuno	419
	Planeta	238	1853	Bermeja	134		Cayo Sal	846
1833	Negrito	490	1854	Caleta del Rosario	15		Casilda	371
1834	Rosa	322		Cayo Livisa	261	1861	Manatí	396
	Joaquina	479		Matanzas	113		Juanita	69
	Manuelita	200		Pinar del Río	185		Yateras	40
1835	Amalia	193		Ortigosa	202		Maniabón	49
	Carlota	253		Güines	161		Santa María	621
	Chubasco	72		Manimani	103	1862	Cabo Indio	281
	Holguín	254		Isla de Pinos	242	1863	Agüica	1,031
	Joven Reina	341		Mariel	70		Domínica	353
	María	290		Brujas. Luisa	589		Manaca	418
	Marte	403		S. Espíritus y Trinidad	743		Canao, Sagua y Bomaniel	216
	Julita	340	1855	Santa Cruz	42	1864	Lezo	365
	Tita	393		Punta de Ganado	74		Guadalquivir	469
	Diligencia	205		Guanajay-Bahía Honda	93		Tercer Neptuno	365
1836	Ninfa	432		Nuevas Grandes	25	1865	Gato	140
	Ricomar	186	1856	Bahía Honda	49	1866	Punta Holanda	278
1841	Portugués (Cabañas)	411	1857	Sancti Espíritus	55			
1842	Majana	150		Almedares	21			
Total								26,026

Source: Archivo Histórico Nacional, Madrid, (hereafter AHN), *Ultramar*, 3554, Secretariat of the Government of Cuba, December 12, 1870. For the period 1824–1841, see also AHN, *Estado*, 8040, Statement of Spanish vessels captured by British warships, June 29, 1841. There are slight differences in the number of slaves carried by some of the vessels and the year of apprehension.

ish government, which, in exchange for supporting her, insisted that Spain agree to sign a more effective treaty against the trafficking in slaves, who continued to reach Cuba in their thousands (about 66,000 between 1821 and 1831) in the face of official complacency (Pezuela 1868, 2: 287). The Treaty of 1835 introduced major changes for *emancipados*, amending Article VII of the 1817 Treaty. From that point on, slaves on board any condemned ship would be handed over to the government whose cruiser had seized it, and not to that of the territory where the Commission that tried it was located. The government in question was then required to set and keep these people free, providing news of their situation when required to do so by the other contracting party (Ferrer de Couto 1864: 113–32). In this way, only if they were captured by a Spanish vessel would the slaves remain the responsibility of the Cuban authorities. The Government Secretariat in Cuba was to keep a register of *emancipados*, which would be given to Britain every six months. In short, the new treaty sought to incorporate more wide-ranging legislation than in 1817, which served as a channel of permanent pressure for the British authorities. Because Spain had hardly any vessels engaged in the pursuit of slave trade, virtually all *emancipados* subsequently became the responsibility of the British government. In fact, after 1835, British cruisers focused their efforts on African waters and the Havana Commission hardly delivered more than a few more sentences (Bethell 1966: 84).

The group of Cuban *emancipados* included not just the slaves captured by British and Spanish cruisers between 1820 and 1835 and those that were captured by Spanish vessels afterward, but also those surprised by the local authorities when disembarking or already on land, according to the Royal Charter of 1817. The issue was raised for the first time in 1826, when the *Mágico* ran aground and the crew fled with some of the *bozales* on board. The Mixed Commission declared the vessel a legitimate capture and took the view that the *bozales* on board should be awarded their freedom. The Council of the Indies established shortly afterward, however, that in these cases, the authorities should pursue the slaves on land, without troubling slave owners on their estates, and that it was up to the Captain General to determine their fate.[9]

The first capture made by the Cuban authorities took place in 1841. In May, 413 *bozales* who had been disembarked from the *Portugués* were picked up in Cabañas. The black recaptives were sent to Havana and the appropriate dossier sent to the Mixed Commission, which returned it so that proceedings could go ahead according to the laws of the land. Captain General Valdés declared the slaves free, and his decision was soon approved in Madrid.[10] The case of several hundred children who disembarked in Nuevitas in 1855 illustrates the difficulties and pressure the local authorities came up against on the rare occasions when they were actually willing to comply with the law (Arnalte 2001). There were, therefore, three types of *emancipados*: those who were freed under the Treaty of 1817; those freed under the 1835 Treaty, though they were very few, given the small number of slave traders captured by Spanish vessels; and finally, a third group, who were freed under the internal laws in force in Cuba.

The Living Conditions of Emancipados

The emancipated slaves were distributed among neighbors and corporations in Havana, where they worked as servants, while supposedly receiving religious instruction and learning a trade. Adults were consigned for five years, and women with children who were unable to work and minors for seven. Once this period was over, it was considered that the *emancipados* could fend for themselves and would obtain their charter of freedom and join society as free people.[11]

Of the 2,380 *emancipados* known to exist in 1831, only 374 were consigned to corporations. Several had been handed over to the Ursulinas Convent, the Hospital of San Juan de Dios, and the naval station as stokers and coal heavers on warships. Public works absorbed a large part of emancipated labor. Generals Vives and Ricafort sent them to work on the Fernando VII aqueduct; Tacón had them paving the streets and building bridges, gardens, and the new jail. Of the private individuals who benefitted from the consignations, a group of widows, government employees, and retired military personnel had them employed in diverse tasks. Indeed, there are reports of emancipated cigar makers, water carriers, calash drivers, bakers, washerwomen, and cooks. They were also consigned to the railway companies of Cárdenas, Cienfuegos, and Trinidad, and to the Havana gas company, which in 1845 received fifty. To promote copper mining in Eastern Cuba, *emancipados* were also handed over to several mining companies.[12] Similarly, to stimulate cotton production, a number were consigned to plantation owners in 1865, including to Carlos Manuel de Céspedes, who took them on in Demajagua, where a proclamation of independence was made shortly afterward.[13]

Consignment inevitably gave rise to many abuses. It was renewed indefinitely, and the emancipated slaves never seemed to get the chance to join the community of free blacks. A whole series of businesses sprang up with these black *emancipados*, and their consignation was coveted because it could provide a tempting income for trustees, with cheap labor for planters and profits for the public treasury. The rural employment of an *emancipado* could produce 15 pesos a month in rent, and much more if the person had learned a trade. These problems can be illustrated with examples that shed light on the life of an urban *emancipado*, which, in fact, very much resembled that of an urban slave. The case of Gabino came to light when the British consul in Havana and superintendent of liberated Africans, David Turnbull, called for his release by the authorities. The Mixed Commission had declared his emancipation in 1824 and he had been handed over to Luisa Apreu de Paz, who forced him to work as a water carrier. Gabino handed over his daily wage of one peso to his instructor. After the first five years, his consignation was extended for a further five, and then again for ten more. In those years, Gabino provided his trustee with 5,228 pesos, while she had paid the sum of 612 pesos for him.[14] To restrict such abuses, in 1851, General Concha banned—although probably unsuccessfully—beneficiaries from employing *emancipados* in any other service but their own.

It soon became clear that the enjoyment of rights as free people that had been awarded to *emancipados* would be difficult to achieve, and that their lot would be similar to that of slaves, with whom they were, indeed, equated. Slavery researchers have highlighted the differences that existed in the urban and rural environments. Slaves in towns had a better chance of acquiring their freedom, either by *coartación* (self-purchase) or manumission.[15] Distribution conditions for *emancipados* prohibited the removal of black people from the city or surrounding area without government authorization. David Turnbull ensured that this rule was scrupulously observed until the arrival of General Tacón in 1835. Given the consul's abolitionist stance, the fact that he made a distinction between Captains General suggests that the *emancipados*' situation deteriorated after 1835.

It was at this point that the practice began of demanding between six and nine gold ounce coins per consignation, which British Commissioner Richard Madden denounced as a contravention of the treaty (Madden 1840: 122). Having paid such a large sum for a five-year consignation (a *bozal* slave then cost 20 to 23 gold ounces, trustees considered *emancipados* their property and were of the view that they should get from them the most benefit.

In addition to consignation for large sums, Tacón's arrival marked the beginning of the practice of handing *emancipados* over to inland plantations. Remaining in the capital city was no guarantee for liberated Africans, but at least it gave them a chance to become free men; once sent to the sugar estates, however, the possibility of freedom was lost to them.[16] Tacón argued that keeping "the public peace" had forced him to place *emancipados* on country estates. Once the custom was adopted of consigning *emancipados* for large sums and sending them to the sugar mills, their condition was on a par with that of rural slaves. They lost any advantage that they might have had as urban slaves and were absorbed into slave consignments on estates.

In a way, the situation of the *emancipados* was worse than that of slaves. Indeed, they were deprived of some of the advantages and protection that legislation accorded slaves. Although recent studies have shown that *coartación*, or self-purchase, became gradually more complex and difficult to achieve by slaves, at least it was recognized as a legal possibility (Varella 2010). The opportunity for self-purchase, however, was not within the reach of the *emancipados*, nor could *emancipados* gain their freedom by manumission of the owner, because they were not subject to the will of the trustee, but to that of the government (Valiente 1869: 14; Madden 1840: 118). Without entering the debate about the efficacy of these institutions in promoting freedom from slavery, they did, in principle, provide mechanisms that granted rights to slaves, from which *emancipados* were excluded.

The *emancipados* could not go to the local mayors who were entrusted with looking after the rights of slaves and hearing cases of offences against them. Until 1856, there was no provision that mayors should defend or represent *emancipados* in conciliation or verbal proceedings, or that district attorneys and attorneys for the government should do so in documents brought before judges and ordinary courts.[17] Even then, there was no attempt to defend the right to freedom of *emancipados* who had completed their five years of instruction, and their claims were restricted to cases of abuse.

Abuse and Its Demographic Effects

All kinds of abuses were committed against *emancipados*. One of the most common was known as *plagio*, or plagiarism, and involved claiming a slave who had died was actually an *emancipado*. The *emancipado* then took the place of the dead slave. All that was needed was to change the name when informing the priest and party captain. On occasion, owners did not even wait for a slave to die, but directly reported the death of the *emancipado*. In exchange for payment, the rural judge would confirm the death and the false proof was sent to the political secretary. There were even cases in which the office received death certificates of *emancipados* who had been consigned but had not even left the depot of runaways or been sent to the estate where they were said to have died (Estorch 1856: 6–160; Figuera 1866: 15; Valiente 1869: 18–20).

Although there is little statistical information about *emancipados*, the existence of extremely high rates of mortality during certain periods is evidence of *plagio*. *Emancipados* were counted for the first time in March 1831 (table 6.2).[18] By then,

Table 6.2. *Emancipados* Up to March 1831 and Mortality

	Men	**Women**	**Total**
Existing total in March 1831	1,531	829	2,380
Introduced from December 1824 to March 1831	1,981	1,008	2,989
Percentage by sex	66.29	32.72	—
Dead (or disappeared)	440	179	609
Percentage mortality by sex	70.60	29.39	—
Percentage mortality for the period	21.70	17.75	20.37
Percentage annual mortality rate	3.52	2.88	3.30

Source: AHN, *Estado*, 8033/2.

fifteen vessels had been captured and 2,989 blacks emancipated. At that date, there were 2,380 *emancipados.* A simple calculation reveals that the yearly average of people who had died or disappeared for the period was 3.30 percent, a very modest figure when compared with subsequent periods and with the mortality estimated for slave population. At this stage, the practice had not yet begun of handing over *emancipados* to plantation owners.

We have a relatively complete statement for *emancipados* for 1841, which lists the year of capture of those surviving (table 6.3, page 138). With this information and other fragmentary data, we can estimate the number of *emancipados* who disappeared or died in different periods.[19] Thus it was that in October 1843, when Leopoldo O'Donnell took over, there were 3,743 *emancipados.* If we add these to the 734 apprehended from June 1841 until that date, and deduct the 1,300 to whom General Valdés had granted charters of freedom (as we shall see below), in October there must have been 3,916 *emancipados.* The difference—of barely 170—was the number who had died or disappeared: a low figure, which corresponds to the period of government of General Valdés, who is accredited with strict compliance with the treaties on *emancipados* and control of the most outrageous forms of abuse.

It is interesting to compare this with what happened later. When General O'Donnell reached Havana in October 1843, there were 3,743 *emancipados.* By

Table 6.3. Emancipated Blacks in June 1841

	Ships	Blacks Captured			Handed over to Britain		Deaths		Fugitives		Freed Persons		Unknown		Total on Total on Island		
		M	W	Total	M	W	M	W	M	W	M	W	M	W	M	W	Total
1824	1	92	55	147	—	—	38	10	1		7	13	1	3	45	29	74
1826	4	474	184	658	—	—	190	56	15	1	32	26	1		236	101	337
1828	3	706	308	1,014	—	—	302	86	14	6	6	17	6		373	204	577
1829	4	577	301	878	—	—	198	95	21	5	7	11			252	189	541
1830	2	132	160	292	—	—	64	47	2			8	1	5	65	100	165
1832	3	784	182	966	—	—	382	78	14	4	4	1	5		379	99	478
1833	3	1,040	250	1,290	110	102	337	38	17	1	6	1	40	4	530	104	634
1834	2	356	199	555	94	99	85	18	3	1	1	1			173	80	253
1835	7	1,681	545	2,226	284	288	553	69	16	1	3		1		826	185	1,011
1836	2	392	189	581	—	—	172	46		1					219	143	362
1841	1	360	53	413	—	—	8								352	53	405
		6,594	2,426	9,020	488	489	2,329	543	103	19	64	81	35	12	3,550	1,289	4,837
							+303	+52							–303	–52	–335
							2,632	595							3,349	1,235	4,482

Source: Author's compilation based on AHN, *Estado*, 8040, statement of Spanish vessels captured by British warships, June 29, 1841. In addition to the deaths that appear in the appropriate boxes, 350 notifications of death provided by corporations and individuals lacked information about the year of capture. These are noted in a separate box, added to the total number of deaths, and deducted in the box applicable to existing ones.

February 1848, at the end of his period of command, 229 had been captured and 459 obtained their freedom. When he left, there were just 2,353 *emancipados*: in other words, 1,163, or 33 percent, had disappeared, making a 6.61 percent the annual average of deaths or disappearances during the four-and-a-half years of his command. When Federico Roncali took over, there were 2,353 *emancipados*, but when General Concha arrived in November 1850, there were 2,138.[20] Between the two dates, 387 black slaves had been captured and charters of freedom awarded to 222, making a figure of 2,518 *emancipados* in November, and an average of deaths or disappearances of 6.03 percent during his period of command. In a further example, in 1857, seven expeditions were captured and 2,111 slaves emancipated. After five years, in 1862, only 734 remained; 65 percent had died or disappeared, in other words, a 10.87 percent annual average.[21]

These figures are even higher than the estimated mortality rates for sugar-mill slaves. Indeed, Alexander von Humboldt calculated this at 8 percent (Humboldt 1856: 203), while Manuel Moreno Fraginals set the figure at 6.3 percent (Moreno Fraginals 1978, 2: 88).[22] Some contemporary authors had already drawn their own conclusions (Turnbull 1840: 150). "The truth is that the mortality figure is exorbitant and either reveals abuse or a series of crimes regarding which the hand of justice is not acting with sufficient energy" (Figuera 1866: 14).

Nor did the birth rates bear any relation to those that have been estimated for slaves. According to the figures of the budget for 1856–1857, three boys and eight girls had been born in Cuba; in 1858, three and seven respectively.[23] The *Cuadro estadístico* published in 1862 accounted for 21 boys and 18 girls under the age of one year, which represented a birth rate of 5.86 percent, of a total of 6,650 *emancipados* (n.a. 1862; Gutiérrez de la Concha 1861: 16). Moreno Fraginals estimated, for the slave population, rates of 19 percent between 1835 and 1841 and 28 percent between 1856 and 1860, when the rise in the price of slaves promoted the adoption of a reproduction policy (Moreno Fraginals 1978, 2: 88).

The population census of 1861 was the only one to compile data on *emancipados*. In the eastern part of Cuba, distanced from the authorities in charge of distribution, their number was insignificant and they were concentrated in Santiago de

Cuba, where they worked in the copper mines. The only jurisdiction in the east with a high number of *emancipados* was Puerto Príncipe—to which the 448 slaves captured by the *Blasco de Garay* had been sent—with 8.39 percent of the total. A total of 35.84 percent of emancipated people were located in the jurisdiction of Havana. In Sagua, Colon, Cárdenas, Santiago de las Vegas, Jaruco, Guanajay Matanzas, Remedios, and Güines, all of which were major sugar-producing areas, there were also large percentages. In general, in 1861, *emancipados* could be found in areas of intense economic activity, where there were also large numbers of slaves (Roldán de Montaud 1982: 589–92).

British Abolitionist Pressure and the Emancipados

Emancipados found it extremely difficult to acquire the coveted charter of freedom, the document that would guarantee their civil condition as free people. Reluctance to declare *emancipados* exempt from government guardianship persisted. Only at particular moments were there signs of more willingness on the part of some authority, and generally only in response to an increase in British abolitionist pressure. The *emancipados* as a group were indeed the object of British pressure from the time the group first formed until it finally disappeared in 1870. Although the Spanish government was guarantor of the freedom of *emancipados*, the British government was in a position to demand observance of this guarantee in compliance with the Treaties of 1817 and 1835. A similar situation opened a window of opportunity used by Britain to intervene in internal Cuban affairs regarding slave trade and slavery.

Whenever the British authorities accused the Cubans of permitting African slave trading, the Spanish government invariably claimed that it was doing everything in its power to put an end to this pernicious form of commerce. The *emancipados* as a group afforded the only real target of pressure. If Britain could tear away from slavery this group of black *bozales* (who were, after all, slaves who had been introduced into Cuba illegally), then this measure could be extended to the rest who had not been discovered, but were continually being disembarked on Cuba's coasts.

By June 29, 1841—fifteen years after the first slaves were captured—only 64 men and 81 women of the respective figures of 6,554 and 2,426 *emancipados* had received charters of freedom. As might be expected, there was more of a tendency to release women and *emancipados* who had been in service for a longer period. Indeed, of the 64 men, 52 had been captured before 1829 and the rest before 1835. As the average lifespan of an adult slave in the *ingenios* was fifteen years, the *emancipados* who gained their freedom were those who were no longer very capable of working. In any case, receiving the charter of freedom did not guarantee they would actually be released. Indeed, when in 1854 General Concha ruled that all consignations of *emancipados* should be renewed, applications for renewal were even made for *emancipados* who were already supposed to have received their charters of freedom, which obviously meant these had been given to other people—that is, if they had been given at all.

In the early 1840s, British abolitionist pressure grew more intense. In November 1840, Turnbull arrived in Havana, having been appointed consul precisely for his abolitionist fervor. Once he was in Cuba, the issue of emancipated people was to become one of the sticking points in the dispute between Britain and Spain on slave trading. At the consul's behest, in December, Britain tried to impose the signing of an agreement to emancipate all slaves illegally introduced as of 1820.[24] In view of the average lifespan of slaves, the initiative essentially meant the total abolition of slavery. Although Spain resisted, Britain did obtain a greater commitment by bringing the treaties to bear.

In May 1841, General Valdes arrived in Havana with instructions that slave trading should be severely punished. In the same month, Britain suggested to Spain that *emancipados* be brought before the Mixed Commission with a view to ascertaining their situation and preferences for being transferred to a British colony.[25] Britain had abolished slavery in 1833 and the transition from slave labor to wage-earner in the West Indies was causing disruption with the resulting decrease in production. To alleviate the problem, "apprentices" had been taken from British enclaves in Africa, as well as hundreds of black *emancipados* by the Mixed Commission of Sierra Leone. Naturally enough, there was also an attempt to attract emancipated

Cubans. However, Spain could not accept the proposal, because it was tantamount to allowing a foreign authority to examine the condition of *emancipados* in compliance with the Treaty of 1817, which stipulated that they be handed over to the government where the Commission was based. Whereas in the early 1830s, the Spanish authorities in Cuba had tried to get rid of emancipated people, they no longer seemed willing to manage without them. Moreover, they were convinced that if they were to give in concerning the case of emancipated people, it would prove impossible to fight against any inquiry into slaves. Although Valdés was determined to put an end to slave trading, he also wished to defend the institution of slavery, which he saw as essential to maintain the colony.[26]

In a bid to remove any reason for complaint while forestalling further demands, Valdés undertook to provide *emancipados* with charters of freedom within five years as of January 1842, as consignations ran out.[27] Between January 1842 and September 1843, when he left his command, he had delivered 1,300 charters.[28] For the first time, the name they bore was genuine, because in that period, any *emancipado* who had served the four-year term under his purchaser was collected and set free (Pezuela 1878, 4: 360; Franco 1980: 374). The British commissioners acknowledged that emancipated people were now receiving their charters of freedom.

To reassure plantation owners, who were convinced that Spain would be forced to abolish slavery, and to prevent the annexationist tendency toward the United States among them, in 1843 the new Spanish government changed tack and sent General Leopoldo O'Donnell to Cuba. Shortly after his arrival, the slave revolt known as the "Conspiracy of *La Escalera*" took place; it was brutally suppressed by the General, with hundreds of slaves murdered (Hernández Sánchez Barba 1957: 241–329; Paquette 1988). As it was claimed that free people of color had been involved, and that the release of *emancipados* had contributed to the growing unrest among slaves, in March 1844, O'Donnell suspended the granting of charters of freedom and the delivery of the lists of freed *emancipados*, which Valdés had been sending to the British commissioners. In April, he notified the government of the measures adopted to maintain order: once the initiated proceedings were over, a gradual and careful expulsion was to take place, not only of all those involved, but of all those of the same race. He also deported vast numbers of the *emancipados* who had received charters of freedom from his predecessor, and had been allowed to remain on the island, where "the right with which they had been made acquainted in the midst of the slaves, had proved so disastrous."[29] The government in Madrid approved the decision to expel the culprits and accepted that any blacks who so wished could be sent to Fernando Po at their own expense.

Since suspending the delivery of charters of freedom might lead to complaints by Britain, from September 1844 onward, a number of charters were awarded to a limited number of *emancipados*, who were then handed over to the British authorities, a practice that had systematically been denied by captain generals since 1836. In fact, in the context of this new flare-up of racial tensions, they resorted to this procedure mainly to rid themselves of the more awkward elements of a group considered a social threat. In 1845, 214 were handed over, virtually all those released that year. In the following year, 132 were transferred to British authorities. Once the immediate fears of conspiracy subsided, both the granting of charters of freedom and the number of blacks handed over to the British authorities declined.[30]

British pressure and the horror caused by the slave uprising led to the passing of the criminal law of 1845 to abolish slave trading. The law provided for harsher penalties for slave traders, but did not authorize inquiries to be conducted on properties to determine which slaves had been introduced after 1820. Indeed, for several years, the number of Africans illegally imported annually into Cuba declined dramatically, dropping from about 10,000 in the 1830s and early 1840s to 1,500 immediately after the *Escalera* conspiracy.

In October 1852, complaints from Britain intensified. Its government was convinced that, as long as the sugar estates enjoyed immunity and no register was made of existing slaves, treaties to regulate the slave trade would continue to be evaded. But circumstances soon became favorable for further pressure on the Spanish government. The following month saw the election as U.S. president of Franklin Pierce, known for his markedly expansionist leanings. Supporters of annexation then organized a new expedition which, under General Quitman's leadership, was to support an internal revolt in Cuba. Britain's help was more necessary than ever, and to obtain it, Spain would have to make concessions. Thus, on March 31, 1853, the government ordered that, by the end of the year, all black persons emancipated by Havana's Mixed Commission according to the Treaty of 1817 must be freed. As for slaves emancipated subsequent to the 1835 Treaty, freedom would be given to those who had served five years of consignation and to the remainder as swiftly as possible.[31] The inclusion of *emancipados* who had been emancipated by the Spanish authorities, to whom Britain had no title to lodge complaints, revealed the need for support at an extremely serious moment for Spanish sovereignty in Cuba. The British government was immediately informed of the decision.

General Juan Manuel de la Pezuela arrived in Cuba in December to implement the new policy. He swiftly adopted measures that spread panic among landowners and slaveholders. After announcing that treaties would be strictly observed, his edict that same month declared the freedom of *emancipados* captured before 1835.[32] In January 1854, he published a bylaw regarding *emancipados* that extensively regulated the situation.[33] It established that liberated Africans were all free. Those who had been in the power of the authorities for five years and were sixteen years old would obtain their charters of freedom. They should hire out their labor for a year, during which men would have the right to monthly wages of six pesos and women to four. The wages of those who had not been under the authority for five years would be administered by the Emancipado Protection Board. As normal black wages were about 20 to 25 pesos a month, anyone hiring an *emancipado* would be getting very cheap labor.

When General Pezuela convened the trustees of *emancipados* through the *Gaceta*, only 900 of the 2,098 thought to exist appeared (table 6.4). Very few were actually given their certificate or were able to choose their employer, because, among other reasons, Pezuela was replaced in September (Valiente 1869: 13; Estorch 1856: 15; Roldán de Montaud 1982: 624–27).[34] The *emancipados* were, in any case, forced to continue work on the farms. In this way, the group of free blacks—based mainly in the city—was prevented from joining forces at a moment of acute labor shortage. The *emancipados* became a test for the conversion of slaves into free wage-earners, at a moment when labor was scarce and a time when the immigration of Chinese settlers and even African apprentices was being promoted.

Table 6.4. Slaves Captured by British Cruisers and Cuban Authorities Up to 1854 and Declared *Emancipados*

From captures made by British cruisers	8,769
Apprehended by subaltern authorities	2,479
Handed over to Britain and transported to Trinidad	987
Released up to December 31, 1840	147
Released up to November 30, 1853	2,063
Deaths, fugitives, cimarróns, insane, and taken in by hospices	5,975
Existing in January 1854	2,098

Source: AHN, *Estado,* 8046, statement of *emancipados* apprehended by British cruisers and by the island's subaltern authorities, February 6, 1854.

On May 3, Pezuela issued an edict empowering the authorities to enter estates to check the identity of black people and announced the creation of a slave register and the freedom of all those not included on it. Rumors began to spread that Pezuela wished to *Africanize* the island and that Britain and Spain had agreed to put an end to slavery (Urban 1957: 29–45). The fear that abolition would soon be decreed led to a growth in annexationism. To restore confidence, Pezuela was replaced by General Concha, who immediately abandoned the antislavery policy inspired by Britain. Once the danger of federal government intervention in the island's affairs had passed and the plantation owners were reassured, there was no longer any need to placate Britain on the issue of *emancipados.*

Concha repealed the May edict and abandoned the slave register. He replaced Pezuela's bylaw on *emancipados,* which plantation and slave owners so disliked, with a new one in December. In Pezuela's bylaw, *emancipados* who had served for five years were freed, and the government only intervened in their recruitment to prevent any reduction in the labor force and to protect them; in Concha's bylaw, *emancipados* became apprentices for five years and were then considered *colonos,* subject to contracts which the government renewed every three years, and for wages that were comparatively far lower than those that existed on the free labor market (Rodríguez San Pedro 1865, 2: 601–04). These *colonos* were subject to a regime similar to that which existed for the contracted Chinese, with the added disadvantage that there was no limit on their contract. Despite British opposition, the bylaw remained in force until 1865. A solution to the *emancipado* issue was only sought years later, when the need for a gradual abolition of slavery was finally taken seriously.

The 1860s and the Moret Law

Gradually, signs of change appeared. Annexationism gave way to the predominance of reformist positions among Creoles, slave trading was condemned, and the search began for a gradual solution to the slavery issue (Corwin 1967: 134). Under a system of servitude, it was hard to endow agricultural work with a sense of dignity, and not surprisingly, the desired attempts to bring in white settlers to farm the land failed. On the other hand, the turn of events in the United States was decisive in the adoption of abolitionist positions in Madrid. When, in April 1862, Abraham Lincoln signed a treaty giving British cruisers visiting rights, the slave trade that had developed under the American flag was doomed. From that point onward, the Spanish government could no longer resist the pressure to put an end to the slave trade, because if the abolitionist North were to win the Civil War, the United States would use the slavery issue as a pretext to intervene in Cuba's internal affairs.

In a society where slaves were destined to become wage-earning rural workers, there was no point in holding in a condition of slavery a group with free status, which had been reduced to this condition precisely because of its potential dangers for destabilizing the system. At the moment when the gradual abolition of slavery was contemplated, it seemed appropriate to begin with this group of genuine "government slaves." At the end of 1862, after consultations with the Council of State, regulations were issued to put an end to the *emancipado* problem: *emancipados* who had served their first consignation would be divided into three series, which would receive their freedom that year and the two following years.[35] However, the scope of this freedom was once again restricted, with blacks remaining subject to the tenant farmer bylaw. In fact, the opposition of the plantation owners and the scarcity of labor hampered implementation of the measure and British consul complaints about failure to comply with pledges continued.

Once the war in the United States was over, the moment arrived to end the slave trade. It was obvious that nobody would believe the government genuinely proposed to put an end to the trade at the same time that it benefited from the results; there was a need to convince people both at home and abroad—as Overseas Minister Antonio Cánovas argued—that the government was determined to prepare a peaceful solution to slavery. Thus on August 10, 1865, the Council of State approved a new regulation of *emancipados* that was more in keeping with the spirit of the treaties before the Treaty of 1854. The new legislation stepped up guarantees designed to prevent the most common abuses. A list of *emancipados* and another of trustees had to be sent to the Royal *Audiencia*. The attorney for the government could visit the *emancipado* depot whenever he deemed it necessary.[36] In short, the role and management of the governor general was controlled. On the other hand, the figure of the emancipated tenant farmer or *colono* disappeared, because it was established that a month after the five years of consignation were complete, the names of *emancipados* would be published in the *Gaceta*, and they would be treated like the other free people of their race. General Dulce, however, decided not to implement the new bylaw. He insisted that five years was insufficient for black apprenticeship, because they were "indolent and lazy . . . court cases or inmates of jails." Indeed, at that time, most *emancipados* were on estates and the general was aware of how difficult it would be to oppose plantation-owner pressure.[37]

Madrid was quick to respond. On October 28, 1865, General Dulce was ordered to send the blacks captured on the *Gato* and any that were seized in the future to Fernando Po, where they would be set totally free.[38] Thus an end was put to the problem for the future. In fact, however, after the *Gato* expedition, only one further disembarkation of *bozales* was recorded (table 6.1). Existing *emancipados* would then enter the depot when their consignation ended to be declared free. The power exercised by captains general to consign *emancipados* was revoked. Concerned not to deprive plantation owners of their labor during the harvest, Dulce once again ignored the government's stipulations. Finally, he gave in: several months later, on March 4, he ruled that the *emancipados* belonging to the thirty-three oldest expeditions should present at the depot, where they would receive their charters of freedom. From November 1865 until May 1866, 421 charters were awarded to the 6,650 existing *emancipados*. Subjected to government and plantation-owners' pressure, in the following months, his successors continued to grant the charters, although at an extremely slow pace.

In September 1868, a revolutionary movement overthrew Queen Isabella II, and shortly afterward a proindependence revolt began in Cuba. The insurgents adopted the abolition principle, forcing the Madrid government to take steps to prevent the United States from considering this a state of war and intervening in the conflict. In May 1870, Overseas Minister Segismundo Moret wrote to the captain general: "France and Britain will not help us whilst we have slaves, and this word [slavery] gives America the right to dangle a sword above our heads" (Thomas 1973, 1: 341). Despite opposition from Cuban slave owners, in July 1870, the Spanish *Cortes* approved the Moret Law, which prepared for the abolition of slavery. In Article V, it declared free all the slaves belonging to the State and those who, by "title of *emancipados*, were under the State's protection."[39] The fact that a law to abolish slavery should deal with a group that was legally free revealed the extent to which the freedom of *emancipado*s was merely nominal and that the 1865 bylaw had not been implemented. Indeed, in the midst of the conflict, the awarding of charters had been suspended and did not resume until September 1869, when the expeditions apprehended in 1841 and 1842 were declared exempt from government dependence. In February 1870, the same was applied to those captured between 1843 and 1849, and in June to those seized between 1849 and 1853 (Roldán de Montaud 1982: 638). The Moret Law was therefore not a novelty, but the culmination of a process already underway. It speeded up the pace at which government exemptions were decreed: on October 7, a charter was awarded to the 2,033 people captured between 1855 and 1858; on October 27, to the 2,459 seized in 1858, 1859, and part of 1860; and in December, to those captured between 1862 and 1866, who were the last ones. A total of 3,192 *emancipados* had been released (Corwin 1967: 249). But the Cuban authorities demanded that, when they obtained their freedom, they should hire out their labor for a six-year period for wages that were below market rates, and allowed their charters of freedom to be guarded by their owners by way of guarantee for compliance with their contract—a guarantee that was tantamount to sentencing the *emancipados* to slavery. The Madrid government strongly opposed the measure and on September 28 ruled that the clause be removed. In the meantime, however, 1,777 such contracts had already been signed. No greater criticism could have been voiced than that of abolitionist Rafael María de Labra:

"The contracts of 1870 are plainly and simply slavery; but slavery of a hypocritical and cowardly kind. By the ingenious means of these contracts, Cuba's *emancipados* will fall once again into the moulds of their former servitude, in this clever way of eluding the precepts of the preparatory law. Do we really need forced labour, even if it is remunerated? Then let's not talk about freedom" (1873: 19–22; trans.—I. M.).

Notes

1. Complete text appears in J. de la Pezuela (1863, 2: 286–91).

2. Liberated Africans existed in the British Caribbean after slave trade was abolished in 1807; see Alvin Thompson (2002).

3. See also the papers presented at the conference "Liberated Africans as a Human Legacy of Abolition: An International Workshop to Mark the Bicentennial of British and American Abolitions of the Slave Trade," Berkeley, CA, May 1–3, 2008.

4. Archivo Histórico Nacional (AHN), *Estado*, 8017. Record of the Mixed Commission, Havana, July 10, 1824, and AHN, *Estado*, 8031.

5. AHN, *Ultramar*, 3549/19, Vives al secretario de Estado y Despacho, 6 de enero de 1825.

6. AHN, *Ultramar*, 3547/7, Exposition Council of Havana, October 13, 1826; and Council of State Agreement, February 4, 1828; and Fontana (1975: 89–98).

7. AHN, *Estado*, 8034/6, Count of Villanueva's note to British commissioners, January 23, 1833, and response. On the negotiations, see Murray (1980: 277–79) and R. M. Adderley (2006).

8. The price of *bozales* ranged from 200 to 300 pesos. In these circumstances, authorities were more concerned to prevent the growth of the free population than any potential loss of labor.

9. AHN, *Estado*, 2022/3, Consultation of Council of the Indies, September 7, 1826.

10. AHN, *Ultramar*, 3548/4, quoted in the opinion issued by the Overseas Council, April 22, 1853; see Eréncun 1858, 2: 1436–37.

11. One example of the distribution conditions in AHN, *Ultramar*, 3549/19. In Brazil, the consignation lasted 14 years, virtually the full duration of a slave's useful life; see Galloti Mamigonian (2009: 236–37).

12. *Defensa de la verdad y de los mineros de la isla de Cuba*. Havana, 1839, p. 66.

13. Archivo Nacional de Cuba, *Gobierno Superior Civil*, 1581/41814 to 41829.

14. AHN, *Estado*, 8057, Turnbull to the Prince of Angola, December 21, 1841, and 8019, complaint lodged by the British plenipotentiary to the Secretary of State in favor of Gabino, March 22, 1842. For recent research on Gabino's case, see O. Gandío Moráguez (2008).

15. For *coartación*, see R. R. Madden (1849: 133–44) and Varella (2010).

16. AHN, *Estado*, 8034, Note from British Judge Commissioner to Tacón, December 9, 1834; *Estado*, 8035, Villiers to Isturiz, May 27, 1836; and Tacón to the Secretary of State, August 31, 1836; also, Pérez de la Riva (1963: 262).

17. Decree of June 27, 1856, in F. Eréncun (1858, 2: 1444).

18. AHN, *Estado*, 8033, exp. 2, general statement showing number of *emancipados* from the fifteen ships that had been captured by British ships from 1824 to date of publication, March 12, 1831.

19. On the reasoning below, see Roldán de Montaud 1982: 582–89.

20. AHN, *Estado*, 8044, Concha to Secretary of State, June 9, 1851.

21. AHN, *Ultramar*, 4666, letter from General Dulce, dated December 1862.

22. The commissioners' figures, quoted by Kenneth Kiple (1976: 53).

23. Biblioteca Nacional de España, Madrid (hereafter BN), ms. 13853, Budget corresponding to *emancipados* for the years 1856–57–58.

24. AHN, *Estado*, 8040/7, Draft agreement on slave emancipation, December 17, 1840. It was proposed that the powers of the Mixed Commission should be increased, to declare the freedom of slaves suspected of being illegally introduced; see Turnbull (1840: 342–48).

25. In April 1840, a similar request had already been made.

26. AHN, *Estado*, 8035, Valdés to the Secretary of State, May 31, 1841.

27. AHN, *Estado*, 8040, Valdés to the Secretary of State, July 31, 1841.

28. AHN, *Estado*, 8040, Valdés to the Secretary of State, April 30, 1842, and *Ultramar*, 4039, O'Donnell to the Secretary of State.

29. AHN, *Ultramar*, 4620/33, O'Donnell to the Secretary of State, April 26, 1844.

30. AHN, *Estado*, 8037, and *Ultramar*, 4046, List of the Cuban slaves who received charters of freedom between 1845 and 1851, sent to the British plenipotentiary on March 26, 1852.

31. AHN, *Ultramar*, 4666, Note from the Count of Alcoy, March 4, 1853.

32. BN. ms. 13853, 73–75.

33. Bylaw of January 1854 in BN. ms. 13853, fols. 79–82, *Ordenanza de Emancipados de 1 de enero de 1854*, fols. 79–82.

34. BN. ms. 13853, pp. 84–88 and 101–97.

35. AHN, *Ultramar*, 4666, Consultation of Overseas Section of the Council of State, November 14, 1862, and Rodríguez San Pedro (1865, 2: 606–7), Royal Order of December 12, 1862.

36. AHN, *Ultramar*, 4666, Regulation for the regime of emancipated blacks, August 10, 1865.

37. On Dulce's attitude and the new bylaw, see Roldán de Montaud 1982: 633–34.

38. As well as facilitating relationships with Britain, the decision was intended to alleviate the shortage of labor on the Spanish possession in the Gulf of Guinea (de Granda 1984: 562–63; Roldán de Montaud 1982: 635).

39. *Gaceta de Madrid*, 1870, no. 187, 07/7, p. 2.

Works Cited

Adderley, Roseanne M. 2006. *"New Negroes from Africa": Slave Trade Abolition and Free African Settlement in the Nineteenth-Century Caribbean.* Bloomington: Indiana University Press.

Aimes, Hubert. 1967. *A History of Slavery in Cuba: 1511 to 1868*. New York: Octagon Books.

Arnalte, Arturo, 2001. *Los últimos esclavos de Cuba: Los niños cautivos de la goleta Batans.* Madrid: Alianza.

Bethell, Leslie. 1966. "The Mixed Commissions for the Suppression of the Transatlantic Slave Trade in the Nineteenth Century." *Journal of African History* 7: 79–93.

Carter, Marina. 2003. *The Last Slaves: Liberated Africans in 19th Century Mauritius*. [Port Luis, Mauritius]: Centre for Research on Indian Ocean Societies.

Conrad, Robert. 1973. "Neither Slave nor Free: The Emancipados of Brazil, 1818–1868." *The Hispanic American Historical Review* (Durham, NC), 53 (1): 50–70.

Corwin, Arthur F. 1967. *Spain and the Abolition of Slavery in Cuba: 1817–1886*. Austin: University of Texas Press.

Erénchun, Félix. 1857–1861. *Anales de la isla de Cuba: Diccionario administrativo, económico, estadístico y legislativo*. 4 vols. Havana: Imprenta La Habanera.

Estorch, Miguel. 1856. *Apuntes para la historia de la administración del Marqués de la Pezuela en la isla de Cuba, desde el 3 de diciembre de 1853 hasta el 21 de septiembre de 1854*. Madrid: M. Galiano.

Ferrer de Couto, José. 1864. *Los negros en sus diversos estados y condiciones tales como son, como se supone que son y cómo deben ser*. New York: Hallet Breen.

Figuera, Fermín. 1866. *Estudios sobre la isla de Cuba: La cuestión social*. Madrid: Impr. del Colegio de Sordo-Mudos y de Ciegos.

Fontana, Josep. 1975. "El problema de los 'emancipados' cubanos ante el Consejo de Estado español (1828)." *Revista de la Biblioteca Nacional José Martí*. 3rd series, 17 (2): 89–98.

Franco, José Luciano. 1980. *El comercio clandestino de esclavos*. Havana, Cuba: Ciencias Sociales.

Granda, Germán de. 1984. "Negros emancipados cubanos en Fernando Poo." *Revista de Indias* 54 (174): 559–66.

Grandío Moráguez, Oscar. 2008. "Gabino: A Liberated African Story." Unpubl. paper delivered at "Liberated Africans as Human Legacy of Abolition: An International Workshop to Mark the Bicentennial of British and American Abolitions of the Slave Trade," University of California, Berkeley, May 1–3.

Gutiérrez de la Concha, José. 1861. *Memoria sobre el ramo de los emancipados de la Isla de Cuba*. Madrid: La América.

Hernández Sánchez Barba, Mario. 1957. "David Turnbull y el problema de la esclavitud en Cuba." *Anuario de Estudios Americanos* (Seville) 14: 241–329.

Humboldt, Alexander von. 1856. *The Island of Cuba*. New York: Derby & Jackson.

James, Anand. 1991. *The Emigration of Liberated Africans to British Guiana, 1841–1852*. Turkeyen: University of Guyana.

Kiple, Kenneth. 1976. *Blacks in Colonial Cuba (1774–1899)*. Gainesville: University Presses of Florida.

Klein, Herbert S. 1986. *La esclavitud africana en América latina y el Caribe*. Madrid: Alianza Editorial.

Labra, Rafael María de. 1873. *La abolición de la esclavitud en el orden económico*. Madrid: Noguera.

Madden, Richard R. 1840. *Poems by a Slave in the Island of Cuba, Recently Liberated.* London: T. Ward and Co.

———. 1849. *The Island of Cuba: Its Resources, Progress, and Prospects, Considered in Relation Especially to the Influence of Its Prosperity on the Interests of the British West India Colonies*. London: C. Gilpin.

Mamigonian, Beatriz Gallotti. 2005. "Revisitando o problema da 'transição para o trabalho livre' no Brasil: A experiência dos africanos livres." In *Tráfico, cativeiro e liberdade (Rio de Janeiro, séculos XVII–XIX)*, edited by M. Florentino. Rio de Janeiro: Civilização Brasileira, 389–417.

———. 2009a. "Conflicts over the Meanings of Freedom: The Liberated Africans' Struggle for Emancipation in Brazil, 1840s–1860s." In *Paths to Freedom: Manumission in the Atlantic World*, edited by R. Brana-Shute et al. Columbia: University of South Carolina Press.

———. 2009b. "In the Name of Freedom: Slave Trade Abolition, the Law and the Brazilian Branch of the African Emigration Scheme (Brazil-British West Indies, 1830s–1850s)." *Slavery & Abolition* 30 (1): 41–66.

Martínez-Alier, Verena. 1979. *Marriage, Class and Colour in Nineteenth-Century Cuba: A Study of Racial Attitudes and Sexual Values in a Slave Society*. London: Cambridge University Press.

Martínez-Fernández, Luis. 1995. "The Havana Anglo-Spanish Mixed Commission for the Suppression of the Slave Trade and Cuba's Emancipados," *Slavery and Abolition* (London) 16 (2): 205–25.

———. 1998. *Fighting Slavery in the Caribbean: The Life and Times of a British Family in Nineteenth-Century Havana*. New York: M. E. Sharpe.

Moreno Fraginals, Manuel. 1978. *El ingenio: Complejo económico social cubano del azúcar.* 3 vols. Havana: Ciencias Sociales.

Murray, David R. 1980. *Odious Commerce: Britain, Spain and the Abolition of the Cuban Slave Trade*. Cambridge, UK: Cambridge University Press.

n.a. 1862. *Cuadro estadístico general que demuestra la población total de la isla de Cuba.* [Havana]: Imprenta del Gobierno.

Paquette, Robert L. 1988. *Sugar Is Made with Blood: The Conspiracy of La Escalera and the Conflict between Empires over Slavery in Cuba*. Middletown, CT: Wesleyan University Press.

Pérez de la Riva, Juan, ed. 1963. *Correspondencia reservada del Capitán General Don Miguel Tacón con el gobierno de Madrid: 1834–1836*. Havana: Consejo Nacional de Cultura-Biblioteca Nacional José Martí.

Pezuela, Jacobo de la. 1863. *Diccionario geográfico, estadístico, histórico, de la isla de Cuba*. 4 vols. Madrid: Imprenta de Mellado.

———. 1878. *Historia de la isla de Cuba*. 4 vols. Madrid: Bailly-Baillière.

Rodríguez San Pedro, Joaquín. 1865–1869. *Legislación ultramarina concordada y anotada*. 16 vols. Madrid: Imprenta de Viota, Cubas y Vicente.

Roldán de Montaud, Inés. 1982. "Origen evolución y supresión del grupo de negros emancipados en Cuba (1817–1870)." *Revista de Indias* 57 (169–170): 559–641.

———. 2011. "En los borrosos confines de la libertad: El caso de los negros emancipados en Cuba, 1817–1870." *Revista de Indias* 71 (251): 159–92. doi:10.3989/revindias.2011.007.

Schuler, Monica. 1980. *"Alas, Alas, Kongo": A Social History of Indentured African Immigration into Jamaica*. Baltimore, MD: The Johns Hopkins University Press.

———. 2001. "Liberated Africans in Nineteenth-Century Guyana." In *Slavery, Freedom and Gender: The Dynamics of Caribbean Societies*, edited by Brian L. Moore et al. Mona, Jamaica: University of the West Indies Press, 133–160.

Thomas, Hugh. 1973. *Cuba: la lucha por la libertad 1762–1970*, 1: *De la dominación española a la dominación norteamericana, 1762–1909*. Barcelona: Ediciones Grijalbo.

Thompson, Alvin. 2002. *Unprofitable Servants: Crown Slaves in Berbice, Guiana 1803–1831*. Mona, Jamaica: University of the West Indies Press.

Turnbull, David. 1840. *Travels in the West: Cuba, with Notices of Porto Rico, and the Slave Trade*. London: Longmans.

Urban, C. Stanley. 1957. "The Africanization of Cuba Scare, 1853–1855." *Hispanic American Historical Review* 37 (1): 29–45.

Valiente, Porfirio. 1869. *Réformes dans les îles de Cuba et de Porto-Rico*. Paris: Impr. Centrale des Chemins de Fer, A. Chaix et Cie.

Varella, Claudia. 2010. *Esclavos a sueldo: La coartación cubana en el siglo XIX*. Unpubl. PhD. diss. Universitat Jaume I, Castelló de la Plana, Spain.

Archival Materials

Archivo Histórico Nacional, Madrid, (AHN), *Estado*; *Ultramar*.

Archivo Nacional de Cuba, *Gobierno Superior Civil*, 1581/41814 to 41829.

Biblioteca Nacional de España, Madrid (BN), ms. 13853.

Defensa de la verdad y de los mineros de la isla de Cuba. Havana. 1839.

Gaceta de Madrid, 1870, núm. 187.

Plantation Laboratories

Industrial Experiments in the Cuban Sugar Mill, 1830–1860

Daniel Rood

On a bright, muggy morning in June of 1841, laborers gulping down a quick mug of *guarapo* at the local beverage stand on Havana's Obispo Street would have seen some curious goings-on behind the counter. José Luis Casaseca, head chemist of the recently inaugurated Instituto de Investigaciones Químicas, had set up an improvised laboratory at the drink stall together with his friend, the engineer and lithographer Carlos Roca. The ad hoc laboratory included a pneumatic engine, a small-scale sugar mill designed for experimental purposes, and a hydrometer on loan from Casaseca's colleague, the pharmacist Joaquin Cabezas.

The "pneumatic engine" was an air pump that created a vacuum in an enclosed jar. Inside, the juice crushed by the mill could be analyzed with full control of variables—a pure environment intruded upon only by the tools of quantification wielded by the sugar chemist. The hydrometer, a graduated glass stem with a bulbous bottom end, could tell an experimenter the relative proportions of sugar and water in the fluid by how deeply the hydrometer floated when dropped upright into the cane juice (McCulloh 1848: 3–5, 55). With such a method, the pair of scientists hoped to calculate the relative quantities of crystallizable sugar, water, mineral salts, and organic byproducts present in different varieties of cane. By revealing these proportions as they stood directly after the grinding of the cane and prior to the multistage evaporation phase of production, Casaseca's experiments would make possible a more precise estimate of the amounts of sugar sacrificed to the imperfections of the manufacturing process.[1]

To ensure the most accurate results, Casaseca wrote, it would have been preferable "to carry the pneumatic engine to a plantation and there conduct the delicate experiments of a laboratory."[2] Unfortunately, the harvest season had ended. The closest the chemist could come to reproducing the ideal conditions of a plantation laboratory, by this time well established as a site of experiment, was to use cane from garden-size plantings on the outskirts of the city, cane that was usually cut, carried to the *guarapería* on Obispo Street, and there sold out of the stall as a sweet, refreshing source of calories.

The plantation laboratory had been by necessity moved to this location.[3] The proprietor of the drink stall may have found his morning routine intruded upon, perhaps brushing by the chemist in the bustle of the morning rush, muttering a quick "*con permiso*" as his hip set a test tube wobbling on Casaseca's lab table. The physical intimacy of molasses hawker and sugar chemist, or said another way, of the market and the laboratory, demonstrates the changing place of scientific experimentation in Cuba's plantation-centered society.

A sign of the changing times, the rigged-up, outdoor, in-store chemistry laboratory might have attracted a few gawkers on their morning errands, but this would have been more of an annoyance than anything else for the chemist and the lithographer. It is not that "science" was a new arrival in Cuba—far from it.[4] However, the experiments related to the sugar export economy fifty years prior had been island-stopping spectacles, sharing the special glow and slow pace of an important saint's day. By the middle decades of the nineteenth century, though, acts of capitalist knowledge production like this experiment had been transformed from occasional performances to daily practices of the slave-centered Atlantic economy. Research had come to be seen not as an interruption to the business day, but as an integral element of the quotidian, hum-drum production and sale of commodities. To the Enlightenment world's public demonstrations of electromagnetism's mysteries and crowd-awing balloon launches (DuBois 2004: 91)[5] were added the humble and barely visible data-gathering labors of the industrial era. A normalized, dispersed, experimental spirit sought to turn every coffee- or flour-laden clipper ship into "a floating observatory," and every sugar mill into a laboratory. Experimenters aimed to accumulate capital through the accumulation of knowledge to maximize efficient production of a good destined for the world market: the industrialization of experiment.[6]

I use the term *industrial* to suggest the predominance of the following characteristics: first, the experiments of the midcentury plantation laboratory were linked closely to the activity of commodity production. Second, the experiments' sustained, durable interventions in the business of manufacturing sugar means that they were industrious in character. Third, the plantation experiments developed within the context of the large-scale, mechanized production of a standardized commodity: sugar. As this chapter will show, in the age before large corporations, with their extensive R&D budgets and in-house staffs of laboratory technicians, industrial experimentation did exist, but it looked different. And some of its most important practices were developed on slave plantations.

The plantation was reshaped by the epistemological dictates imposed by mass production, becoming the most important space of knowledge production created to respond to new challenges that had arisen for the sugar export economy after about 1830.[7] These new challenges were layered atop those long presented by the particular exigencies of sugar making. Since sugar cane had to be ground within hours after it had been cut, and boiled immediately after that to precise temperatures, the organization of labor and the flow of materials from the field through the factory had an urgency that other forms of capitalist production did not. The margin for error was small. Once the fire was raging and the cauldrons were heated, any interruptions, from the perspective of the planter, would be costly in terms of labor, fuel, and sugar. In the sugar industry, then, there was an increased incentive to industrialize knowledge production: to blend experimentation and other data-gathering efforts into the flow of production. As the grinding, boiling, and drying of sugar became increasingly mechanized by the 1850s, the precise tempos became ever more sacred. The growing capital-intensive and large-scale character of sugar production made any interruptions to the flow of production frightfully cost-prohibitive.

In this chapter, I trace the transformation of the mid-nineteenth-century Cuban sugar plantation into a place of experimentation, a laboratory subsidized by planters, merchants, financiers, and the colonial government with the goal of making over the island's slave-centered mode of production according to the priorities (quantity, efficiency, scale, and speed) of the Industrial Revolution that had been transforming the ways and means of commodity production in other parts of the Atlantic world.

The first section of the present chapter discusses how the Cuban planters, scientists, and government bureaucrats dedicated to this transformation reached out to Europe, North America, neighboring Caribbean islands, and beyond for foreign expertise, capital, and hardware. Instead of viewing technological advance as *either* a foreign import or an indigenous development, I show how the plantation became, among other things, a filter through which innovations both foreign and domestic could be assessed. The technological transformation of the grinding, boiling, and draining aspects of sugar manufacture was a mix of local inventions and importations from Europe and elsewhere. Even if originally "invented" in Europe, each of the most important innovations was subjected to extensive trials on tropical sugar plantations in Martinique, Guadeloupe, Louisiana, Bourbon, and especially Cuba. The marketability of new technologies depended on their having endured the ordeal of the sugar harvest. Engineers, capitalists, planters, chemists, and government officials circulated throughout these plantation islands, the United States, and western Europe. In their travels, they participated in experiments, wrote official and private reports, and corresponded with one another, collaborating in the refinement of the new hardware of sugar production, making it fit to bear a price tag and claim a place in the brochures of iron-working firms.

Furthermore, in the debates that inevitably arose around the incorporation of productive or organizational innovations, participants wove claims through contrasting scales of legitimation: the genre (the reports, memorials, and newspaper columns discussing plantation experiments) seemed to require that the authors telescope smoothly between an authority grounded in local expertise and that to be found in being up-to-date with the latest publications of scientific organizations in Europe and the Americas.[8] In this way, both the vectors of invention and the modes of argumentation characteristic of the plantation laboratory make difficult the project of territorializing the sources of innovation, or the personnel involved, as *either* metropolitan or colonial, *peninsular* or *criollo*, *yanqui*, or *cubano*. Legitimacy to a certain extent depended on their ability to be both, or neither.[9]

Whereas the technocrats were peripatetic, and the knowledge that they produced deterritorialized, ungrounded, and mobile, they also found that local particularities mattered immensely. Ultimately, new data had to be squeezed from unique plantation contexts, in particular times and places. The second section explores how the plantation laboratory became a space of collaboration and contest among different figures of the Atlantic industrial world. Chemists, engineers, and statisticians worked alongside planters, colonial bureaucrats, sugar masters, and slaves in the hectic rush of the Caribbean sugar harvest. Such figures as the chemist in the Cuban sugar mill and the railroad engineer overseeing slaves and Chinese laborers in the laying of tracks from plantation to port were new figures on the stage of the Atlantic socioeconomy. This plantation technocrat was a novel character, whose appearance qualitatively transformed the Atlantic world. He was often a professional scientist, a technocrat mediating between capital and the State, but he could also be a planter. Fluency in the language and the practices of industrial experiment in the plantation laboratory, and participation in the counterpoint of groundedness and migration that I just described, were deciding qualifications.

The final section reviews how capitalist knowledge production had been transformed and how these changing practices were part of a broader transformation of Cuban society in the middle decades of the nineteenth century, as the island was changed from "*la isla de ensayos*" to an *isla de experimentos*.[10] The plantation experiment became normative, an expected and indispensable phase of much economic activity. Not only had the experiment proliferated from the plantation into other areas of Cuban society, but the spectacular character attendant on earlier scientific experiments had been mostly sloughed off. The practice of the plantation-experiment had also ushered in novel understandings of what the plantation should be: a space productive not only of massive quantities of high-quality sugar, but also of precise scientific data, on which a secure future for enterprise could be erected.[11] The scale of capital investment characteristic of the industrial age imposed a new level of demands on the breadth and precision of knowledge, or at least a feeling that such was necessary; expensive projects dedicated to lowering the costs of production through improvements in the manufacture, marketing, and transport of sugar confronted Cuba's capitalists with demands for knowledge and preliminary preparation of unprecedented rigor and scale.

As the example of the chemist working alongside the *guarapo* seller that began this chapter makes clear, the experiment had been transformed from spectacle to side-work, blending into the landscape of the market, at times dissolving into the continuous stream of a thoroughly capitalist plantation society.

Global Literacy and Local Knowledge

By the 1840s, a standard practice of experimentation on the plantation had evolved. These experiments tended to center around the Real Junta de Fomento. The Junta (renamed the Direccion de Obras Públicas after the effective dismantling of the Junta in 1854) was the main official agency responsible for the disbursal of funds allocated for activities thought to benefit the Cuban economy. Constituted by peninsular merchants, Creole planters, and a newer membership of scientific experts, and headed by the Intendente and the Capitan-General, the Junta was essentially a public-private advisory board charged with the economic and infrastructural development of the colony.[12]

Government-sponsored and controlled institutions such as the Junta and the Sociedad Económica de Amigos del País had dedicated themselves to strengthening the Cuban export economy since their inception in the 1790s, focusing mostly on the reduction of commercial restrictions in the importation of slaves and the exportation of sugar. The Junta's turn to improving the technics of sugar production and transport through the promotion of specialized, professional, scientific-technological institutions such as the Instituto de Investigaciones Químicas, the Escuela de Maquinaria, the Comisión de Estadística, and the Academia de Telégrafos Eléctricos signaled a shift in the interests of the Junta and the island's wealth-holders more generally, from mercantile to industrial concerns.[13]

For inventors, capitalists, importers, engineers, and other figures involved in the technological development of sugar manufacturing and its ancillary activities, the Junta had become an indispensable source of support. Typically, inventors of the latest technologies went to the Junta for financial aid. To evaluate the innovation and arrive at a decision about the sort of support they should offer, the Junta distributed new technologies to major plantations, where they were put to various tests. The Junta would then select two or three of its members, often planters themselves, who together formed a temporary commission, a formal investigative sub-committee of the Junta, to visit the sites of experiment and evaluate the submissions.

Thus, many plantation experiments were undertaken by a collaborative network consisting of the colonial state, newly professionalized industrial researchers such as chemists and engineers, and elite sugar planters. Together they formed in effect a thick filter through which innovations, foreign and domestic, were made to seep. Marrying scientific and technological concerns in a thoroughly transnational network, the plantation technocracy can be thought of as sharing elements both of a bourgeois republic of letters and an informal association of itinerant craftsmen. Made up of Creole planters, Spanish colonial officials, Louisiana sugar masters, French or North American chemists, and others, this network had a global reach, collecting machines, techniques, literature, and technological intelligence from the Caribbean, North America, Europe, east Asia, and the new sugar islands in the Pacific. The development of new technologies was the result of transnational collaborations that crossed the borders of empires and nation-states. Furthermore, an applicant's being up-to-date on the most recent of European chemical experiments and manufacturing breakthroughs was a crucial criterion of evaluation.[14]

This requirement accentuated the already globalized membership of the plantation laboratory.

At the same time, plantation experimenters continuously acknowledged the inescapable confines of geography: from the microclimate of Guanajay, to the climate of opinion among planters in Güines, specificities of the Cuban local surged insistently to the surface of experimenters' discourse. Knowledge was grounded in the local, tight, sweaty spaces, the intimacies particular to the boiling and grinding houses of the sugar plantation. The plantation laboratory was a new kind of space, for the crystallization of the new kinds of Atlantic industrial identities that is my project to illuminate. In the case of the plantation experiments, knowledge and novel subject positions were produced by way of a rich dialectic, a complicated back-and-forth play between global literacy and local expertise.

Casaseca's reports to the Junta offer many examples of such play. One instance arose when a new product called "Dr. Stolle's Arcanum" grabbed his attention.[15] A German merchant of La Sociedad de Koble Luling y Compania imported the product, which the inventor claimed was superior to the lime conventionally used as a clarifying agent in the sugar-manufacturing process. The arcanum was poured into the cane juice in its first stage of heating, clinging to the many nonsaccharriferous particles suspended in the juice (such as the fragments of solid cane pulverized by the mill that had sneaked through the filter, known as *bagacillo*) so they would sink to the bottom or float to the surface as scum that could be skimmed off to leave the cleansed cane juice in the pan (Moreno Fraginals 1978, 1: 92–94).

Lime, either imported from England or the United States or mined from local quarries and cooked in lime kilns had been the clarifier of choice since the turn of the century.[16] Dwindling resources of both wood to fuel the kilns, and lime, however, encouraged Casaseca and other members of the Junta to search for a substitute.[17] Instead of mining scarce lime, and dedicating costly labor-power to the painstaking process of charcoaling valuable lumber, Casaseca hoped that plantations would be able to purchase arcanum from a chemical factory in Germany. The proposed experiment, then, aimed to substitute a synthetic compound produced by the burgeoning heavy chemicals industry in Germany for the scarce natural resources of Cuba. The Junta, surely sharing Casaseca's hopes, agreed to collaborate in "submitting the product to testing on a grand scale."[18]

Casaseca used the experiment to establish his authority in the Paris-centered world of applied industrial chemistry. As I explain in more detail below, the German entrepreneur's innovation turned out to be a flop, and Casaseca took the opportunity to issue stern advice to European scientists: "I strongly believe that European chemists should renounce the use of all sulfides," he warned, "that they only recommend because of their ignorance of the frightful rapidity with which cane juice transforms *under the influence of the tropical climate*."[19] The chemist thus chastised his metropolitan colleagues for their failure to take into account the Caribbean climate and how that might affect chemical processes carried out in open-air cauldrons. In his report, Casaseca enacted the tension between global literacy and local expertise: driven by an interest in a German product, and preparing for a visit to the French Academy of Sciences, Casaseca nevertheless employed his locally based knowledge to legitimate his rejection of the new clarifying procedure.

Moreover, the European scientists whom Casaseca apostrophized in his report suffered from insufficient knowledge of the technics of production prevailing in Cuban boiling houses. Although "Dr. Stolle's arcanum" might have performed well in German refineries, neither the importing merchant nor the German chemist Stolle seemed to have foreseen that the arcanum, and the method for applying it, would be inapplicable in Cuba's average boiling house.[20] Although many of the larger sugar mills had undergone considerable modification, and had installed state-of-the-art, steam-heated vacuum pans to evaporate and refine sugar, a typical Cuban plantation of the early 1840s still processed sugar through a system known as the *Jamaica train*.[21] Immediately after the juice was extracted by passing the canes through a roller mill, it was transported to the boiling house, which held the Jamaica train: a linear series of open-lid cauldrons heated by one fire and a reverberatory furnace that conducted the heat underneath them. Each batch of cane juice passed through the cauldrons in succession—first the clarifying pan, then two evaporating pans, and finally the strike pan, in which the cane juice was transformed into granulated sugar. This moist, brown, granulated sugar (*mascabado*) was then packed into cone-shaped receptacles with a hole at the apex, and hung upside-down to drain off the molasses, leaving white sugar in the cone. After two to three weeks, it was ready to be packed into boxes and shipped.

In models that had preceded the Jamaica train, each cauldron had had its own furnace and fire. The governing concept of the Jamaica train was to economize on wood by sacrificing dexterity. In essence, it welded a succession of individual processing units into a single clumsy but fuel-efficient machine, each of the cauldrons was now one of the consecutive elements of a unitary apparatus, soldered to a single heat source and thus fixed to the singular time-frame characteristic of sugar-making.

Stolle's method, on the other hand, depended on exact temperature control of the individual pans. "To reduce the heat in the last cauldron [which would have been necessary for the arcanum to have been an effective purifier,] the entire boiling process would have to have been suspended," Casaseca complained. Since the levels of sucrose present in sugar cane decline quickly and steadily after grinding, the readers of his report would have been aware, such a delay would have ruined the cane juice waiting to be boiled in the other cauldrons. Continuous flow of production was a primary concern, a fundamental *chemical* necessity, not merely an economic goal, as it was in other kinds of production.

In his report to the colonial government, then (which was also published in the government's official newspaper, *La Gaceta de la Habana*), Casaseca claimed superior knowledge of local phenomena, both climatic and technological, chiding European scientists to the effect that their pretensions to universal knowledge fell short of the especially important case of Cuba.[22]

In other cases, however, awareness of the latest foreign news in the chemistry and engineering of sugar refineries wielded considerable influence in itself. Francisco Oger, the accountant of the Junta, had the power to consign to oblivion the work of inventors by refusing monetary support or publicity.[23] He did so on one occasion on the grounds that the petitioner, Mariano Vieta, was not up-to-date on the scholarly conversations among chemists, manufacturers, and planters in the Atlantic world. If Vieta had read Casaseca's Paris *Memoria*, Villa Urrutia's recent

Informe, the French manufacturer Charles Derosne's manual, or the other works of an emergent canon of sugar technology, he would not have promulgated the "the mistaken principle that it is the quantity and not the quality of the product that most concerns planters . . . Surely without having read or meditated upon, as he should have, the fundamental principles upon which Derosne and Company depend to develop their systems," Oger concluded, "Vieta approaches the Junta with the request that [he be given] the moderate (for him) sum of $100,000."[24] Although literacy in the emergent Paris-centered culture of academic chemistry was a criterion, it is crucial to note that all of the pieces of literature Oger mentions were based on plantation experiments in the colonial world. Their arguments were products of the daily labors in the bustling plantation laboratories of Cuba, Martinique, Jamaica, and Bourbon. The grounds on which Oger based his rejection thus suggest that global literacy and grounded knowledge operated in tandem. Neither one nor the other was independently sufficient. On the contrary, both were considered to be fundamental aspects of the plantation experiment, unavoidable prerequisites for officially sanctioned participation in the sugar-refining industry in Cuba—in the end, they were twin imperatives for the development of new knowledge in an industry crucial to global capitalism.

R. S. McCulloh, a North American chemist and also a refiner at the U.S. Mint, traveled to Cuba in the 1840s under the auspices of the U.S. Bureau of Standards as part of a larger investigation into frauds being practiced in the importation of foreign sugar. The Treasury Department had evidence that merchants were bringing cane juice into U.S. ports but passing it off as molasses. The former was simply crystallizable sugar in solution, and could still be processed into value-added white sugar. On the other hand, molasses was simply the brown stuff that had dripped through the crystals in the draining phase of processing, and would never crystallize. Under both U.S. and Spanish regulations, the cane juice was charged a higher duty than molasses since potentially it was of greater value.

Due to the inherent sensitivity of saccharine substances to changes in temperature and climate, and to its rapid deterioration over time, McCulloh had to travel personally to Louisiana and Cuba. He tried to avoid the trip, but discovered through an interesting type of experiment that experiments on sugar and its byproducts would have to be performed at the point of production. Wanting to ascertain the effects that a sea voyage would have on dried and sliced sugar cane, McCulloh wrapped a few samples and shipped them from Cuba to Philadelphia. Unwrapping the slices after his arrival, he found them desiccated and useless. "These results should therefore settle the point," McCulloh announced, "that dried cane . . . cannot be exported without loss, to be manufactured in foreign countries by the process of maceration [soaking or spraying of the dried cane, also called *lixiviation*, *percolation*, or *imbibing*]. Many have thought that the cane sugar industry could be thus completely and advantageously revolutionized. But . . . [such a scheme is] no longer worthy of serious consideration" (McCulloh 1848: 191–93). The U.S. Treasury Department's official chemist, like his counterpart Casaseca, conceded that the Cuban plantation was indispensable as a site of experiment and of sugar manufacture, drawing diverse industrial Atlantic world characters to the boiling house and consigning the metropolitan laboratory to an auxiliary role. McCulloh initially thought of geographical rootedness as a variable to be experimented with, but learned that the plantations of the tropics were an undeniable constant to which experiments on sugar cane would long be tied.[25]

Even in the context of a single request to the Junta, plantation experimenters telescoped repeatedly between local knowledge and global literacy. For example, the Havana-based planters' partnership Drake and Company,[26] in search of new methods for producing rum, promoted Fawcett's of Liverpool, a maker of steam-powered sugar-manufacturing devices.[27] Santiago Drake translated and submitted to the Junta a letter from Mr. Fawcett describing his product. Fawcett included in his informational packet to Drake extracts from two letters he had received from "A. Campbell Esqr. resident proprietor of the Copse Estate" in Montego Bay, Jamaica, whose own correspondence included the text of a report composed by his employee "Mr. M Clark resident Engineer & joint patentee" on the Jamaican plantation.

By calling himself "resident proprietor," Campbell emphasized that he was no absentee planter, but a man intimately involved in the day-to-day operations of his plantation, whose technical authority was thus reliable.[28] Campbell's employee Mr. Clark also emphasized his familiarity with particularities specific to the Caribbean sugar mill by labeling himself the "resident engineer." The migrant engineer was spatially fixed by this label—he sought to create the impression that he was part of the plantation. At the same time, his identity as "joint patentee" drew him back to the status associated with the Liverpool manufacturing firm. In Clark's self-imposed "cross-cutting identity," forged out of equal parts colonial savvy and metropolitan standing, we are given another example of the rich play between local and global founts of authority that put wind in the sails of these Atlantic experts.[29]

Drake's petition to the Junta was characterized by multiple overlapping, intercalated points of view, vectors of knowledge crisscrossing and cross-referencing on a global scale. At the same time, each character in the petition's layered narrative frame lodged his claims to authority in microsites of plantation experiment: first, as Campbell reported, an English invention was shipped to Jamaica in the care of a traveling engineer (Clark), who together with a Jamaican planter (Campbell) carried out experiments on the Montego plantation. Then the two men wrote reports that were put together, the planter's report embracing, based on, and framing the report of the engineer. This document was then sent back to Liverpool, from where the proprietor of the ironworks (Fawcett) wrote his own cover letter glossing and framing the Jamaican reports. Fawcett sent this document to Drake's plantation in Cuba, where the equipment would presumably undergo further experimentation before being purchased and imported from Liverpool, accompanied by British traveling engineers who would erect it and temporarily operate it on the purchaser's plantation. To set the plan in motion, however, Drake appealed to the colonial state in Cuba, reinscribing the packet of documents he received from Liverpool, framing them within his own narrative of Cuban economic development, and forwarding it to the Junta. Woven together by repeated acts of collation,[30] Liverpool, Jamaica, London, Cuba, and other locales were constituted as nodes of experimentation and vectors of narration by the physical movement of experts, commodities, laborers, and texts, fluidly within and outside the worlds of slavery.

Such a complex narrative frame mirrors the tensions (itinerancy and fixity, global circulation and local savvy, skeptical engineers and striving planters, verbose chemists and silenced slaves) out of which knowledge was produced in the slave-holding Atlantic world of the industrial era. The new subject-positions of the Atlantic industrial slaveholding world thus were not positions at all, but itineraries. For the planters, bureaucrats, chemists, machinists, and engineers whose voices we hear in the documents, tropical authenticity and metropolitan repute were a persistent duality, keeping the site of knowledge production unsettled. Furthermore, we are also witness to the global scale at which innovation unfolded, with experiments, tweakings, and retoolings taking place in various regions of the world. A proprietary model of scientific activity, in which innovative ideas are attributed to "Europeans," "the metropole," or even, on occasion, "the periphery," or "the colony," is hopelessly inadequate to capture this reality. The situation is much more accurately modeled by these woven *expedientes*, which is why I have chosen to describe their structure in such detail.

As Jonathan Curry-Machado points out in his exciting new research on British engineers in Cuba, traveling engineers were the key agents of industrial technology transfer, since they had knowledge both of the point of machine production in England and how best to adapt it to fit the local needs of the machine consumer in Cuba. They often pioneered innovations while on the island, based on what they learned there. The seasonal nature of the work allowed them to travel back to producer areas and fill orders that planters placed with them (Curry-Machado 2011: 87). Since Cuban planters and scientists collaborated actively with British engineers in the fine-tuning of sugar-refining apparatus, these inventions themselves should be thought of as collectively authored, as the products of peregrination.

The negotiations of power and knowledge that went on in this Atlantic, migratory world were simultaneously characterized by mobility and groundedness. At the same time, they depended on an awkward but richly productive intersubjectivity that daily unfolded in the pressed and stressed spaces of the plantation laboratory as these Atlantic industrial subjects reformulated their relationships of authority and expertise in relation to one another.

Normativity Achieved: Life in the Isla de Experimentos

By the middle decades of the nineteenth century, the industrial experiment (as a knowledge-producing practice closely wedded to commodity production) had been transformed from an occasional spectacle to a daily reality of the slave-centered Atlantic economy.

In an article discussing new sugar-milling equipment, a reporter for *El Diario de la Habana* unwittingly revealed the key role that plantation experiments had come to play in Cuba's plantation society. The piece compared two "*trapiches de antifrotraccion*" (new methods), one invented by the Cuban José Francisco Oton and another invented by a French resident of Havana named Pedro Pouchaud. Although they guarded high hopes for Oton's model (which they had seen in operation in his workshop), they could not help but compare it unfavorably with the competing invention by Pouchaud, on the grounds that the latter had "corroborated [his claims] with the experience of two consecutive harvests, on a plantation of some magnitude, thereby proving its utility," whereas Oton "has not been able to submit to significant experiment [*esperiencia*] a machine whose system and locomotion present in theory and in test-runs considerable advantage."[31]

The experiment practiced in the safety of Oton's workshop was equated to "theory," a subset of scientific knowledge insufficient for the writers of the piece. The mill had not yet been adequately constituted as an object of knowledge. It could not be seen or known in the way that Pouchaud's quite similar machine could. The workshop-based *ensayo* had been consigned to the purgatory of the theoretical in an age overwhelmed and inspired by the efficacy of the empirical. The experiment, then, was not defined by its removal to a controlled laboratory or workshop atmosphere but by its insertion into the ongoing flow of commodity production. And like never before, an experiment or no experiment often meant the difference between a deluded visionary and a well-grounded entrepreneur who should be rewarded for the sensible risk he was taking. By the early 1840s then, the *isla de ensayos* had been transformed into the *isla de experimentos*. The contributors to *El Diario de la Habana* who reported on economic and scientific developments on the island had come to see experimentation in the sugar mill itself, in the blazing heat and real-time action of the harvest season, as normative.[32] The absence of such experimental data was not grounds for dismissal of Oton's system—how could they dismiss it, *El Diario* writers seemed to be saying, when they lacked the information needed to evaluate it at all?

In 1844 the Junta received a request from Doctor Mariano Vieta to support his "secret" for manufacturing sugar, which he claimed would increase the yield of white sugar coming out of cane juice by 30 percent. The Junta responded with interest, appointing Joaquin Santos Suarez and the Marqués de Duquesne to carry out or witness an experiment. The two-man commission visited Vieta on his plantation El Fenix, conducting various tests over two days, but left unsatisfied, stating in no uncertain terms that they could not squeeze the necessary data out of Vieta's subpar equipment: "We are convinced that so long as these tests are not executed on a better-equipped plantation, our report will be lacking in due precision, and we will cease to deserve the confidence with which [the Junta] has honored us."[33] The results gotten under such circumstances would be lacking in accuracy, the commission concluded, and they decided that further experiments would be carried out on a neighboring plantation, one that possessed "a good mill or machine and the other tools necessary to be able to calculate the percentage increase offered by the invention."[34] Their disdain for Vieta's technology did not bode well for the latter's invention. Maybe he read the writing on the wall, because, as Duquesne tactfully phrased it, "Mr. Vieta has not been able to grace us" with his presence on the neighboring plantation, an absence that heightened Duquesne's original skepticism regarding the "secret" improvement. Vieta's invention was ultimately rejected by the Junta.[35]

The practice of the plantation-experiment itself had transformed understandings of what the plantation should be: it was expected to be a space productive of precise scientific data, helping to lay a solid foundation on which a future for capitalist enterprise could be erected. Of the many benefits accruing to modernized equipment, its ability to serve up dependable, precise statistical information *about itself* held a prominent place in the minds of the commission's members.

This expectation was revealed by Justo Cantero, especially in his estimates of the annual yield of Domingo de Aldama's Matanzas plantation, Santa Rosa, relating to which he made the following caveat: "Perhaps this sugar-mill will not offer the regularity presented by those constructed expressly for a determined number of boxes of sugar." In this case, innovation itself made systematic quantification and forecasts an inexact science, "since [Aldama was] introducing various modifications because the growth in output demanded enlargement of the boiling and draining houses (Cantero [1857] 2005: 141)." Nevertheless, Cantero revealed that in his survey of the island's largest sugar plantations, he had become accustomed to the provision of exact production figures and even implied that annual output of boxes was incorporated into the design of the mill ahead of time.

Casaseca showed the same concerns as the commission that rejected Vieta's boiling house as an inadequately appointed site of experimentation. In his investigations into the "musty smell" and sour taste that marred Cuba's rum exports, he asked the Junta to connect him with some plantation distilleries, "that have good Arristola stills or are constructed by the same design, since in my opinion these are the best on the island and the most in conformity with science." Casaseca specified the new steam-powered continuous column stills, which he thought most conducive to rigorous data collection. Thus the mechanized plantation was treated simultaneously as an object subject to quantification and as a precision measuring tool in itself. Plantation experimenters understood the ideal plantation to be a place characteristic of the mechanical reproduction of variables, not the trial-and-error, dash-of-salt method of the *isla de ensayos*.[36]

For Juan Ramos, a Puerto Rican inventor, the legitimacy of his experimental results was ensured not by the excellence of the sugar mill on which he carried out his trials, but by his own ability to replicate the actual conditions of production prevailing there, whatever they may have been. To quantify the improved yields that his mill offered, he worked in tandem with the planter, setting up his experimental model beside the equipment normally used on the plantation, also using the same cane, labor, weather conditions, and so forth. This way, he could be sure to reproduce with precision the key variables, laying a solid and trustworthy empirical ground for his comparative experiment.[37] Trying to revise the relationship between commodity production and knowledge production, Ramos chose to mirror the productive apparatus already operating in the plantation's boiling house, hoping to fabricate a refined reflection of such antiquated techniques. The spatial intimacy of knowledge production and commodity production (the experimental sugar-processing train and the "real" train involved in refining sugar for export) ensured the reproduction of variables and the precision of calculations that could not have been provided in the safety of an urban laboratory in Havana or Europe. "To get as close as possible to the productive process, without actually interfering," is a statement that encapsulates quite well the spirit of industrial experiment under examination in this chapter. The method continued to be an important aspect of his transnational marketing strategy. In a widely read journal for New York City merchants, there appeared an article called "Muscovado Sugar," which read as follows:

> A new method of manufacturing sugar has been discovered and patented by Don Juan Ramos, of the island of Porto Rico, by the agency of which Muscovado sugars may be manufactured in increased quantities of superior quality, and at much less expense than before. The improvement consists entirely in the use of an ingredient for the cleansing of the liquor, and so wonderful are said to be its effects that at a trial made in the presence of a number of planters, and subjected to the most rigorous tests, the new mode of manufacture showed a saving of 41 per cent.[38]

Although Mariano Vieta's petition had been rejected by the Junta for the absence of reliable data, his collaborator, the planter Juan Fuste, thought he had certainly done one thing right. Fuste emphasized that "as my harvest season had already begun, I requested that he carry out his experiments in such a way that I not have to interrupt the manufacturing process nor incur any kind of expense, which he promised to do, and has kept his promise religiously." The experiment thus became part of the fast-paced flow of production particular to sugar manufacture, as Vieta set up his apparatus alongside that in Fuste's boiling house, so the latter could continue operating throughout the experiment.[39]

Owing to the particular logistics of the sugar industry there was increased incentive to industrialize experimentation—to incorporate it into the flow of production. With the progressive mechanization of the grinding, boiling, and drying of sugar that had advanced considerably by the 1850s, the precise tempos became ever more sacred, and as production grew ever more capital intensive and large scale, any interruptions to the flow of production, such as those we saw in Casaseca's experiments with "Dr. Stolle's arcanum," became frightfully cost prohibitive.

The need for unobtrusive quantification given rise to the increasing capital requirements of mechanized, mass production inspired the planter Pedro Diago to develop his own quantitative method for calculating soil productivity without compromising the precise tempos imposed upon slaves and slave owners alike by the chemical finickiness of sugar cane.[40] In Diago's early career as a planter, the only method known for figuring out how many *arrobas* (1 *arroba* = 25.3 lbs.) of cane could be grown per *caballeria* (23 acres) of land was to cut a sample batch of cane from a given quantity of land and weigh it. This method was flawed because soil quality from different sections of the plantation could vary widely. Inconsistent soil makeup made precise generalization impossible. Nor could one exactly cut cane from all the different areas of the plantation, for this was an unjustifiable waste of the valuable crop.[41]

Many years of measuring had taught Diago that 130 *arrobas* of raw cane consistently yielded 4 *arrobas* of manufactured sugar. With Diago's ratio in hand, Casaseca was able to calculate the average agricultural productivity of an entire plantation, by way of the following simple formula: b/a = x (*b* representing the boxes of sugar, *a* the quantity of land, and *x* the number of boxes of sugar per *caballeria*). Knowing the total boxes of sugar to leave the plantation, and the number of *caballerias* planted, one could deduce the weight of the cane grown per quantity of land.

When Casaseca coupled this calculation with his projects for improved soil classification (hence his collection of soil samples from various plantations as part of the same project), he was able to get an island-wide picture of productivity of the lands, all without disturbing the daily business of production. The chemist, Casaseca, and the planter, Diago, collaborated successfully, creating a statistical method for the plantation laboratory that allowed investigators to blend smoothly into the labor process.[42] "The experiment" as a social practice of knowledge production in this case dissolved itself into the flow of production: the ideal of the plantation-as-laboratory.[43]

Conclusion

The spirit of industrial experiment is perhaps most vividly evoked in Casaseca's *guarapo* stand experiments on Obispo Street. His sidewalk experiments that day were carried out in the midst of the urban din of midcentury Havana. His report to the Junta, written on the eve of his departure for Europe, where he would survey prevalent beet sugar manufacturing techniques and present his latest studies to the Academy of Sciences in Paris, compared his findings to a data set consisting almost entirely of plantation experiments: Peligot's experiments, not to mention the findings "in New Orleans of the pharmacist Monsieur Avequin," and the "various experiments, that according to my wishes, my assistant Don Juan Miguel Asbert carried out in April of 1841," on four of the largest and most technologically advanced plantations on the island.

Having collected and analyzed the work of various plantation experimenters (pharmacists, chemists, engineers, planters), he compared their findings with his own sidewalk experiments on sugar cane taken from semiurban gardens, and was able to make the disconcerting conclusion that the backwards state of many Cuban plantations was to blame for the loss of up to 68 percent of the crystallizable sugar concealed in ripe, uncut cane. Casaseca rigged up an improvised laboratory on the streets of Havana, not with any goal of demonstrating his scientific prowess, but on the contrary aiming to blend in with the flow of pedestrians and cart traffic, with the calls of street vendors and the impassioned strains squeezed from the accordions of passing musicians. Trying to efface his presence rather than promote it, Casaseca sought to operate inconspicuously in the midst of the production and purchase of sugar, slaves, and other commodities, delving into the hidden essence of one of the world's most important plants and evaluating the manufacturing techniques used in Cuba, to improve the island colony's position in a competitive world market.

Notes

1. In his report, Casaseca compared his own findings to those of other chemists, who had found the sugar canes contained approximately 70 percent water, 20 percent sugar, and 10percent fibrous material. *Archivo Nacional de Cuba* (ANC), *Fondo Real Consulado y Junta de Fomento* (JF), *Legajo* 95, *Expediente* 3996, 1842.

2. ANC, JF, *Leg* 95, 3996, 1842. Casaseca was off to Europe soon, and wanted to have his experiments in Cuba finished, as he was planning to present the results at the world-renowned French Academy of Sciences. Thus the importance of being in conversation with the leading French chemists of the era, such as Eugene Melchior Peligot.

3. For a fascinating account of the mobility of both laboratory equipment and experimental practices in the nineteenth century, see Brian Gee (1989: 37–59).

4. See especially Maria González-Ripoll Navarro (1999). For a more general picture of Havana as "a port of entry and exit of the circulation of techno-scientific ideas and practices, a nexus between local knowledge . . . and knowledge produced overseas," see Leoncio López-Ocón and María Isabel García-Montón (2000: 284).

5. Compare to Manuel Moreno Fraginals' account of the 1791 experiments testing out a sugar mill designed to be driven by the motive force of a giant pendulum (1978, 1: 85). See also "Invencion de la navegacion con vapor en España en tiempo de Carlos V." *Diario de la Habana*, January 14, 1843, and John A. Heitmann (1987: 10).

6. For standard accounts of the industrialization of research, normally posited as a phenomenon beginning in the last two decades of the nineteenth century, see Georg Meyer-Thurow (1982: 363–81) and Alfred Chandler (1990).

7. In particular, it faced increasing competition from European beet sugar (which brought the engineering and experimental spirit of the English and French industrial revolutions to refining), the rise of new cane sugar plantations in places like India, the Pacific islands and East Africa, and a long-term dip in prices. Finally, changing understandings of political economy led to increased commodity exchange *across* imperial boundaries, intensifying competition among manufacturers. For a succinct summary of these changes, see Dale

Tomich (1991: 297–319). For the price swings that have been characteristic of the modern market in sugar, see Noel Deerr (1949, 2: 527–33).

8. The contrapuntal character of the experiment reports reminds one of Fernando Ortiz's description of the founding opposition of Cuban society: sugar versus tobacco (2002 [orig. 1940]).

9. Which is not to say that national, linguistic, and racial identities did not matter. In an insightful piece, Martha Hodes challenges the notion that the constructed, inconstant character of race, often proven by showing how racial ideas vary across geographical space, somehow mitigates racism's social power. On the contrary, she concludes, it is precisely in the flexibility and adaptability of racial thinking that its "abiding power" resides (2003: 84–118).

10. The idea of an "*isla de ensayos*" is borrowed from the title of Gonzalez-Ripoll's important book by the same title, which covers various forms of social, political, economic, and technological innovations that happened between 1790 and 1815. The idea of an "*isla de experimentos*," meant to suggest a time in which the scientific experiment had become a normative, everyday part of social practice for those involved in the sugar export economy, is my own concoction.

11. Manuel Moreno Fraginals (1978, 1: 167–68) made the case that sugar mills were hampered by the wildly fluctuating data that observers recorded. He found the absence of standardization, predictability, and replicability exasperating.

12. For a succinct explanation of the responsibilities undertaken by the Junta de Fomento, see Leví Marrero (1984, 10: 41–42); see also Moreno Fraginals (1978, 1: 106–12). For the relatively privileged position of Cuban Creole elites within the power structures of the Spanish Empire, see Manuel Moreno Fraginals (1995: 157–68).

13. Compare to the rise of specialized organizations that replaced the old philosophical societies in nineteenth-century England (Bernal 1954: 552–53). Industrial chemistry, as a profession and as an independent discipline, was just then taking shape in England and France (Knight and Kragh 1998). The establishment of such organizations signaled a new phase *not* participated in by the much-studied Francisco Arango y Parreño. The founder of the Junta and perhaps the foremost proponent of a Cuban economy focused single-mindedly on sugar export, active between approximately 1780 and 1820, Arango y Parreño showed only mild interest in the logistics of production (García Rodriguez 2005: 24).

14. Recent scholarship has highlighted the transnational circuits in which nineteenth-century sugar technologists traveled (García-Muñiz 1999; Curry-Machado 2011).

15. ANC, JF, *Leg* 97, 4067, "Expediente sobre el Arcanum del Doctor Stolle [of Berlin] para la clarificacion del guarapo de la caña de azucar," 1843.

16. Lime was widely used as a purifier in the late eighteenth century, separating out troublesome byproducts in soap boiling, glass making, and iron and lead smelting, among other branches of industry; see Archibald and Nan Clow (1952: 474–75, 517) and Deerr (1949, 2: 578–79).

17. Plentiful evidence of wood shortages in nineteenth-century western and central Cuba has been well analyzed in Reinaldo Funes Monzote (2004).

18. ANC, JF, *Leg* 97, 4067, "Expediente sobre el Arcanum," 1843.

19. ANC, JF, *Leg* 97, 4067, "Expediente sobre el Arcanum," 1843, emphasis added—D. R.

20. By 1860, the end of our period, one-quarter of all sugar mills were still using animal power and open-lid evaporation in the "Jamaican" style, but such mills produced only 10 percent of the island's sugar. Semimechanized and completely mechanized sugar mills accounted for the lion's share (Santamaría and García 2004: 189–90). In 1843, however, this process of mechanization was less widespread, and Casaseca, not being a fortune teller, had no way of knowing that the Jamaica train would be obsolete in twenty years. He wanted to assist average planters rather than only the wealthiest minority. At the same time, he did encourage planters to modernize their equipment.

21. Oddly, the Jamaicans whom Cubans credited with development of the technology in the 1780s called it the "French method." Moreno surmises that this type of boiling train had its origins in the French Caribbean, but that Cubans learned it from Anglophone planters. For once, no one seems interested in taking credit for methods of sugar processing.

22. For a similar anti-European, pro-American bias among U. S. naturalists in the early nineteenth century, which also prioritized intimacy with the particulars of New World nature over Europeans' propensity for armchair philosophizing, see Andrew Lewis (2005: 663–96).

23. For analyses of State-controlled knowledge production in the colonial setting, see, for example, William Beinart (1989: 143–62) and Irene Silverblatt (2004). For the role of the State in new sciences of quantification *within* western Europe, see Ken Alder (1995) and Andrea Rusnock (1995).

24. ANC, JF, *Leg* 95, 4007, "Expediente promovido por el Doctor Dn Mariano Vieta para que la Junta le compre su secreto de elaborar el azucar con un 30% en el producto común," 1844.

25. It seems that there were at least two other attempts in the 1840s to transport unground cane, on these occasions from Martinique to France; both yielded inconclusive results. Daubree and Davier both tried the method of drying the cane to preserve it, and revivifying it with systematic lixiviation upon its arrival at the French refinery. Fermentation of the dried cane slices was inevitable on a transatlantic journey (Deerr 1949, 2: 548, note). Widespread success was never achieved, meaning that in the sugar industry, a core-periphery dynamic never fully developed, since extensive in-country manufacturing remained a chemical necessity.

26. A merchant and the patriarch of the Drake family, Santiago (James) Sr. had emigrated from England, arriving in Havana in the 1790s. After marrying into a family of elite planters, he diversified his economic interests by purchasing sugar plantations. The family soon expanded their mercantile and planting interests into Matanzas and Sagua la Grande, remaining an important conduit between Cuban Creole planters and Anglophone merchants and financiers (Ely 1960: 55–85).

27. ANC, JF, *Leg* 94, 3969. "Expediente formado en virtud de carta del Sr Dn Santiago Drake, acompañando copia de otras tres que tratan sobre el aparato de Mr. Fawcett para elaborar azucar," 1829. Fawcett, Preston, and Company "played a preponderant role in the mechanization of Cuban sugar-mills," selling fifty eight- to twelve-horsepower steam engines designed to be hitched to horizontal cane-grinding mills, which they also manufactured and sold to Cuban planters with considerable success (Moreno 1978 1: 207–08).

28. For the classic denunciation of "absenteeism" among Jamaican planters, see Orlando Patterson (1969: 33–51).

29. For the idea of "cross-cutting identities," see the introduction to James Sidbury (1997: 1–10).

30. In the Cuban National Archive, this stack of inter-referential, collated documents is literally woven together with string into a single *expediente.*

31. *Diario de la Habana*, January 1, 1843. The piece says that Oton's mill uses a technique to make up for the absence of mechanized driving power. Many planters, unable or unwilling to commit to a fully mechanized productive system, picked and chose. They thereby created a hybrid or creolized technology, for example incorporating parts of the Derosne system into their Jamaica trains already in operation. For some fascinating reflections on how such phenomena characterized Cuban plantation society, see Antonio Benitez-Rojo (1992).

32. Recall that Casaseca felt compelled to apologize for the fact that his sidewalk experiments had not been performed on a plantation.

33. ANC, JF, *Leg* 95, 4007, "Expediente promovido por el Doctor Dn Mariano Vieta," 1844.

34. ANC, JF, *Leg* 95, 4007, "Expediente promovido por el Doctor Dn Mariano Viet*a*," 1844. Vieta's alleged increased yield "is due to double-crushing the cane and soaking the *bagazo* in warm water." The soaking technique was tried again later, and found wanting.

35. ANC, JF, *Leg* 95, 4007, "Expediente promovido por el Doctor Dn Mariano Vieta," 1844.

36. ANC, JF *Leg* 95, 3995, "Expediente promovido por el Sr D José Luis Casaseca, en solicitud de alguna recompensa por el proceder que ha inventado para quitar a los aguardientes el olor a mosto," 1841.

37. ANC, JF, *Leg* 97, 4066, "Expediente promovido por Dn Pascasio Ruiz de Cordova a nombre y como apoderado de Dn Juan Ramos, vecino de Pto Rico, proponiendo vender a la Junta un proceder inventado por este para la elaboracion del azúcar," 1853. For the important place that the principle of replicability held in "the new chemistry," see Jan Golinksi (1995: 82).

38. *Hunt's Merchant Magazine* (1854) 30: 267.

39. ANC, JF, *Leg* 95, 4007, "Expediente promovido por el Doctor Dn Mariano Vieta," 1844.

40. Diago was a key figure in mid-nineteenth-century programs to improve sugar manufacturing and Cuba's transportation infrastructure; see Santamaría and García (2004: 172). His brother, Fernando, was also an important player. See Marrero (1984, 10: 49).

41. The use of calculation and estimates as a substitute for costly or obtrusive research was a feature of many statistical undertakings of the Enlightenment era. Many chemists emphasized the value of methods subtle enough that they did not "interfere with the workings of nature" (Roberts 1995: 516). So Diago's method could be justified in terms of both cost and rigor, as I have argued here. For a similar project undertaken by late-eighteenth-century German forest scientists, see Kathryn Olesko (1995: 105–6).

42. ANC, JF, *Leg* 95, 4027. "Tareas del instituto de investigaciones químicas," 1848. Casaseca was trying to bring the exact calculability of the plantation laboratory out to the field, to the agricultural phase of production, to be able to calculate the productivity of different types of soil, which itself requires bringing the field to the laboratory (in the form of soil samples). But we would be missing the point if we simply pigeonholed Casaseca as an important forerunner of agricultural reformers such as Reynoso, although he was. He

thought of farm and factory as a unity, as opposed to the epistemological disaggregation they underwent after the transition to the *central.*

43. Moreno reads Casaseca's notable absence from the boiling house as grounds for dismissal of the data based on this part of the chemist's research (Moreno 1978, 1: 249). It is on the very same grounds that I find Casaseca's collaboration with Diago so worthy of attention.

Works Cited

Alder, Ken. 1995. "A Revolution to Measure: The Political Economy of the Metric System in France." In *The Values of Precision*, edited by Norton Wise. Princeton, NJ: Princeton University Press.

Beinart, William. 1989. "Introduction: The Politics of Colonial Conservation." *Journal of Southern African Studies* 15 (2): 143–62.

Benitez-Rojo, Antonio. 1992. *The Repeating Island: The Caribbean and the Postmodern Perspective.* Durham, NC: Duke University Press,

Bernal, John D. 1954. *The Scientific and Industrial Revolutions.* Vol. 2 of *Science in History.* Cambridge, MA: MIT Press.

Cantero, Justo Germán. 2005. *Los Ingenios: Collección de vistas de los principales ingenios de azúcar de la Isla de Cuba* (orig. 1857). Madrid: Consejo Superior de Investigaciones Científicas.

Chandler, Alfred. 1990. *Scale and Scope: The Dynamics of Industrial Capitalism.* Cambridge, MA: Harvard University Press.

Clow, Archibald, and Nan Clow. 1952. *The Chemical Revolution: A Contribution to Social Technology.* London: Batchworth Press.

Curry-Machado, Jonathan. 2011. *Cuban Sugar Industry: Transnational Networks and Engineering Migrants in Mid-Nineteenth-Century Cuba.* New York: Palgrave.

Deerr, Noel. 1949. *The History of Sugar.* Vol. 2. London: Chapman and Hall.

DuBois, Laurent. 2004. *Avengers of the New World: The Story of the Haitian Revolution.* Cambridge, MA: Harvard University Press.

Ely, Roland. 1960. *Comerciantes cubanos del siglo XIX.* Havana: Ed. Liberia Martí.

Funes Monzote, Reinaldo. 2004. *De bosque a sabana: Azúcar, deforestación y medio ambiente en Cuba: 1492–1926.* México, D.F.: UNESCO; Siglo Veintiuno (XXI) Ed.

García-Muñiz, Humberto. 1999. "Louisiana's 'Sugar Tramps' in the Caribbean Sugar Industry." *Revista/Review Interamericana* 29 (1–4). *http://cai.sg.inter.edu/revista-ciscla/volume29/garcia.pdf.*

García Rodriguez, Gloria. 2005. "Ensayo Introductorio: Tradición y modernidad en Arango y Parreno." In *Francisco de Arango y Parreño: Obras,* edited by G. García Rodriguez. Havana: Imagen Contemporanea, 1–56.

Gee, Brian. 1989. "Amusement Chests and Portable Laboratories: Practical Alternatives to the Regular Laboratory." In *The Development of the Laboratory: Essays on the Place of Experiment in Industrial Civilization*, edited by Frank James. London: MacMillan, 37–59.

Golinksi, Jan. 1995. "The Nicety of Experiment: Precision Measurement and Precision of Reasoning in Late Eighteenth-Century Chemistry." In Wise, *The Values of Precision*, 72–91.

González-Ripoll Navarro, Maria. 1999. *Cuba, la isla de los ensayos: cultura y sociedad, 1790–1815.* Madrid: Consejo Superior de Investigaciones Científicas.

Heitmann, John A. 1987. *The Modernization of the Louisiana Sugar Industry, 1830–1910.* Baton Rouge: Louisiana State University Press.

Hodes, Martha. 2003. "The Mercurial Nature and Abiding Power of Race: A Transnational Family Story." *The American Historical Review* 108 (1): 84–118.

Knight, David M., and Helge Kragh, eds. 1998. *The Making of the Chemist: the Social History of Chemistry in Europe, 1789–1914.* Cambridge, UK: Cambridge University Press.

Lewis, Andrew J. 2005. "A Democracy of Facts, an Empire of Reason: Swallow Submersion and Natural History in the Early American Republic." *William and Mary Quarterly* 62 (4): 663–96.

López-Ocón, Leoncio, and María Isabel García-Montón. 2000. "La Habana, un núcleo y portal de la ciencia (1857–1867)." In *La Habana, Puerto Colonial (Siglos XVIII–XIX)*, edited by Agustín Guimerá and Fernando Monge. Madrid: Fundación Portuaria, 283–307.

Marrero, Leví. 1984. *Cuba: Economia y sociedad.* 14 vols. Madrid: Ed. Playor.

McCulloh, R. S. 1848. *Reports from the Secretary of the Treasury of Scientific Investigations in relation to Sugar and Hydrometers, under the Superintendence of Professor A.D. Bache.* Washington, D.C.: Treasury Department; Wendell and Van Benthuysen.

Meyer-Thurow, Georg. 1982. "The Industrialization of Invention: A Case Study from the German Chemical Industry." *Isis* 73 (3): 363–81.

Moreno Fraginals, Manuel. 1978. *El Ingenio: Complejo Económico Social Cubano de Azúcar.* 3 vols. Havana: Editorial Ciencias Sociales.

———. 1995. *Cuba/España, España/Cuba: Historia común*. Barcelona: Ed. Crítica, 157–68.

Olesko, Kathryn M. "The Meaning of Precision: The Exact Sensibility in Early Nineteenth-Century Germany." In Wise, *Values of Precision*, 103–34.

Ortiz, Fernando. 2002. *Contrapunteo cubano del tabaco y el azúcar* (orig. 1940). Madrid, Spain: Ed. Cátedra.

Patterson, Orlando. 1969. *The Sociology of Slavery*. Rutherford, NJ: Fairleigh Dickinson University Press.

Roberts, Lissa. 1995. "The Death of the Sensuous Chemist: The 'New' Chemistry and the Transformation of Sensuous Technology." *Studies in History and Philosophy of Science*, 26: 503–29.

Rusnock, Andrea. 1995. "Quantification, Precision and Accuracy: Determinations of Population in the Ancien Régime." In Wise, *The Values of Precis*ion, 17–38.

Santamaría García, Antonio, and Alejandro García Alverez. 2004. *Economía y Colonia: La Economía cubana y la relación con España, 1765–1902*. Madrid: Consejo Superior de Investigaciones Científicas, Instituto de Historia.

Sidbury, James. 1997. *Ploughshares into Swords: Race, Rebellion, and Identity in Gabriel's Virginia, 1730–1810*. New York: Cambridge University Press.

Silverblatt, Irene. 2004. *Modern Inquisitions: Peru and the Colonial Origins of the Civilized World*. Durham, NC: Duke University Press.

Tomich, Dale W. 1991. "World Slavery and Caribbean Capitalism: The Cuban Sugar Industry, 1760–1868." *Theory and Society* 20 (3): 297–319.

Archival Materials

Archivo Nacional de Cuba (ANC). *Fondo Real Consulado y Junta de Fomento* (JF), *Legajo* 94–95, 97; *Expediente*, 1829, 1842–1848, 1853.

Slavery, Frontier, and Diplomatic Relations

Brazil-Uruguay, 1840–1860

Keila Grinberg and Rachel Caé

This work, which was developed within the scope of broader research on slavery and international relations in South America, defends the hypothesis that slavery, especially the way in which it ended in Brazil and in Spanish-speaking South America, was an important factor in the establishment of diplomatic relations between Brazil and its neighboring countries.

We worked with three arguments in preparing this study. (1) Many slaves, whether or not they were aware that slavery was becoming less legitimate along the borders between Brazil and its neighbors, fled the country and benefited from the concept of "free soil," arguing in freedom lawsuits that on setting foot in countries in which slavery was no longer legal, they too became free. (2) Although this movement led to freedom for a considerable number of slaves, for the slave, freed, and Afro-descendent population living along the Brazilian border, the border also meant re-enslavement, since it was frequently invaded by people who kidnapped the so-called "people of color" to be baptized in Rio Grande do Sul as slaves later to be sold. (3) Principally after 1850, the re-enslavement invasions configured a new frontier for slavery, since the Atlantic slave trade of Africans had already ended.

During the nineteenth century, territories and borders began to be concretely established between the independent states that made up South America. In the case of the Brazilian border at the Rio da Prata, this demarcation also involved a discussion of the legal legitimacy of slavery, since in December, 1842, the Eastern Republic of Uruguay decreed the abolition of captivity on its territory. The study of the concept of *frontier*, which is essential to developing this issue, involves understanding this space as a zone or region existing along two sides of a dividing line, which is difficult to precisely define. But, beyond this, it is necessary to understand it based on a temporal understanding of the "complexity of historical factors that explain economic occupation of this given space and the political implications arising therein" (Golin 2002: 16), as a space that is extraordinarily dynamic and contradictory, and also marked by relations of force and power between two states in formation, which had different positions regarding slavery.

Therefore, in this article we propose a definition of the scenario at three moments to analyze the diplomatic relations between Uruguay and Brazil during the decades of 1840 and 1860, within the context of the abolition of slavery in the former, and the promulgation of the Eusébio de Queiroz Act of 1850, which extinguished the Atlantic slave trade to Brazil. The first period, *Conditional Freedom* (1842–1851), was marked by the abolition of slavery by the government of Uruguay, which stimulated an increase in runaway slaves to Uruguayan territory and constant complaints from Brazilian slave owners. The second, *Recognized Freedom* (1851–1860), began with the signing of the slave extradition treaty between Brazil and Uruguay. It was characterized by discussions, at the levels of both the provincial government of Rio Grande do Sul and the Imperial government, on the condition of the slaves who crossed the border and on new interpretations given to the law to regulate these cases following the termination of slave trading on November 7, 1831. The third period, *Threatened Freedom* (1860–1870), is marked by accusations by the Uruguayan government regarding the robbery of blacks from its territory to be enslaved in Brazil.

We contend that although there was intense trafficking in slaves between Brazil and Uruguay even before the independence of the two countries, slaves used the border area after 1842 for the express purpose of reaching freedom; likewise, after promulgation of the Eusébio de Queiroz Act and the signature of the slave extradition treaty in 1851, Uruguay, which had been the destination of runaway slaves, began to be invaded by slave catchers in search of people to enslave and sell in Rio Grande do Sul. This is how the region began to assume a new identity, beginning in the 1850s, as an enslavement frontier, here understood according to the concept formulated by Joseph Miller (1996: 140–53) and extensively used in Africanist historiography (Lovejoy 2002; Candido 2006). Although we will not go into it in depth in this article, we intend to later explore the connections between the processes of enslavement in Africa, principally by the Portuguese, during the nineteenth century, and the incidents of enslavement and re-enslavement that took place in the frontier regions between national States, as analyzed in our study.

Independence, Slavery, and Abolition in South America

By 1800, almost 1,000,000 enslaved Africans had been brought to Spanish America. Brazil had already received a total of 2,500,000 enslaved Africans, and another 1,500,000 would arrive in the nineteenth century. Thus, a total of 4,000,000 enslaved Africans were brought to Brazil—that is, some 40 percent of all the people brought to the Americas from Africa. At the beginning of the nineteenth century, slavery was deeply rooted in Brazil and in Spanish America, and more Africans were arriving in these places than ever before (Andrews 2004).

The expansion of coffee growing in Brazil increased the demand for slaves, with owners willing to pay high prices for African slaves. At the same time, after the revolution in Saint Domingue (Haiti) during the last decade of the eighteenth century, and at the end of the slave trade in the North Atlantic in 1808, the ports of arrival in South America grew in importance, with more merchants trying to sell their slaves in the region. This was the case for cities such as Montevideo and Buenos Aires, the entry to the Rio de la Plata, from where African slaves were sold and distributed to places like the mining areas in Peru.

The largest number of African slaves circulating between the Portuguese and Spanish imperial borders coincided with the beginning of independence movements in South America. Right after Argentina made its first attempt to become independent, in 1811, it tried to abolish the slave trade. In 1812, it ruled that all those who were born in the new country would be free, even if they were the children of slaves. Even though this decision was later reversed, and final emancipation of slaves in Argentina only took place in 1853, it was clear from the beginning that the process of independence in Hispanic America, in spite of the opposition of slave owners and merchants, would sooner or later lead to the abolition of slavery. In 1825, almost all the countries in Hispanic America had banished imports of slaves from Africa and had passed emancipation laws, whether gradual or immediate (table 8.1).

As we know, the opposite happened in Brazil. Independence did not bring discourse favorable to the abolition of slavery. The general political discourse of the 1820s to 1840s reinforced the need for African labor for the country's devel-

Table 8.1. Independence and the End of Slavery in South American Countries, 1810–1888

Country	Independence	End of Slave Trade	Law of Free Womb	Abolition of Slavery
Uruguay	1825			
(from Brazil)	1825 (1838)	1825	1842	
Columbia	1819	1821	1821	1852
Argentina	1816	1813 (1838)	1813	1853
Peru	1821	1821	1821	1854
Venezuela	1811	1821	1821	1854
Bolivia	1825	1840	1831	1861
Paraguay	1811	1842	1842	1869
Brazil	1822	1831 (1850)	1871	1888

Source: Andrews (2004: 57).

opment. At the same time, slavery played an important role in the self-image of an independent Brazil. Brazilian civilization, very socially hierarchical, was based on African slavery and saw itself as dependent on African labor. At least until the 1850s, when the Atlantic slave trade was prohibited and the prices of slaves rose significantly more than they had since the 1820s, slave ownership was common among the free population, as it had been for some time, as shown by different scholars of this topic.

This short and somewhat schematic contextual table takes us to the frontier between an independent Brazil and its neighboring countries. Between the different free womb acts during the 1820s and the final abolition of slavery in 1840s and 1850s, the number of slaves rapidly diminished throughout the countries of Hispanic America. During that same time, the Brazilian population of enslaved Africans increased significantly. It is estimated that some 760,000 Africans entered the country between 1831 and 1850 (Eltis 1987: 243–44). At the time of the 1872 census, some 18 percent of the population of Rio Grande do Sul was composed of slaves; the number was estimated to be 98,450 slaves in 1874. Throughout the nineteenth century, the province ranked sixth in the number of slaves in the country (Reis 2000: 91).

This situation meant that each proposal or measure relative to the emancipation of slaves in any country in South America that bordered Brazil was seen as a threat to the Brazilian authorities—especially those of Rio Grande do Sul. In reality, this situation had existed since the end of the eighteenth century, when, by force of the Royal Charters of 1773 and April 14, 1789, the right of asylum in Spanish lands was extended to enslaved blacks and mulattoes who entered its territories, granting freedom to those who crossed the borders (Isola 1975). In 1813, there are records that the problem worried the Portuguese authorities, as attested by the claim by the Portuguese government for the return of slaves who had taken refuge in Brazil in the territory of the United Provinces of Rio da Prata. This example shows that political emancipation and the idea of individual emancipation in the nineteenth century were being understood by slaves on the frontiers as a way to achieve personal freedom. Escapes by slaves had been occurring since at least the

1810s, and, in growing numbers, from the 1820s to the 1860s, due to the different wars that had been taking place in the region. As occurred in several other places in the Americas, slaves joined the troops fighting for independence in hopes of earning their liberation. The same thing happened in the wars for independence in Brazil, Argentina, and Uruguay.

After the approval in 1831 of the first law to abolish the slave trade in Brazil, which would become known as "just for the English to see" legislation, this movement by Brazilian slaves became more intense. The law stated that all slaves who entered Brazilian territory "coming from outside" would be free. How and whether the slaves knew of the 1831 law is another matter, and hard to evaluate. But it is interesting to note that several Brazilian slaves (or those who were based in Brazil), after having recrossed the border back into Brazil from Argentina or Uruguay, went to the courts to claim their right to freedom, basing their arguments on the law of 1831.

Slavery and Diplomatic Relations between Brazil and Uruguay

In 1828, following the independence of Uruguay, the presence of Brazilians along the old Banda Oriental (eastern bank of the Uruguay River) caused diplomatic problems between the two countries. The Uruguayan government complained of Brazilian interference in local politics; dried beef manufacturers put pressure on the Rio Grande government to oppose the presence of ranchers who took their cattle to the eastern side. The result was suppression of the transfer of cattle—and consequently, of slaves—from Rio Grande do Sul to Uruguayan territory, which was reinforced by the Uruguayan decree of November 16, 1835, which prohibited the entry of Africans into the country (Petiz 2006: 41).

However, measures such as these were hard to implement. From the start of the Farroupilha war in 1835, the number of ranchers from Rio Grande who crossed the border in search of security had been growing. The presence of Brazilian ranchers in Uruguay along the border with Brazil was so great that in 1857, they occupied 30 percent of all the Banda Oriental (Leitman 1979: 169).

During this period, Uruguay was in a period of civil war, which became known as the Great War (1839–1852). The *Blanco* party, supported by the Argentinean federalists under the command of Manuel Oribe, and the *Colorado* party, partisans of José Fructuoso Rivera, fought for control of the government. In December 1842, Rivera was defeated in the province of Entre Rios. The invasion by Manuel Oribe's troops and the advance to Montevideo made it necessary to incorporate more soldiers. This war-related problem led the *Colorado* government to create new military mechanisms concerning private property, which required more enlistments among the captive population. Thus, between 1842 and 1851, the Republic had two de facto governments, one in Montevideo and another in Cerrito, each with its own policies regarding slavery (Maiztegui Casas 2004). With Rivera's proclamation in 1842 of the abolition of slavery in Uruguay, the situation became even more complicated. Even before the promulgation of the law, the Uruguayan government ordered a draft of slaves for military service; the owners of the drafted slaves would receive 300 pesos for each, and the slaves would immediately be given their letter of liberation, with the obligation to serve in the army for four years.

At the same time, the government in Montevideo warned the Brazilians to "guarantee their property," as reported by the diplomat Duarte da Ponte Ribeiro, who was at that time on a mission in Uruguay and Argentina. He emphasized that

> [in] a circular letter dated in the month of June 1842, the government of Montevideo declared that with the Republic threatened with a foreign invasion, the subjects of other nations should take the necessary measures to ensure their property, for which the government could not be held responsible in the event of turmoil caused by an invasion of the republic. When it made this declaration, it was known that the purpose was to use slaves, considering them to be property for use in the war; but our Agent asked for an explanation, and when it was not given, he took the silence as an affirmation that this included the slaves (Brazilian), and protested against it. (Petiz 2006: 43)

Since this measure mostly affected the Brazilian owners who had property in the eastern area, it led to strong complaints by the owners from Rio Grande. They tried to remove their slaves from the country, and were aided by employees of the province of Rio Grande do Sul and the imperial government, which supported the southern slave owners, protecting the slaves in Brazilian war ships.

For the imperial government, recruiting provided a clear incentive for slaves to flee from Rio Grande do Sul to Uruguay. There was also a rumor that the government of Uruguay was planning to instigate the British minister to send British ships to take over Brazilian ships that were transporting slaves. Rumor or not, the fear that this caused in the office of the Brazilian chargé d'affaires in Montevideo was unquestionable. In December 1842, after abolition, fearing "insults" by the English, who were more dedicated to repression of the Atlantic slave trade, and to save the slaves who were the property of the subjects of the Brazilian Empire, more than 200 slaves were transported to Santa Catarina in the warship *Sete de Abril*.[1]

With confirmation of the emancipation of the slaves in 1842, including slaves belonging to Brazilian owners, there were new complaints. The Uruguayan government responded that it had warned of "the risk which the residents of Rio Grande were facing, as the owners of this property, who should remove them from the country and that if they preferred to keep them there, then they were risking the current losses."[2]

But Rivera was not the only one to recruit slaves. As soon as he established himself in the eastern territory, installing the government of Cerrito, Manuel Oribe, who proclaimed the abolition of slavery in the part of the Uruguayan territory he occupied in 1846, had also used the enlistment of slaves to fill out the ranks of his army. The owners were promised an indemnification at an "opportune time," but in 1847, complaints grew from Brazilian slave owners who wanted their slaves returned. The vast majority of these owners did not receive satisfactory replies from the Cerrito government, which refused to turn over runaway slaves who were serving in the country's army. As in the previous decree, in 1842, the imperial government affirmed that the measures implemented by the republic encouraged Brazilian slaves to run away, which did, in fact, happen. Silmei Petiz found a variety of documents, including notices from police chiefs and orders by the president of the province, dated between 1848 and 1849, telling of slaves escaping from Rio Grande do Sul abroad.[3]

The formal establishment of Uruguay as a nonslave territory led to a variety of diplomatic questions, which did not go unnoticed by the slaves who lived along the border. They perfectly understood the phrase used by the Uruguayan government, that "blacks were changed from being things to being people by those who could change this condition for them; and they could not, without grave injustice, return to the state of slavery." By passing over the border they sought to achieve freedom.[4] All this led to serious problems for the slave-owning empire in the process of consolidating its national territory and facing increased concern about establishing treaties to prevent these cases. The treaties of 1851 between Brazil and Uruguay were signed in this context.

Brazil was called to intervene in the conflict between the *Blancos* and the *Colorados*, and its participation was decisive for the victory of the latter. This made it possible for Brazil to propose five treaties, in which Brazilian preeminence over Uruguayan political questions was clear. Among these was the extradition treaty, through which Brazil could request the extradition of criminals and of slaves who had fled to Uruguay.

Besides this treaty, the following were also signed: the "Perpetual Alliance Treaty," in which Uruguay established the right of Brazil to intervene in its internal conflicts; the "Commerce and Navigation Treaty," which allowed navigation on the Uruguay River and its tributaries, and exemption from customs charges for Brazil in its exports of dried beef and live cattle; the "Assistance Treaty," through which Uruguay recognized its debts to Brazil; and the "Border Treaty," through which Uruguay waived its territorial claims to areas north of the Quaraí River and recognized for Brazil the right to exclusive navigation on Lake Mirim and the Jaguarão River, which are natural borders between the two countries. These treaties were the first to be established between the Empire of Brazil and Uruguay after independence. In a letter to Paulino José Soares de Souza, future Viscount of . . . Uruguai, Andrés Lamas, the Uruguayan consul in Rio de Janeiro during this period, noted that he considered the text on extradition of slaves to be an imposition.

The signing of the extradition treaty for slaves between Brazil and Uruguay on October 12, 1851, inaugurated the second period of the scenario under analysis. The treaty applied to the slaves who crossed into Uruguayan territory without their owners' permission, under the conditions that possession of the runaway slave had to be proven, and that expenses would be paid by the claimant. Also in 1851, the *Colorado* government—even though it recognized the Brazilian right to recapture runaway slaves and impeded entry into the country of individuals who were enslaved in Brazil—resisted allowing searches for slaves within its territory, except in those circumstances that explicitly matched the conditions of the treaty, as shown in the circular letter of December 6:

> 1. It is absolutely forbidden to introduce, under any pretext and in any location in the Republic, any individuals that do not have a certificate of freedom, until the Legislative Body has adopted a provision on this matter to resolve it as it sees fit.
>
> 2. Slaves that have entered as runaways into the territory of the Republic after November 4 [last November] will no longer be returned.
>
> 3. Claims will be granted when made by the President of the Province of Rio Grande do Sul, and the slaves are Brazilian subjects established in said Province, by the slave owner, or by whomever is duly authorized to represent him. . . .
>
> 4. The claim shall be accompanied by titles and documents which, according to the laws of Brazil, serve to prove the property under claim.[5]

This circular letter began a series of diplomatic clashes, whose agents were the Uruguayan government, the Rio Grande slave owners, and the provincial authorities of Rio Grande do Sul and the imperial government, in Rio de Janeiro, which shows that the disputes between the two countries were far from settled by the signing of the treaty. During the next year, a complaint from the Uruguayan government reported in the Foreign Relations Ministry report of 1852 again declared that slaves who had escaped into the territory before the ratification date of the respective treaty of 1851 were not to be claimed, and if they were, they would not be returned. According to the government of the republic, this treaty could only be in effect from that day on.

Likewise, again according to the Uruguay note, the owner could no longer, by himself or by sending someone else on his behalf, capture his slave within that territory. A proceeding would have to be begun, and only through this proceeding would the slave be returned. All runaway slaves who were captured by Brazilians inside Uruguayan territory, by anyone who had violently (or by other means besides extradition) taken them from there, were to be returned to Uruguay, pending their legally and regularly settled return.

It is important to point out that the treaty did not cover a series of situations that began to arise over time. For example, in 1856, the subdelegate of Sant'Anna do Livramento consulted the president of the province of S. Pedro do Rio Grande do Sul regarding some doubts as to how freedom would be granted (1) to slaves who, for any reason, passed over the border, as for example while chasing an animal that crossed into the republic's territory; (2) to slaves of owners whose properties were partly located in Brazil and partly in Uruguay; or (3) to slaves who, contracted in the Uruguayan state, returned or passed back into the province.

Regarding the first question, the decision was that since the village of Livramento was located a short distance from the border, slaves who in a continuous act while on domestic service crossed over that border could not be considered free. Also slaves who tried to take advantage of this circumstance, instead of being considered freed, would be treated as runaways. In general, it was only when the slave was forced by his owner to work in a neighboring territory that he could be freed; when he was there against the will of his owner, as in these exceptional cases, the principle that the freedom of the land frees the slave who touches it could not be applied. With regard to the second question, it was decided that they also could not be considered freed, since in this case the continuity of territorial property meant the continuity of its domestic jurisdiction. Third, slaves who were contracted or performed authorized service for their owners in the neighboring territory and who returned to the province of Rio Grande do Sul were to be considered freed.[6] The circumstance that the border between the two countries was very large and open, and in it, there were farms located partly in Brazil and partly in Uruguay, made it evident that it was impossible to admit that in every case in which a slave stepped into Uruguay, he was to be considered free.

For the president of the province of Rio Grande do Sul, these issues touched on the interests of owners in the region. At the Imperial Court, the situation was different. During this same year of 1856, the president of the Court Relations Tribunal, no less than Eusébio de Queiroz, consulted with the State Council, asking whether "a slave residing in a foreign country could enter the Empire, and not only remain enslaved, but even be sent back to his owner by the courts in his country." The reason was the arrival at the Relations Tribunal of the case of a slave who had committed a crime, and whose owner was domiciled in Uruguay. The opinion issued by the State Council, in a decision considered notable at that time, which led to Notice 188 of May 20, 1856, presented the following conclusions:

1. The Law of November 7, 1831 did not only have the intention of ending the slave trade for new Blacks, but also of reducing the number of slaves in Brazil and also of those freed by the Law;
2. Its provision inevitably included the case of slaves who, with the consent of their owners, had gone into foreign countries and then re-entered the Empire (Soares 1938: 79–83).

The note by the State Council was criticized by owners residing in the province of Rio Grande do Sul, who lived with the impacts of the Farroupilha war and the other constant wars in the region, which contributed to an intensive movement of land owners and their slaves from one side to another of the border between Brazil and Uruguay. To a large part of the elite in Rio Grande do Sul, the authorities' failure to take the situation of the border into consideration was compromising on the principle of expropriation. This Notice of May 1856 confirmed a principle accepted in international law, under which a slave who stepped on free soil would acquire the right to freedom.

This was a principle that initially was not inserted into the application of the law in 1831, but which, with the new situation in the 1850s, was being added to the understanding of the law. Even against the protests by slave owners and by the president of the province of Rio Grande do Sul, even after the opinion was amended by two others, on July 20 and September 10, 1858 (which emphasized, again, the need to return the runaway slaves), the Notice of 1856 began to be a part of all requests for freedom by slaves who crossed the border into Uruguay. In practically every case, the Supreme Court (Tribunal da Relação), according to the understanding of the Law of November 7, 1831, granted the request of the slave. This fact even gave rise to rumors that the Brazilian authorities were looking kindly on the freeing of slaves in those circumstances.

And this was not by chance: in 1858, responding to a consultation made by the president of the province of Rio Grande do Sul about a situation in which slaves mortgaged in Brazil were taken to Uruguayan territory, Eusébio de Queiroz and the Viscount of Uruguay wrote the following opinion (later approved by the emperor and referenced by José Maria da Silva Paranhos, minister of foreign affairs):

> The slave does not know of the transactions in which he is the object; he does not enter them, nor can he examine them, he obeys his owner. If the owner brings him to the Eastern State, whatever the obligations contracted, whether or not there is a mortgage, by that simple fact, the slave acquires his freedom, is free in this republic [of Uruguay], is freed in Brazil. Both governments are obliged to maintain the right they have granted him; one cannot claim his return; or the other grant it. This interpretation is so exact that the imperial government . . . [in a previous case] determined

> the following: Finally, those slaves who, working as contracted, or in work authorized by their owners on the indicated territory, return to the province of Rio Grande do Sul are freed; therefore, by the general principle presented above, the fact of being or having been with consent of their owners in a country in which slavery has been abolished, immediately gives the slave the condition of freed[om].[7]

Beyond the complaints by the Uruguayan government regarding attempts by Brazil to circumvent the extradition treaty, the 1850s also saw the stage set for another concern, which characterizes the third period of the scenario analyzed: the stealing of Africans and their descendants on the borders between Brazil and its neighboring countries. The documentation analyzed, beyond demonstrating the intense traffic of slaves across the borders, calls our attention to the increasingly frequent cases of kidnappings, especially of children, beginning in 1850.

From 1853 on, several accusations had been made regarding this issue, and this continued at least until the 1860s. The purpose of these robberies was to enslave, or re-enslave, free blacks so that they could be sold in Brazil. According to the documentation, many were children, brought to the province of Rio Grande do Sul to be baptized as having been born from slave wombs. Several accusations by Uruguayan authorities were made on this matter, as was shown in the reports by the minister of foreign relations of 1859, 1860, and 1861.

In the first, the minister referred to a complaint by Uruguay regarding the "robbery of persons of color to be sold" in Rio Grande do Sul. In one of the cases mentioned, it was alleged that a house was robbed by two Brazilians, who took a three-year-old child; in another case, the claim was that "close to Aceguá, two minor children of color were stolen, who were later sold as slaves in Rio Grande," and their family members now wanted "their rescue and return." The minister also said that "It was verified in part of this accusation that one of these minor children, who had been sold under the name of Domingos and declared that his name was João Serapio, was judicially placed in the village of Piratinim."[8]

In 1860, the Ministry of Foreign Relations report noted that the political head of the department of Salto informed the government that

> from an establishment in the field, which belonged to him, a Black woman named Carlota and four minor children of color, who had been born in the Republic, and of which the youngest was only five months old, had been stolen and taken to Brazil to be sold as slaves by D. Marcellino Ferreira, a Brazilian subject. . . . He then returned to the Republic and was arrested by the competent authority, and declared that he had in fact taken those persons to Brazilian territory with the intention of selling them as slaves, and offered to return them in a few days[;] . . . far from keeping his promise . . . Marcellino Ferreira managed to escape August 29 from the prison where he was being held, and evade the police on his way to the border.[9]

In 1861, the minister reiterated that "the imperial government has called the attention of the president of the province of São Pedro do Rio Grande do Sul to the robbery of minors of color in the Eastern State, to be sold in Rio Grande as slaves."[10]

Conclusion: A New Enslavement Frontier?

Although there is still little documentary evidence in this respect, it is possible that several of these slaves had been sent to the Court and to the Paraíba Valley. If so, the intensification of complaints about the robbery of blacks in Uruguay to be enslaved in Brazil during this period fits in the rearrangement of production in the Brazilian Empire after 1850, with the end of the Atlantic trade to Brazil. Besides the fact that the regions in the north and far south had begun to export captive labor to Rio de Janeiro, the Republic of Uruguay itself had become the target for the capture of slaves. Another hypothesis, which also has yet to be verified, was that these robberies were being influenced by the flight of slaves from the province of Rio Grande do Sul in previous periods. A large number of the claims for the return of runaway slaves had not been settled.

Even when they knew where their slave was, most often serving in the Uruguayan army, the slave owners were unable to secure their return, since the Uruguayan government considered that as soon as a slave entered the military, he became free, and therefore, could not be extradited. We still do not know how long these claims and extradition requests could have taken to be resolved, which means that it is not unfeasible that some of these robberies were undertaken to recover property lost in this manner.

The robbery of free Uruguayan blacks was thus part of the supply of the internal market for captives, and was essentially a new, albeit illegal, network of the slave trade. In a context in which the African frontier was closed and the Atlantic trade could no longer provide labor, the southern borders of the Brazilian Empire became enslavement frontiers. Ironically, for slaves who ran away from Brazil and never returned, or who successfully claimed their freedom in the courts, the border meant freedom. But for the many who were kidnapped and forced to cross the border into Brazil as slaves, the border became synonymous with slavery.

Notes

1. Brazilian Diplomatic Missions. Montevideo—Notices 1842.
2. Ibid., 44.
3. Ibid., 53–56.
4. Ibid., 44.
5. *Foreign Relations Ministry Report of 1856.* Itamaraty Historical Archives, Rio de Janeiro.
6. Ibid.
7. Opinion of the State Council on March 20, 1858, Brazil—Uruguay. Extradition of Slaves. Itamaraty Historical Archives, 5/58.
8. *Foreign Relations Ministry Report*, 1859, 92.

9. *Foreign Relations Ministry Report,* November 10, 1860.

10. *Foreign Relations Ministry Report,* 1861, 54.

Works Cited

Andrews, George Reid. 2004. *Afro-Latin America, 1800–2000.* Oxford, UK: Oxford University Press.

Candido, Mariana. 2006. *Enslaving Frontiers: Slavery, Trade and Identity in Benguela, 1780–1850.* Unpubl. PhD diss., York University, Toronto, Canada.

Eltis, David. 1987. *Economic Growth and the Ending of the Transatlantic Slave Trade.* Oxford, UK: Oxford University Press.

Golin, Tau. 2002. *A fronteira: Governos e movimentos espontâneos na fixação dos limites do Brasil com o Uruguai e a Argentina.* Vol. 1. Porto Alegre, Brazil: L&PM.

Isola, Ema. 1975. La esclavitud en el Uruguay desde sus comiezos hosta su extinción (1743–1852). Montevideo, Uruguay: Facultad de Humanidades y Ciencias.

Leitman, Spencer. 1979. *Raízes sócio-econômicas da Guerra dos Farrapos.* Rio de Janeiro, Brazil: Graal.

Lovejoy, Paul. 2002. *A escravidão na África: Uma história de suas transformações.* Rio de Janeiro: Civilização Brasileira.

Maiztegui Casas, Lincoln R. 2004. *Orientales: Una historia política del Uruguay.* Vol. 1. Montevideo, Uruguay: Planeta.

Miller, Joseph. 1988. *Way of Death: Merchant Capitalism and the Angolan Slave Trade, 1730–1830.* Madison: University of Wisconsin Press.

Petiz, Silmei de Sant'Ana. 2006. *Buscando a liberdade: As fugas de escravos da província de São Pedro para o além-fronteira (1815–1851).* Rio Grande do Sul, Brazil: Universidade de Passo Fundo.

Reis, João José. 2000. "Presença Negra: Conflitos e encontros." *Brasil: 500 [quinhentos] anos de povoamento.* Rio de Janeiro: Instituto Brasileiro de Geografia e Estatística, 79–91.

Soares, Antonio Joaquim de Macedo. 1938. *Campanha jurídica pela libertação dos escravos (1867 a 1888).* Rio de Janeiro, Brazil: José Olympio.

Archival Materials

Brazilian Diplomatic Missions. Montevideo—Notices 1842.

Itamaraty Historical Archives, Rio de Janeiro. *Foreign Relations Ministry Report of 1856, 1859, 1860, 1861.*

Itamaraty Historical Archives, 5/58. Opinion of the State Council on March 20, 1858, Brazil—Uruguay. Extradition of Slaves.

Ruling the Household

Masters and Domestic Slaves in the Paraíba Valley, Brazil, during the Nineteenth Century

Mariana Muaze

Babylonia, Friday, March 30

My dear Marianinha,

I am writing to let you know how we are doing. We and all in our family are well and with peace of mind. Your grandma is feeling better, even though she is extremely weak and apprehensive. Your aunt Matilde has been sick, but nothing too serious. . . .

Your father and friend of the heart,
Velho.[1]

The councilman José Maria Velho da Silva, the author of this letter, belonged to a Portuguese family of lesser nobles who migrated to Brazil in the second half of the eighteenth century and accumulated great wealth. He established himself at the Rua dos Pescadores, Rio de Janeiro. His uncles Manoel and Amaro Velho da Silva were important slave traders and amassed a large fortune through this commerce and by engaging in large-scale trade. They acquired privileged social status, especially after the arrival of the Portuguese royal family in 1808.[2] Even though José Maria inherited the family business, he opted to lead a bureaucratic career, becoming, due to his family's prestige, first the jewel keeper of the Imperial Chamber, and then a chamberlain.[3] His cousin and wife, Leonarda Maria Velho da Silva, was lady-in-waiting of Empress Thereza Cristina, following the footsteps of her sister, Maria Eugenia, and her mother, Dona Leonarda, who served the Princess Carlota Joaquina while she stayed in Brazil.

José Maria's oldest daughter, who is referred to in his letters as Marianinha, married Joaquim Ribeiro de Avellar Filho in a ceremony at the imperial residence of Quinta da Boa Vista, November 17, 1849. As a condition of accepting the marriage proposal, José Maria demanded that the groom's father, Joaquim Ribeiro de Avellar, a wealthy coffee planter in the region of Paty do Alferes in the Paraíba Valley, secure the noble title of baron for him. The groom's father owned over 700 slaves and occupied political positions in the local government of Paty do Alferes and Vassouras.[4] The groom's father accepted the demands of the bride's family. To obtain the title then, the groom's father made many contributions to the construction of a hospital named after Emperor Pedro II and utilized his prestige and a network of influential politicians in the Court to become the Baron of Capivary in time for his son's marriage.

Right after the marriage, Mariana and Joaquim stayed in the city of Rio de Janeiro, which was referred to as the Court at the time. However, in around 1853, the couple moved to the countryside, to the main residence of the Ribeiro de Avellar's family—a rural estate called "Pau Grande." The couple had to move to the country because Joaquim's father, the baron, was not in good health, and the son had to take care of the administration of the family property. From then on, Mariana Velho de Avellar and her parents started to write to each other very often, approximately two or three times a week. Even though this practice was common in Europe of the mid-nineteenth century among members of the literate social classes, who also had the free time to write, it was not such a common practice in Brazil (Vincent-Buffault 1996).[5] And if we consider the high rate of illiteracy and the precarious mailing system of the society in general, it is interesting to note the high frequency with which Mariana wrote to her parents.[6]

The epistolary dynamic of intimate character established by the correspondents sought to alleviate the longing one felt toward the other. At the same time, it served to build a self-image influenced by absence, by waiting for replies, and by the desire to see each other again. The frequent exchange of letters between the parties continued for many years, only interrupted by the death of the father, José Maria, in 1860 and of the mother, Dona Leonarda, in 1871. After her mother's death, Mariana, who became the viscountess of Ubá in 1887, recovered all her writings, keeping them with other family mementos, such as photos, diaries, and notebooks. From this correspondence only 31 letters written by Mariana to her parents survived, dated from 1860 to 1864, and 70 from her parents to her from 1853 to 1866. The stories developed by the writers of these letters, who represented the Brazilian aristocracy, exposed the everyday life of families who dealt closely with domestic slavery and reveal their family perspective.[7]

My interest in working with these letters is to elucidate the role women played as the "ladies of the house." This effort aligns with the perspectives and methodologies of microhistory, which sees the family as a key to understanding the functioning of the aristocratic families of the imperial era in Brazil.[8] However, we cannot understand the female obligations mentioned in the letters merely as natural to their condition; rather, they are representations of the way they wanted to be seen. According to the new social habits, these representations were based on the idea that they should take multiple roles, such as zealous mother responsible for her children's education; lady of the house, the household manager; and wife, demonstrating a taste for socializing, refinement, submission to her husband, and fear of God.

Many roles emerged from the dialogues established in the letters. In this study I became particularly interested in analyzing the responsibilities of the ladies of the house in relation to their domestic slaves. My intention was to see if I could gather from the narratives a sense of how an environment of mediation and conflict made their coexistence possible (Reis 1989). Their relationship was marked by opposing feelings of affection, hatred, gratitude, resentment, care, and vengeance, which together were part of the privately instituted social order typical in slave societies (Alencastro 1997).

To promote understanding of this study, it is necessary to point out the ambiguities that characterized how the wealthy landowners exercised their dominion over society. Influenced by paternalistic practices, they created a system of interchange of favors supported by a vast web of benefit distribution that generated dependency among its members and only recognized social relations from the top down. The place each individual occupied in this structure depended upon his or her personal relations within the traditional hierarchical relations of dependency (Chalhoub 1998).

This logic of domination was part of the Imperial society at all social levels. In the private sphere, it regulated the relations between masters and their domestic slaves. However, in practice, the everyday routine allowed a dialogue to be established between these unequal groups. Without necessarily breaking the rules of social hierarchy, these subaltern groups developed strategies of submission that would grant them some small privileges. Even though the letters, written by the family and analyzed here, reproduced the aristocratic view of the social structure, it was possible to find examples of strategies the domestic slaves used to gain the trust of their masters and enjoy some small benefits, manumission being the one most desired.

As a result of the tension that existed in the system of domination imposed by the masters and the strategies developed by the slaves to survive in this system, a social dynamic emerges, marked by a feeling of mutual fright. A slave who started to become part of the group that enjoyed benefits from the master would become attached to that group and terrified of losing his or her place in it. At the same time, the masters would have to maintain constant vigilance, since in general, slave rebellions were led by those who were closer to their masters (Slenes 1997, 236; see also H. M. Castro 1993).

Ladies of the House: The Feminine Contribution to the Maintenance of Order

The analysis of the main themes exposed in the letters studied showed that they commonly exchanged information on a variety of topics, such as political disputes and decisions, social events, and visits received. They would also comment on the growth and development of the children, news from the imperial Court, and the health of family and friends. Even though the handling of domestic slaves was not among the main topics discussed by Mariana and her parents in the letters, their words in many ways revealed how the aristocracy had established routines with their slaves that were marked by strategies of dominance, instances of resistance, distribution of favors and small privileges, and the use of a symbolic violence (Chartier 1995). From the letters, we were able to learn about aspects of the family routine, such as the treatment given to the domestic slaves, the daily chores of the maids and how they cared for the children, and the general maintenance of the household. All of this allowed us to reflect on the relationship between masters and the selected group of slaves who had permission to work inside the house.

Based on the passages that discuss the household routine and the role played by the ladies of the house, represented in the letters between Mariana and her mother, Dona Leonarda, it is possible to understand what was expected from these wealthy women in the 1800s. They were supposed to administer the house efficiently, performing tasks such as those related to the children's education, to the purchase and supply of food and domestic goods, and to the management of domestic slaves, which was crucial for the satisfactory functioning of the household. For these women, to be able to run the house efficiently meant, ultimately, being able to select domestic slaves well and train each of them in a specific skill. The need for specialized labor favored their circulation from the Court to the province—the countryside—and back: "Mom, lend me your cook, Luiz, so I can treat my guests as I must and wish. I also would like him to teach my 'bichos de cozinha' [unskilled cooks] how to prepare some of the goodies I've been deprived of."[9] The most experienced and skilled domestic slaves were frequently borrowed by Mariana Ribeiro de Avellar from her parents, the Velho da Silva family. "May God and our Lady grant you every wish, my good mother, for the relief you gave me by lending me your great maid, *who, when she behaves well, is priceless*" (emphasis added—M. M.).[10]

In these words we see how important and valuable was the "good slave," who, according to the ladies' perception, was one who would combine competency in her service with modesty and good behavior. Skill and obedience therefore were seen as the two sides of the same coin and should balance out positively in the system of slave domination. In the passage cited above, however, Mariana expressed how complicated it was to combine the two traits in the daily routine of domestic slavery, because sometimes the responsibility to behave well and work accordingly fell to the servant. Her comment shows that a degree of consideration was allowed toward the more skilled and experienced slaves, due to the service they provided. As a strategy, then, the maid would use her good service as a means to increase her value to the lady and maybe gain some privileges as a result.

With the exception of minor episodes such as the one mentioned above, there was no specific and detailed account of domestic slave disobedience in the letters. The writers had little or no interest in commenting on or describing the many instances of slave resistance or what happened with the slaves and their lives. In the narratives of the aristocracy, the relationships were vertically stratified in a way typical of their system of domination and according to the established hierarchical logic.

It is interesting to note that Mariana's concern to receive her guests well shows that her family had already adopted the change of *habitus* demonstrated by the privileged elite of the imperial society in the second half of the nineteenth century.[11] In this context, etiquette and the so-called civilized ways started to be more valued as an element of prestige and the social hierarchy necessary among the wealthy.[12] As a result, the demand for more refined domestic services increased: recipes for sophisticated sweets and other dishes, different ways of cutting meat, new ways to set tables and display china, and so on. It was during this time that many books and manuals were translated and published in Brazil, which aimed, through the rules of etiquette, to instruct and guide the wealthy families concerning the new savoir-vivre. The feminine press was also fundamental in the task of disseminating these new habits to the wealthy families.[13]

As a result of the new habits and codes of conduct, a cook, a maid, a housemaid, a page, and other domestic slaves already accustomed to serve well became valuable assets to the wealthy ladies who had to display a habitus according to their place in the social hierarchy. On this topic, Dona Leonarda wrote to her daughter, "Yesterday was the dinner at Jacintinha's, my guests were invited and went. The dinner was served *a la russe*, trying to imitate the great dinners. Jacintha showed to Dona Maria José her outfit full of valencienes. And you thought she was not fond of luxuries. It's better to shine than show off."[14]

The concern with serving well stimulated the movement of domestic slaves from the Court to the province and revealed that for wealthy families, more refined conduct became an element of social differentiation.

To maintain an efficient management of the household, these women created a support system that included not only loaning slaves to each other, but also the purchase of slaves for others. In a letter dated August 8, 1864, Dona Leonarda, the mother, mentioned that she had just bought an excellent female slave for Dona Antonia Mascarenhas Salter, cousin of Joaquina Ribeiro de Avellar Filho, for the amount of 1:550$000, including the payment of all taxes. Her words express her pride in concluding a great business deal and describe the abilities of the maid: "She has cooked dinner for two days and I was satisfied with it, so I hope your taste matches with mine. Her ironing skills for men's clothes are excellent, and she can do the washing and bake as well."[15]

Among other qualities of a maid, she also emphasized her robust figure, her cheerfulness, and her gratitude for being purchased, which, by Dona Leonarda's standards, showed her to be a good slave. According to her account, she had gone personally to the slave auction house to buy the slave, who had been sent to the auction house after her former master, a Portuguese man named Manoel Peixoto, returned to his home country.[16] Afterward, she asked her daughter to check on the slave: "I would like you find out if the servant is pleasing her new mistress and I ask you to observe her performance at the first dinner she prepares."[17] This event shows that women bought slaves themselves. They also had autonomy to deal with certain amounts of money to purchase domestic slaves and other items for the house, since they were better suited for the task.

In the letters, other passages, like the example cited earlier, showed that the circulation of slaves could take the opposite direction—from the province to the city. In this case, the most requested service was for wet nurses. It was not hard for Mariana, who owned many slaves, to find someone who was in a condition to serve as wet nurse. "Mother, would you do me a favor to tell Juca that I offer him Felisberta who already breastfed my two daughters. She is not as good as Bernarda in taking care of the house but is careful, clean and older. I just think that her due date will be after Carolina's."[18]

When in need of a wet nurse, it was very important that the due dates for the lady and the slave be as close as possible. Mariana also demonstrated her preference for wet nurses who she knew well, in an attempt to avoid problems of disease, lack of proper hygiene, promiscuity, and poor nutrition.[19] From the second half of the nineteenth century, the medical and scientific community—influenced by the ideas of Rousseau concerning the importance of maternal breastfeeding to strengthen the bond between mother and child—already defended the act of breastfeeding by the mother. Even so, it would take a while before the wealthy families adopted this practice, since they could use slaves to nurse their children. No wonder it was very common to find ads in most of Brazil's daily newspapers of the time, seeking or offering the services of wet nurses.

There were many instances recorded involving the handling and training of domestic slaves, which shows that this was a recurrent task for the "ladies of the house." However, this daily duty was only mentioned in the letters on exceptional occasions, when there was a need to borrow a servant, during someone's illness, or when there was some other setback. During one of her long stays in Petrópolis, Dona Leonarda cancelled her visit to the property of Pau Grande to return to the Court to train a new *mucama*, or personal servant. She apologized to her daughter for the inconvenience and added, "The new *mucama* is only twenty-four years old and doesn't know a thing. During the days she stayed here, together with the other servants she messed everything up, so I need to check on them, otherwise I might lose the few that I still have."[20] In the management of the household, it was necessary to be able to deal with the unforeseen to keep it running well: "You see, Mom, in the middle of all this confusion, my washer fell sick and I had to make Felipa do the laundry and Bernarda the ironing."[21]

The domestic routine could be affected by the illness of a skilled black servant. In a letter to his daughter, for example, the councilman José Maria writes the medical recommendations of Dr. Peixoto for the treatment and recuperation of the slave Sebastião, his master mason: he should not be exposed to rain or sunshine, he should refrain from taking walks, eating too much fat, and drinking alcohol; if possible, he should drink milk. According to the medical beliefs of the time, the atmosphere in the countryside was healthier than the city, which was usually affected by epidemics. Sebastião remained at the country home to receive all the necessary care. The councilman also recommended: "Do not exaggerate taking care of Sebastião, to not spoil him, otherwise he will be lost. He should be given something to do in order not to lose the habit, since his major flaw is laziness."[22] In this case, the zeal shown for Sebastião could be an act of gratitude for services provided to the family, or because of his high value in the market, since he was a skilled worker.

The uniform and harmonious aspect of the narratives presented by the authors of the letters in relation to problems involving their slaves in some ways minimized the conflicts related to their relationship, reproducing the dominant discourse of the slave society. However, the choice of tasks to be completed, where slaves would live, the number of hours they had to work, permission to practice their religion, the possibility of living with their own family, the establishment of godparent relationships, permission to accumulate money—all of these were part of a system of negotiation between slaves and masters.[23] For those who worked and lived with their masters, the possibility of earning benefits was greater. The more precarious the conditions in which the slave lived, the more he or she would value any benefit received from the master. On the other hand, to earn the trust of a master could signify a breakup with the rest of the slave group. As a result, slave owners tried to maintain an unstable balance of the privileges given, always reminding the slaves that they could be revoked (Chalhoub 1990; Reis 1989).

The slaves had to learn the rules of this social construction to take advantage of it. Often, the flights and small acts of disobedience or unruly behavior were not necessarily an attempt to break away from the system, but a way to increase their value and importance within it. In this way, it is necessary to see the power relations between domestic slaves and masters as a two-way street, although certainly less favorable to those without their freedom.

Although social relations were limited by the hierarchical structure of society, the proximity of living in the same house allowed masters and domestic slaves to develop affections, complicity, and loyalty.

> It was so big and valuable, the favor you did by lending me Felisberta to look over Maria Izabel that the importance of her service surpasses my natural difficulty to write. I'm very, very grateful for such a delicate gesture. . . . My gratitude to you and your husband comes from the bottom of my heart. Felisberta fulfills religiously and perfectly her duty, always making an effort to please us, so much that she returns to you leaving us missing her dearly. I wish her all the good because she deserves it. If was not for the doctor's recommendation, to send her back to the country, with your permission, I would keep her with me. . . .
>
> With love I send you a hug as well as to Mariquinhas, Julia, Lulu, Antonio Ribeiro, also a hug to José Maria, D. Antonia and D. Maria. My respects to Mrs. Mariana, Mr. Braz, and to Mr. Joaquim Mascarenhas. Love to my brother and compadre. Say hello to Janjana, Maria Gertrudes, and Bernarda.
>
> With all my heart,
> Your very thankful sister and comadre,
> Carolina Velho.[24]

This letter, which completes the one analyzed before that mentions Felisberta and suggests that she had gone to the Court in 1862 to breastfeed Maria Izabel, the first daughter of José Maria da Silva Velho (Juca) and Carolina Monteiro Velho. Three years later, because of health problems, she returned to the country home, which confirms the practice of sending captives to the province for convalescence. Carolina's expression of praise for Felisberta as a "good slave" went beyond satisfaction with the efficiency she demonstrated performing her duties; it was mixed with feelings of affection, which we sense in her statement: "I wish her all the good because she deserves it."

A second daughter, named Mariana to honor her aunt, was born in 1866, and the viscountess once more answered the family's request and sent another servant named Bernarda. On August 4, 1866, her brother Juca would write,

> . . . Marianinha is doing fine and Bernarda is performing her duties very well and pleases us very much. She is very respectful and grateful for the news you sent of her son and for the care you dedicate to her Feliciano. *Let us know of Felisberta, whom we regard as a friend, and never cease to remember her earnest and dignified conduct, nor her many demonstrations of concern and friendship toward us while she took care of Maria Izabel: what a beautiful person! Send her our regards and tell her we always remember her with pleasure. . . .*
>
> Your brother and sincere friend
> José Maria.[25]

Once more, the compliments dedicated to the personal servants expressed two important qualities sought out by the masters: competence in performing their duties, and good behavior, shown here in the form of gratitude to the mistress. In the epistolary narratives, attitudes of submission and recognition of the hierarchy that existed between slaves and masters were emphasized. As a return for the good services provided, the social actors of these letters utilized a system of interchanges of favors. Mariana Velho de Avellar promised to take care of Feliciano, son of the slave Bernarda, who was a baby when the mother was sent to the city to serve Mariana's brother.

To fulfill her brother's request, Mariana separated Bernarda from her newborn son in the same way she had previously separated the slave Felisberta from her son. In this regard, we must consider the situations of the slave families. As Manolo Florentino and José Roberto Goes demonstrated, imperial society did not consider it a crime to separate enslaved parents from their children, siblings, or mates. A substantial number of the slaves on the plantations lived within an intricate network of godparentage that was fundamental to build ties of solidarity that could ease their lives as slaves. To the slaves, these godparentage links worked as an important pillar of their community. Establishing godparentage connections was the same as establishing allies to deal with the daily hardships and sufferings of their lives. To the owners, the slave family was an essential instrument of control to maintain peace in the *senzalas*, the slave quarters. To manage the plantations, the master had to focus not only on economic issues, but on controlling the slaves by using strategies of dominance, and a main strategy was giving permission to the slave to have a family (Florentino and Góes 1997, 30).

It might seem at first, after reading the letter above, that the negotiation between the slave wet nurses and their mistresses was conducted in an environment of harmonious relations, but it was not. In reality, when Mariana promised to care for the slave's son, she was actually utilizing a strategy of dominance. High infant mortality affected all social groups at the time, but especially the slave population, due to the precarious conditions in which they lived and worked. Therefore, Bernarda knew she probably would never see her son again and feared for his health. However, if she resisted or refused to obey her mistress, it would create an environment of conflict that could result in the loss of privileges she had earned for herself and her son for being a reliable domestic servant. So, as a strategy, she accepted her mistress's request, hoping that it would result in a better fate for her son Feliciano.

As we can see, to analyze the relationships between slaves and their masters in the 1800s, we must understand that the boundaries of these relations were extremely ambiguous. As we have already mentioned, living and serving in the master's house allowed the emergence of affections such as those expressed by Mariana's brother, Juca, toward Felisberta. In a passage from a letter of March 20, 1867, the young Maria Izabel sent a piece of fabric large enough to make a dress, as a gift to Felisberta, whom she referred to as "mommy Beta."[26] Acts such as these expose the complexity of the historical construction of the affections in the private life of the slave society. In a letter sent on December 3, Dona Leonarda said:

> After having finished writing the letters to be sent tomorrow morning and while at the window watching the rain, we were surprised to see the arrival of Daniel, who at once told us that everyone was well. But since nothing is perfect, *he told us of Simão's death. We were very sad because he was a good slave and my granddaughter, Mariquinha, liked him a lot. He also served me well as my valet de chamber when I stayed in Botafogo. Joaquim will feel sad as well, especially he because was accustomed to him.* But let's finish with this sad news and talk about more cheerful things.[27]

Dona Leonarda's concern when seeing Daniel's arrival at night to bring the mail made her think that something might have happened to a family member. After finding out that everyone was okay, she became calmer. Her words express the relief of knowing that all was well and demonstrate that her concerns are limited to her family members, exposing clearly the distinction between the two worlds of domestic life. When she feels sorry for Simão's death, her emphasis was on the good work he had provided to them (what every master expected), and the affection he had earned from members of the family. Having access to the private domains of their masters facilitated the development of small demonstrations of affection or feelings, intimacy, gratitude, and an interchange of favors, that if well used by the slaves, could earn them important breaches in the system. To be recognized by the master or mistress as a good slave, who correctly fulfils the expected social role, the slave sometimes reached the edge of the system, but did not necessarily break its vertical structure (Reis and Silva 1989).

Sharing the household with the domestic slaves did not leave the owners untouched. In several photographs from the 1800s, children appear accompanied by their wet nurses, demonstrating that the black nanny was not only accepted, but an important element of child rearing, as well as part of the private domestic life of her master. In the many letters Mariana wrote to her parents, she constantly mentioned the old slaves who probably had taken care of her: "I miss very much Baba, Nana, Rita, Deolinda, Sabina, and Bartholomeu" (Petrópolis, December 2, 1860). "Joaquim sends regards to Mother and I do it to Babá, Nana, Ritinha and Deolinda" (Petropolis, May 10, year unknown).

Mariana even wrote to her mother about Deolinda, expressing her happiness about the slave's recovery from an eye problem. She also commended her parents for paying for the medical treatment that gave the slave the capacity to return to her services as a seamstress, which required good, sharp eyesight.[20] The analysis of these letters leads us to agree with Robert Slenes, who argued that the domestic slaves were usually selected from among members of the old slave families, who had demonstrated loyalty to their owners (1997).

The conditions of domestic slavery permitted the development of affections and demonstrations of allegiance toward the masters that could be rewarded with manumission. The opening of the master's will was usually a moment of great hope for the slaves, since it could bring their dreamed-of freedom. Dona Mariana Luiza da Gloria Avellar, Joaquim's aunt and one of the owners of the plantation Pau Grande, in her testament bequeathed all her movable and immovable properties to relatives and godchildren. In relation to the slaves, it said:

"The following female slaves are freed: Guilhermina *crioula*,[29] Jesuína *crioula*, Emilia.

To Deolinda and her son Hermes, also freed, I bequeath the amount of forty mil reis.[30]

I emancipate the male slave José Feliz.

The executor will pay to my sisters the amount equal to the value of two female slaves that I am emancipating: *Balbina and Maria do Bom Jesus.*

I leave a gold chain, earrings, and all the clothing to be shared among the slaves that I have freed: Guilhermina, Jesuina, Emilia, Militana, and Deolinda."[31]

As he had promised his sister, the Baron of Capivary, brother of Dona Mariana, granted freedom to four female slaves—Ilíada, Prudentina, Florinda, and Leonidia—of the 700 or more distributed through his six plantations. In the fifteen years between Dona Mariana's will (1848) and the Baron's will (1863), there were important political, economic, and social changes, resulting from, among other factors, the end of the transatlantic slave trade (1850). According to the studies of Ricardo Salles, after the 1860s, the slave population declined in the plantation areas of the Paraíba Valley. This process affected the relations between master and slave, establishing what the author refers to as a more mature slave community. It was based on a new dynamic that strengthened slave families, increased the number of Creoles in relation to African slaves, and better balanced the gender ratio of slaves in captivity. In this new context, it is interesting to point out that the number of manumissions diminished: "Wealthy planters, especially the ones who owned large plantations and had other means to control their slaves, became more reluctant to free them. When freedom was obtained, it was the result of greater efforts on the slave's part than before 1850. From being a practice strongly used as a concession from the master, the manumissions became more and more a conquest of the slave" (Salles, 2008, 256).

The relation between the number of slaves owned and the number of those freed by the baron was typical for the time; the rate of manumissions granted by slaveholders was low, especially among wealthy planters. However, the baron's testament calls attention to the case of America Luiza da Conceição, a servant on one of the baron's properties. Besides being freed, America Luiza's was the only one to inherit property goods: the usufruct of land with coffee plantations, a house, a pension of 10 *contos de reis*, and forty-four slaves, including adults, children, and her two young daughters, Maria and Margarida Baiana.[32] The baron's great concern with America Luiza's well-being was probably the result of their intimate relationship. They could have been father and daughter, or even lovers—most probably the latter, since the baron requested the return of the properties, including the slaves, to his son Joaquim Ribeiro de Avellar, after America's death, without regard for the woman's future descendants. If she were his daughter, he would probably not do that, since the properties and goods would be used to guarantee a safe future for his illegitimate grandchildren.

Many times, manumissions stated in wills were not honored by the family or even by the executors nominated by the testator. Afraid that this could happen in his case, the Baron of Capivary warned: "I hope that my heir remembers all that he owes me, so he does not fail to attend to my requests."[33] Even so, his testament was contested, and America Luiza received only nine slaves of the forty-four originally bequeathed to her. There were instances in which the master revoked the concession of manumission to certain slaves. Dona Mariana Luiza da Gloria Avellar's testament, cited above, called for the manumission of three female slaves: Militana, Balbina and Maria do Bom Jesus. However, she changed her mind, and in the end sold them to the Baron of Capivary, the first for 700$000 and the other two for 200$000, since she shared their ownership with her sisters. Right afterward, she justified herself by declaring: "If I do this, it is because of their misconduct."[34]

Dona Mariana da Gloria's action demonstrated a pedagogical purpose, not only to the women who lost the benefit, but to all other domestic slaves, who would learn how much power the masters had over their lives. From the slave owner's perspective, the concession of freedom (and any other privilege earned through the interchange of favors) must be understood as a gift, a very generous one. Dona Mariana da Gloria therefore utilized this tool to punish the slaves. By selling the slave women, she revoked part of her will without having to make changes in it, since she could not free someone she did not own anymore. By a simple gesture, legitimated by the slaveholding system, she changed again the future of these women.

As we can see, regarding the policy of exchanging favors, if necessary, force was used. In this society, besides the physical violence, there was symbolic violence that imposed the dominance of the masters and reminded the slaves all the time of their place in this system. In conclusion, it is possible to say that for the dominant class, a "good slave" was the one who understood well how the system worked and behaved accordingly. In this sense, the slave family played an important role in maintaining peace in the slave quarters, even though the masters also used other instruments of control. When Dona Mariana da Gloria revoked the manumission of the female slaves to teach them a lesson, she was acting according to the practices of the paternalist system, demonstrating how wealthy women also followed the rules to maintain the order. The vertical structure of the imperial society was also reproduced in the family, where the women were submissive to the men, extended families were more powerful than nuclear ones, and the wishes of the master were to be obeyed by the slave. The slave tried to survive by devising strategies of submission that could bring them some benefits or privileges to ease their life as a captive. From these daily social dynamics emerged affections, complicities, and feelings that were extremely ambiguous, but that when exposed and analyzed, help us understand the complexity of the relationship between masters and their domestic slaves.

Notes

1. José Maria Velho da Silva's letter to Mariana Velho de Avellar. All letters quoted throughout this chapter, unless otherwise cited, are part of the private collection of Roberto Meneses de Moraes.

2. For more information on the Velho da Silva family and how they built their wealth, see Muaze (2008, Ch. 1).

3. The desire to become part of the Court bureaucracy was not motivated only by the desire for a prestigious position—it was also an attempt to change the public image of slave traders during the course of the termination of the transatlantic slave traffic. Until 1831, slave traders had an important economic role of supplying Brazil with slave labor; as a result, the traders had high social status. However, once the slave traffic was prohibited, these men started to be seen as pirates or outlaws. At the same time, it would not be in the interest of the Crown to let these men invest their money someplace else, so they were incorporated into the bureaucracy to keep them in Brazil.

4. To learn more about slavery in the Paraíba Valley, see Salles (2008) and Marquese, Rafael, and Tomich (2009).

5. Vincent-Buffault sees this kind of intimate writing as expanding in Europe during the second half of the eighteenth century. The rise of the bourgeoisie and their way of life makes it possible to express feelings of individuality and intimacy outside of the family circle. The old aristocracy then incorporated this practice of intimate writing.

6. In the nineteenth century, Brazil was a nation with a high rate of illiteracy, mostly among women. Rio de Janeiro, the capital, had the highest literacy rate, but even so, only 29 percent of its population could read and write. Therefore, the family studied was almost an exception, since the majority of their women, for three generations, had been educated, even learning other languages (Alencastro 1997, 475, table 6).

7. To read more about practices of intimate writing and reading, see Gomes (2004), Darnton (1992), Chartier (2001), and Mignot, Bastos, and Cunha (2000).

8. According to Revel, in microhistory's methodology, the study of the detail or the individual improves understanding of the collective thinking of society (Revel 1998; Levi 1992, 133–62; Vainfas 2002).

9. Mariana Velho de Avellar's letter to Leonarda Maria Velho da Silva. Petrópolis, November 13, 1862.

10. Ibid.

11. The concept of *habitus* used in this chapter refers to the one developed by Norbert Elias (1993–1994). In Europe, the changes in social habitus were related to the rise of the bourgeoisie and capitalism. In Brazil, it did not happen in the same way, because the elite merely adopted the daily practices of consumption and behavior of the bourgeoisie, without Brazil becoming a capitalist country. For more on this topic, see Muaze (2008).

12. To learn more about the Brazilian elite of the 1800s, see Mattos (1990).

13. To mention only some of the works available in the archives and public libraries of Rio de Janeiro: Roquette (1997), Rieusseyroux (1877), Boitard (1872), and Bassanville (1878).

14. Leonarda Maria Velho da Silva's letter to Mariana Velho de Avellar. Rio de Janeiro, April 12, 1869. With the change of habitus of the mid-nineteenth century, dinners served *à la française* were replaced by the *à la russe* style. In the first, the food was served all together, regardless of the type of food. In the latter, the food was served in courses, with different kinds of china, silverware, wine, and decoration.

15. Leonarda Maria Velho da Silva's letter to Mariana Velho de Avellar. Rio de Janeiro, August 8, 1864.

16. For more on slave auctions in Rio de Janeiro, see Karasch (2000), specifically chapter 2.

17. Leonarda Maria Velho da Silva's letter to Mariana Velho de Avellar. Rio de Janeiro, August 8, 1864.

18. Mariana Velho de Avellar's letter to Leonarda Maria Velho da Silva. Petrópolis, May 25, 1862.

19. For an analysis of the debate about maternal breastfeeding in the nineteenth century, see Muaze (1999).

20. Leonarda Maria Velho da Silva's letter to Mariana Velho de Avellar. Petrópolis, Tuesday, December 22, year unknown.

21. Mariana Velho de Avellar's letter to Leonarda Maria Velho da Silva. Petrópolis, February 15, 1862.

22. José Maria Velho da Silva's letter to Mariana Velho de Avellar. June 26, year unknown. About the feeding of slaves and their health, see Karasch (2000), especially chapter 5.

23. This system of negotiation between slaves and masters is discussed by many historians who specialize in the study of slavery: Slenes (1997), Florentino and Góes (1997), Guedes (2008), and H. M. Castro (1993).

24. The godfather of a child is known as *compadre* by the parents of this child, and the godmother is known as *comadre*. Carolina Velho's letter to Mariana Velho de Avellar. SC, January 18, 1865.

25. Emphasis added—M. M.; José Maria Velho da Silva's letter to Mariana Velho de Avellar. Corte, August 4, 1866.

26. José Maria Velho da Silva's letter to Mariana Velho de Avellar. Court. March 20, 1867.

27. Emphasis added—M. M.; Leonarda Maria Velho da Silva's letter to Mariana Velho de Avellar. Petrópolis, Saturday, December 3, at 9 p.m., year unknown.

28. Mariana Velho de Avellar's letter to Leonarda Maria Velho da Silva. Petrópolis, November 16, 1862. It is interesting to note that in the testament of Dona Leonarda Maria Velho da Silva, Deolinda was listed as one of her slaves, priced as 800$000. The Will of D. Leonarda Maria Velho da Silva, Rio de Janeiro, March 16, 1871 (Arquivo Nacional).

29. The terms *crioula* and *crioulo* were used to denote that the slave was born in Brazil. The words *africano* and *africana* or the names of some African nations, such as *mina, benguela,* or *cabinda,* were used to distinguish those who were not from Brazil.

30. A unit of Brazilian money during the nineteenth century.

31. Emphasis added—M. M.; D. Mariana Luiza da Glória Avellar's testament. Paty do Alferes, 1848.

32. Barão de Capivary's testament, Pau Grande, February 20, 1863. Vassouras: CDH/ Universidade Severino Sombra, (box 242). See also Barão de Capivary's will, 1863. Vassouras: CDH/ Universidade Severino Sombra, (box 116).

33. Barão de Capivary's testament, Pau Grande, February 20, 1863. Vassouras: CDH/ Universidade Severino Sombra, (box 242).

34. Slave sale contract written by D. Mariana Luiza da Glória Avellar, Pau Grande, March 9, 1848 (private collection of Roberto Meneses de Moraes).

Works Cited

Alencastro, Luiz Felipe de. 1997. "A Corte e a modernidade nacional." In *História da vida privada no Brasil,* edited by L. F. Alencastro. Vol. 2. São Paulo: Companhia das Letras.

Bassanville, Mme la Comtesse de. 1878. *Almanach du savoir vivre.* Paris: E. Plon.

Boitard, Pierre. 1872. *O novo manual do bom tom,* 2nd ed. Rio de Janeiro, Brazil: E&H Laemmert.

Castro, Hebe Maria. 1993. *Das cores do silêncio.* Rio de Janeiro, Brazil: Nova Fronteira.

Chalhoub, Sidney. 1990. *Visões de liberdade: Uma história das últimas décadas da escravidão na Corte.* São Paulo: Companhia das Letras.

———. 1998. "Diálogos políticos em Machado de Assis."In *A história contada: Capítulos de história social da literatura no Brasil,* edited by S. Chalhoub and L. Pereira. Rio de Janeiro: Nova Fronteira.

Chartier, Roger. 1995. "Diferenças entre os sexos e dominação simbólica (nota critica)." *Cadernos Pagu* (Núcleo de Estudos de Gênero/ UNICAMP) no. 4: 37–47. www.pagu.unicamp.br/sites/www.pagu.unicamp.br/files/pagu04.04.pdf.

———. 2001. *Práticas de leitura,* 2nd ed. São Paulo: Estação Liberdade.

Darnton, Robert. 1992. "História da leitura." In *Escrita da história,* edited by P. A. Burke. São Paulo: Unesp Editora.

Elias, Norbert. 1993–1994. *O processo civilizador*. 2 vols. Rio de Janeiro: Jorge Zahar.

Florentino, Manolo, and José Roberto Góes. 1997. *A paz das senzalas: Famílias escravas e tráfico atlântico*. Rio de Janeiro: Civilização Brasileira.

Gomes, Ângela de Castro. 2004. "Escrita de si, escrita da história: A título de prólogo." In *Escrita de si, escrita da história,* edited by Â. de Castro Gomes. Rio de Janeiro, Brazil: Ed. Fundação Getúlio Vargas.

Guedes, Roberto. 2008. *Egressos do cativeiro: Trabalho, família, aliança e mobilidade social* (Porto Feliz, São Paulo, c. 1798–c. 1850). Rio de Janeiro: FAPERJ; Mauad X.

Karasch, Mary. 2000. *A Vida dos escravos no Rio de Janeiro 1808–1850.* São Paulo: Cia das Letras.

Levi, Giovanni. 1992. "Sobre a micro-história." In *A Escrita da história: Novas perspectivas,* edited by Peter Burke. São Paulo: Ed. Universidade Estadual Paulista (UNESP).

Marquese, Rafael and Dale Tomich. 2009. "O Vale do Paraíba escravista e a formação do mercado mundial de café no século XIX." *O Brasil Imperial 1831–1870,* edited by Keila Grinberg and Ricardo Salles. Rio de Janeiro: Civilização Brasileira.

Mattos, Ilmar. *O Tempo saquarema.* São Paulo: Hucitec, 1990.

Mignot, Ana C. V.; Maria Helena C. Bastos, and Maria T. Santos Cunha. 2000. *Refúgios do eu: Educação, história, escrita autográfica.* Florianópolis, Brazil: Mulheres.

Muaze, Mariana. 1999. "A Descoberta da infância: A formação de um habitus civilizado na boa sociedade imperial." Unpubl. MA diss. Departamento de História da Pontifícia Universidade Católica, Rio de Janeiro, Brazil.

———. 2008. *As Memórias da Viscondessa: Família e poder no Brasil Império.* Rio de Janeiro, Brazil: Jorge Zahar.

Reis, João José, and Eduardo Silva. 1989. *Negociação e conflito: Resistência negra no Brasil escravista.* São Paulo: Cia das Letras.

Revel, Jacques, editor. 1998. *Jogos de Escalas: A experiência da microanálise.* Rio de Janeiro, Brazil: Ed. Fundação Getúlio Vargas.

Rieusseyroux, Alquié Mme. Louise de Rieusseyroux. 1877. *Lê Savoir-vivre en toutes lês circonstances de la vie.* 14th ed. Paris: F. Ebhard.

Roquette, José Ignacio. 1997. In *Código do bom-tom: Regras da civilidade e de bem viver no século XIX,* edited by Lilia Moritz Schwarcz. São Paulo: Companhia das Letras.

Salles, Ricardo. 2008. *E o vale era escravo.* Rio de Janeiro: Civilização Brasileira.

Slenes, Robert. 1997. "Senhores e subalternos no oeste paulista." In *História da vida privada no Brasil,* 2: *Império: A corte e a modernidade nacional* edited by L. F. Alencastro. São Paulo: Cia das Letras.

Vainfas, Ronaldo. 2002. *Os protagonistas anônimos da história: Micro-história.* Rio de Janeiro: Ed. Campus.

Vincent-Buffault, Anne. 1996. *Da Amizade: Uma História do exercício da amizade nos séculos XVIII e XIX.* Rio de Janeiro, Brazil: Zahar.

Archival Materials

Arquivo Nacional. Rio de Janeiro, 1871. Will of D. Leonarda Maria Velho da Silva.

Centro de Documentação Histórica/ Universidade Severino Sombra. Vassouras, 1863. Will of Barão de Capivary.

Centro de Documentação Histórica/ Universidade Severino Sombra. Pau Grande, 1863. Testament of Barão de Capivary.

Private collection of Roberto Meneses de Moraes.

French Travelers and Journalists Debate the *Lei do Ventre Livre* of 1871*

Claudia Santos

This article presents the views of French travelers and publicists about the 1871 "Free Womb" law (*Lei do Ventre Livre*) in Brazil, which sought to exempt children born of slave mothers from slavery. To investigate this topic I have studied travel accounts by twenty-seven French travelers who were in Brazil between 1850 and 1890, as well as articles written by ten publicists who wrote about the South American empire during the same period. The core idea is that these writers were much more than mere spectators. At a moment when the "question of slavery" was becoming an increasingly international issue, they played an important role in shaping public opinion about the new legislation and the permanence of the institution of slavery in Brazil. Further, this analysis seeks to show the importance of these reports and publications in the construction of certain myths regarded as constitutive of the Brazilian nationality, such as, among others, the myths of racial democracy and of the indolence of Brazilians.

The elimination of the slave trade in the early 1850s—perceived by the majority of the French as a direct result of British pressure—prompted numerous reflections

*Translations from French to Portuguese by Cláudia Santos; translated from Portuguese to English by Scott Feiner.

on the inevitable end of slavery. Undoubtedly, it would not be expected to continue under the same conditions, and from that point on the institution of slavery went through significant changes. However, the end of trafficking would not necessarily lead to the end of slavery, and theoretically, it could last much longer, depending on the birthrate in the slave population.[1]

Certainly, Brazilians had very different expectations with regard to the duration of the institution of slavery, but few could ignore the difficulties of maintaining it indefinitely. Pressure from the British to eliminate trafficking, abolitionist campaigns in Europe, and emancipation in other countries were among the many obstacles to attempts to maintain slavery in Brazil. Even though the majority of the large slave owners wished to keep it as long as possible, the question of its duration would eventually be subject to public opinion. However, this was only stated formally with the enactment of the 1871 law, whose first article declared that any child born to a slave mother was free, from that date on.

What led to the enactment of the Free Womb law at this moment? In general, historians attribute it to the convergence of certain factors: the pressure of "European opinion," the victory of the northern states in the American Civil War, the War of Paraguay, slave resistance, and the political will of the emperor. Disputes arise, however, when trying to determine the weight of each of these factors.

In his assessment of the period prior to the enactment of the Free Womb law, Robert Conrad emphasized the role of the emperor, who, aware of the worldwide changes in the 1860s, sought a solution to the slavery issue that would satisfy the international abolitionists as well as meet the interest of the Brazilian slave owners. The end of the institution of slavery in the Portuguese, French, and Danish empires, and above all, the outcome of the American Civil War, weakened the supporters of slavery around the world. As a result, if Brazil had remained the only independent country in the Americas to continue slavery, it would have faced a serious disadvantage in international relations (Conrad 1972, 90). In his analysis of the debate among state advisors on the subject of slavery reform, Ricardo Salles also attributes the change of position with regard to the Rio Branco law to greater sensitivity to international criticism (Salles 2008).

In the field of international relations, the importance of the issue of immigration needs to be highlighted. At the time, Brazil, as well as other South American countries, was attempting to attract a stream of European emigration, which went primarily to North America. In the 1850s and 1860s, the Brazilian government supported various initiatives to attract European emigrants, under a sharecropping, or as it was then called, a partnership system, and in small farm arrangements (Conrad 1972, 90). Various recruitment and advertising agencies were created under the auspices of the government.[2]

Of the travelers and publicists under discussion here, the performance of both Charles Expilly and journalist Elisée Reclus, along with the Germans Avé Lallemant and J. Von Sturtz, reinforces the idea that the persistence of slavery in Brazil was beginning to be a distinct disadvantage in international relations, especially with regard to the immigration of Europeans to Brazil. In the early 1860s, the two Frenchmen waged a campaign against slavery in Brazil, while simultaneously trying to dissuade Europeans from emigrating to the South American empire.

In June 1862, in one of the largest most widely circulated magazines at the time, the *Revue des Deux Mondes*, Elisée Reclus published an article denouncing the procedures of Brazilian immigration agencies in Europe, focusing on the two major obstacles to the settlement of Europeans in Brazil: slavery and the power of the large land and slave owners.

Recognizing the great interest of the Brazilian authorities in attracting European settlers, Elisée Reclus criticized the absence of concrete measures to limit the influence of slavery on the society and economy of the Brazil, which in his view would complicate the formation of a stream of emigration from Europe to Brazil: "No one is concerned with preparing the land for the arrival of foreigners, whether by the immediate emancipation of slaves, or by the gradual reduction of slavery. Ignoring that a population of emigrants can only thrive by cultivating free soil, they feed the foolish dream of European peasants working peacefully side by side with slaves from Africa" (Reclus 1862, 375–414).

To the readers of the *Revue des Deux Mondes*, Elisée Reclus presented Brazil as a country viscerally connected to slavery, and warned that after the "predictable" outcome of the American Civil War, the South American empire would, in a short time, have the sad honor of being the last slave-based power. Like many other journalists, Reclus compared Brazilian slavery to American slavery, but, unlike most, he stressed the negative aspects of the institution in Brazil. Whereas in the United States, slaveholders were continually confronted with antislavery voices, in Brazil, the entire society was deeply implicated in slavery. In his work, Elisée Reclus criticized any allusion to Brazilian slavery as a mild institution, because to him, the main difference between the United States and Brazil was that in the latter, slavery was not seriously targeted: "In Brazil, the masters can be benevolent, considering that unwelcome abolitionists are not there to threaten their sacred properties" (Reclus 1862, 386).

One of the main goals of Reclus's article was to show that slavery and the power of the major slave and land owners put the lives of European emigrants in Brazil in danger and represented insurmountable obstacles to the emigrants' permanence in Brazil. He thus corroborated the statements of the German Avé Lallemant, who in 1860 in Europe had written about the precarious living conditions of settlers in the colonies founded in the Mucuri Valley in Minas Gerais. The "Mucuri Case," as well as the conflicts on the Ibicaba plantation in São Paulo, were highly publicized in Europe and led some countries to restrict or even prevent emigration to Brazil.[3] Paraphrasing Lallemant regarding the "Mucuri horrors," Reclus warned his readers in France and other parts of the world that this case could be considered neither an isolated situation nor an accident:

> One would think that perhaps the horrors of colonization committed by Mucuri belong to the past and would not be repeated; but in a country under the rule of slavery, such events are part of the natural order of things. . . . In all places in Brazil where field work was reserved for black slaves, Europe settlers should expect a somewhat disguised servitude. . . . The history of colonization, taken as a whole, shows that emigrants from Europe . . . can never hope to be treated as free men, because land ownership, this first guarantee of freedom, is in practical terms out of their reach. (Reclus 1862, 404)

Reclus therefore clearly concludes that while slavery and the power of the major slave owners remained intact, the emigration of Europeans to Brazil would be inadvisable.

Charles Expilly, a French traveler who resided in Rio de Janeiro in the 1850s, published four books in the 1860s about Brazil, which voiced his position against slavery as well as against European immigration to the country. Charles Expilly used the book *La Traite, l'emigration et la colonisation* to request that his country's authorities take steps to prevent French emigration to the Brasil. Expilly cited the "Mucuri disasters" and the Ibicaba conflicts as examples to prove that the French were exposed to real dangers by settling in Brazil (Expilly 1864a, 139–43). In 1864, Expilly also published *Du Mouvement de l'emigration au port de Marseille*, to prove that emigration to Brazil from the port of Marseille was considerable, and that, consequently, it was necessary to create a special commission there to control and prevent this emigration.[4]

Aside from publishing books, Charles Expilly took practical measures against European emigration to Brazil. In 1866, he became deputy commissioner of emigration in Le Havre and afterwards, chief commissioner of emigration in Marseille, a position he was to hold from 1868 to 1870. Expilly's arguments presented to demonstrate the need for a special commissioner's office in Marseille were not based on the number of French who had shipped off to Brazil, even though, due to clandestine operations, the actual figures were higher than those officially released. Rather, his arguments were based on two main ideas. First, the fact that agents of the Brazilian Empire had chosen the south of France as a field of activity after the German and Swiss governments took measures to discourage their efforts could result in the formation of a true flow of emigration. Second, and most importantly, the European emigrant was subject to considerable risks with emigration to Brazil. In this regard he clearly stated the purpose of his actions: "We believe this book will prevent a number of emigrants bound for the South American Empire from settling there. If of 100 people for whom death awaits along the rivers of Brazil, 20 decide to remain in Europe after reading our truthful pages, we will have fulfilled our duty to humanity in general, and to our country" (Expilly 1864a, 101; 1864b, 336).[5]

This campaign against French emigration to Brazil earned Expilly the title of *ennemi du Brésil*, and it was also applied to J. Von Sturtz,[6] former consul of Prussia in Brazil, who struggled to prohibit the emigration of Germans to the South America empire. This title was repeated several times by other French publicists, as well as by Brazilian authorities who—through the diplomatic service in Paris—hired journalists to challenge the articles written by Expilly and Reclus.[7] In these diplomatic documents, the Brazilian government expressed great concern about French intervention in the Mucuri and Ibicaba cases and about the formation of negative opinion of Brazil due to the conflict against Paraguay.[8]

In 1875, this concern with the "enemies of Brazil" was apparent among Brazilian statesmen. In his report to the Ministry of Agriculture on emigration and colonization in Brazil, João Cardoso de Menezes e Souza argued that the major obstacle to European immigration was not slavery, but rather the *ennemis du Brésil*. For Cardoso, promoting European emigration would require the formation of a network of publicity favorable toward Brazil: "I have already pointed out on other occasions, the importance of organizing an advertising network in Europe mainly to establish the truth about colonization in Brazil. Several events were distorted by the *enemies of Brazil* to divert emigration from the Brazilian Empire" (Cardoso 1875, vii; cf. 28–32, 270, 343, emphasis added—C. S.).

Nonetheless, Charles Expilly stated that the struggle was not against Brazil, but against "l'esclavage, l'oppression et la barbarie" (Expilly 1864a, 91). Coincidentally, the publicity network to which Cardoso referred seems to have received the support of travelers themselves, as some travel narratives report that "l'affaire Charles Expilly" was still featured ten and even twenty years after the publication of his last book about Brazil. In 1876, the traveler Emmanuel Liais—a French astronomer who was very close to Pedro II—tried to defend the Brazilian Empire against Charles Expilly's charges (Liais 1882, 209–10), and in 1886, the controversial book by Gustave Aimard still had the same goal (1888, 96).[9]

Thus, analysis of the texts of French travelers and journalists in the 1860s indicates the existence of a campaign against slavery and emigration to Brazil, one that may have played an important role in the discussion of the 1871 law. Finally, the emperor had been called to intercede directly on behalf of immigrants experiencing difficulties in the Mucuri Valley, and certainly he and other members of the political and intellectual elite were aware of these articles in magazines of wide global circulation. From one international viewpoint, Brazil was linked to slavery and appalling living conditions for European settlers. On the other hand, the difficulties with colonization were connected to the slave mentality of the Brazilian elite. In the same year that Charles Expilly published his *La Verité sur le conflit entre le Brésil . . .* , the Société Française pour l'abolition de l'esclavage called attention to the emperor's famous message with regard to emancipation measures, with important consequences for avoiding the issue of slavery. Additionally, the weight of European opinion in the decisions of the emperor was identified and criticized by some contemporaries, such as José de Alencar, who in his article, "Erasmus' New Political Cards," wrote:

> Dear sir, allow me to say, you were the victim of this fascination. By far you smiled at celebrity. . . . For the greedy imagination, foreign fame tastes better and is valued more. Praise, in some of those languages that have become cosmopolitan, spreads around the world and immediately becomes universal opinion. The four winds of the press carry the name in vogue to the edges of the earth. . . . You have already begun to reap the first fruits of celebrity, that are so desired. European journalism now receives from the Brazilian Emperor those lavish tributes of unfailing admiration. . . . The foreigner who you proclaim is one of the wisest and most illustrious rulers. . . . The country suspects that the enthusiasm from overseas is not spontaneous and without hidden agendas, and obtained at the expense of dangerous concessions. . . . Many courtships have already been made by the imperial crown to influence European and American opinion. . . . Releasing a hundred

slaves whose services you had given the nation; distinguishing the leader of a religious order that emancipated the womb with a special caress, encouraging manumission through honorific favors, responding to the charitable aspirations of an abolitionist European society, and finally reclaiming the legislative power for this delicate social reform via the voice of the throne, no doubt you think you have earned the privileges of a philanthropic king. This is a great mistake, sir. . . . These doctrines have seduced you, far away from Brazil and now, the generous impulses of charity, take the unfortunate role of a conspiracy of evil and great, terrible wickedness. (Alencar 2009, 356)[10]

Thus, the intervention of these Frenchmen in the public debate about slavery, colonization, and the Paraguayan War corroborate the interpretation that in the mid-1860s, the permanence of slavery in Brazil began to pose a serious disadvantage in international relations. Perhaps it is not possible to explain the 1871 law exclusively as the result of the emperor's decision, motivated by pressure from the antislavery voice abroad. Undoubtedly, it is necessary to relate the international context to the internal situation and consider, among other factors, slave resistance.[11] But if slave resistance as a factor in the reform of 1871 is at this time not fully documented,[12] there is still sufficient evidence of the impact of both antislavery and anti-Brazilian opinion in Europe during this period. The "enemies of Brazil" campaign sparked swift reaction from the Brazilian government and can be considered to have been a key factor driving the reform of the Free Womb law. Finally, we must not forget that, during the emperor's journey to Europe the same year that the Rio Branco law was passed, Brazilian institutions, facing the charges made by the "enemies of Brazil," clearly assumed—as we will see below—a defensive stance. In this battle, the emperor found several allies among the French. While F. Dabadie, Charles Expilly, and Elisée Reclus—Republicans linked to the 1848 Revolution in France—promoted a campaign against slavery in Brazil, other French travelers and journalists played a key role in defending the process of gradual emancipation beginning with the 1871 law.

In November 1871, less than two months after the enactment of the Rio Branco law, Auguste Cochin—French political writer and author of *L'Abolition de l'esclavage* (1861)—published an article in the famous *Revue de Deux Mondes* titled "L'abolition de l'esclavage au Brésil." The primary purpose of the article was the "clarification of European opinion" that, according to the author, had been deceived by the "overly optimistic defenders of the law of September 28" (Cochin 1871, 711). Cochin took a position contrary to that of the writers who had presented the law as "the great letter of liberation." Thus, despite the title of his article, Cochin sought to demonstrate that the law was too timid a step toward the end of slavery. Why, then, was the title "L'Abolition de l'esclavage au Brésil" chosen? Was the idea so widespread that the law of 1871 represented the end of slavery? Or was the choice of the title merely a rhetorical device to attract his readers? It is quite difficult to answer these questions, especially when we realize that this is not the only ambiguous aspect of his article.

Despite the idea conveyed by the title, the liberal Catholic Auguste Cochin criticized the foundation of the 1871 law, yet avoided direct criticism of the Brazilian government. The emperor—who was in Europe at this time and spoke at length with Auguste Cochin—was presented to readers as a great abolitionist. Moreover, the writer argued that the 1871 law had the merit of achieving reform without resorting to violence. Still, the law was presented as "incomplete and incoherent," according to the Antislavery Society, which was already applying pressure against the Brazilian law: "We are not surprised by the complaints of the Anti-slavery Society of London, composed of the oldest lawyers of the poor slaves, too experienced to trust in promises and half-measures" (Cochin 1871, 711).The main initiative of the law—to liberate children born after 1871—only guaranteed legal freedom on paper because, in fact, they would still be slaves, or "if it makes them feel better, 'servants' for twenty-one years" (Cochin 1871, 715). Considering the other provisions of the law, which for example provided for a national registry of slaves and prohibited the separation of parents and children under age twelve, Auguste Cochin found it incomprehensible that a law was needed to ensure such basic rights.

As a result, he sought to undo the idea that the law was a letter of liberation, referring to the notion of "European opinion," which he intended to clarify: "The European opinion will be shocked to learn that a law was needed, in 1871, to force or prohibit Brazil in regard to what the most basic moral sense imposes in all civilized countries" (Cochin 1871, 712). Even though the law had "condemned, shaken and softened" slavery, Cochin vehemently called for its immediate termination. In this case, his main argument was that only truly bad slave owners might fear such a measure: "Brazil reaps and will continue to reap exactly what it has sown" (Cochin 1871, 715–16).

In his article, Cochin stated that many Europeans believed, or wanted to believe, that the 1871 law meant the abolition of slavery in Brazil. Before the publication of his article, I found no French articles about the 1871 law. In contrast, between 1872 and 1873, eleven writers addressed the issue, and four of them took a position very close to the one condemned by Cochin.

But if the main goal of Cochin's article was to criticize the writers who presented the 1871 law as the end of slavery in Brazil, he corroborated this position, not only with the title of his article, but also with its conclusion: "Among civilized nations, only Spain continues to hold slaves in Cuba and Puerto Rico despite promises of the law and—incredibly—despite requests from the colonies themselves. . . . Spain, the first to reintroduce slavery in modern history, will be the last to erase that blemish, but surely it will be very soon, for better or worse" (Cochin 1871, 717).

Alfred de Falloux—former minister of public instruction for Napoleon III, friend and biographer of Auguste Cochin—also stressed the ambiguity of this article published in *Revue*, while at the same time he sought to explain it as resulting from Cochin's good relationship with the emperor and with "certain Brazilian statesmen." According to the Count of Falloux, the Brazilian Empire had the support and affection of Auguste Cochin, "because the Empire was Catholic and constitutional." Furthermore, D. Pedro II, during his trip to Europe in 1871, had made a point of meeting with the writer, with whom he "talked at length." In contrast, Alfred de Falloux noted that Auguste Cochin "didn't entirely approve of the new law; he considered it too slow, too complicated; it would not fully meet his great expectations." Nevertheless, "Lord Cochin had dedicated an article in the *Revue des Deux Mondes* to him" (Falloux 1884, 130–31).

Cochin's difficulty in reconciling his defense of the empire (and principally the emperor) with his antislavery conviction is also recognizable among other Frenchmen, for example the Republican *quarante-huitard* Charles Ribeyrolles, a revolutionary of 1848, whose ties established in Brazil with Pedro II and other Brazilian statesmen also prevented a radical critique of the institution of slavery. In turn, this moderate antislavery stance—linked to an advertising campaign by the empire—was harshly criticized by other French *quarante-huitards*, such as Expilly and F. Dabadie.

In 1872, the *Revue Maritime et Coloniale* published an article, also titled "L'Abolition de l'esclavage au Brésil," signed simply "L. R.," without a surname. Even with no information available about the author, this article deserves some attention, because it highlights two important issues: the larger efforts to associate the 1871 law with the extinction of slavery in Brazil, and the use of Cochin's article to corroborate this interpretation. This journalist presented the Free Womb law as a major reform to promote the emancipation of slaves and, further, as a measure that would lead to the actual extinction of slavery in Brazil (L. R. 1872, 148). To support this last statement, the author used the conclusion in Auguste Cochin's article (L. R. 1872, 155).

The article by the lawyer Léon Michaux-Bellaire and the travel accounts by Gustave Aimard and Roland de Moustier repeated, in part, the opinions of the unknown author, since, in support of the law of 1871, they eventually credited it with putting an end to slavery in Brazil.

Léon Michaux Bellaire, in 1876, five years after the enactment of the law of 1871, published a book titled *Considerations sur l'abolition de l'esclavage et sur la colonization au Brésil*, seeking to provide legal explanations to the 1871 law. The author began his book by proclaiming the end of slavery in Brazil, while at the same time he emphasized the role of Emperor Pedro II in passing the law: "The law of September 28, 1871 declared the abolition of slavery in the Empire of Brazil . . . the law of September 28, 1871 was not accepted without being challenged, but the principle of emancipation eventually triumphed, thanks to the willpower and firmness of conviction of Emperor Dom Pedro II" (Michaux-Bellaire 1876, 5–8).Only on page 13 does the lawyer detail the true provisions of the new legislation, trying to justify them in the eyes of his readers, who probably thought that the final abolition of slavery in Brazil was a certainty. Reports by Renaud de Moustier (1885, 13–14) and Gustave Aimard (1888, 119, 133) adopted the same procedure.

In Léon Michaux-Bellaire's book, first of all, one must note the mention of British journalists as major opponents of Brazilian law, as he applauded the emperor's support of the 1871 law: "Your devices seem wise, and we cannot support the criticisms that were made, especially by a few English journalists" (Michaux-Bellaire 1876, 34).

First, the author justified the slowness of the Brazilian process, comparing it to policies chosen by France and England to extinguish slavery in their colonies. Then, the author praised the articles of the law that guaranteed the "peaceful and gradual passage of slave labor to free labor" by means of labor contracts—for a period of five years—that would be required from all slaves freed by legislation. To Michaux-Bellaire, these "police measures" were necessary, because, as it was "already proven," the newly freed men would not work after emancipation (1876, 29). Thus, the French lawyer utilized one of the main arguments in defense of gradual emancipation that was heard in the Brazilian debate about the end of slavery, the effectiveness of which had important consequences in the formation of the Brazilian nationality.

In his assessment of the Free Womb law, Michaux-Bellaire identified yet another issue: the guarantee of property rights. The end of slavery could not neglect this right, which made reparations to the owner absolutely necessary (Michaux-Bellaire 1876, 41).

During the 1870s, the Rio Branco law also received the support of French travelers Emmanuel Liais, in 1876, and Paul Bérenger in 1879. According to the former, slavery was to be abolished in Brazil peacefully and within a short time, thanks to the combination of two factors: the provisions of the 1871 law and the "good will" of men who, increasingly, freed their slaves. An astronomer and friend of the emperor, Emmanuel Liais, also provided arguments in favor of the policy of gradual emancipation. First, Brazil was not a large nation suppressing slavery in its colonies; abolition declared precipitously would instantly result in a "complete turnaround of the existing social order, ruin and cataclysm" (Liais 1882, 213). But his argument was based primarily on the idea—widespread among proponents of slavery—that, for blacks, freedom meant idleness. Liais went on to say that the slow process of emancipation was, above all, in the interests of blacks themselves, as, based on his conception of freedom, the end of slavery would result in a miserable life. It should be noted that Liais was one of the most emphatic advocates of the idea of the inferiority of nonwhites, making direct reference to the racists of that time (Liais 1882, 216).[13]

Paul Berenger introduced an argument that also was used many times by advocates of gradual abolition and one with great relevance in the formation of Brazilian society: in the empire, the transformation of labor relations could be realized gradually and peacefully, due to the absence of prejudice against blacks (Berenger 1879, 442).

During the 1880s, the French continued to support gradual emancipation. In 1880, Max Lyon also provided arguments to defend the gradualist option, even though most of the measures outlined in the law of 1871 had remained only on paper. He particularly emphasized the irrefutable right to ownership, noting that in the case of immediate abolition, the State should compensate land owners, which the Brazilian government had no ability to do (Lyon 1880, 7–15).

In 1882, after a short stay in Brazil, Ernest Michel wrote of an intense debate between the proponents of gradual emancipation and those defending immediate abolition: "among the impatient and slow moving, the wise will find the right formula to heal this hideous wound without causing many disorders and achieve a happy transition to free labor" (Michel 1887, 90).

In the context of escalating debate on the issue of slavery and the formation of an abolitionist movement increasingly united around the message of "immediate abolition without compensation," the law of 1871 and the gradualist movement found a strong ally. In 1882, a doctor and friend of the emperor, Louis Couty, argued in Europe against a distinguished French abolitionist for Brazil's right to not decide immediately in favor of complete abolition.

In 1881, Victor Schoelcher, deputy of the Second French Republic and author of the 1848 law abolishing slavery in the French colonies, had stated to an audience of more than 200 people at a banquet commemorating the abolition of slavery in French colonies that there was only one only way to achieve the emancipation of slaves in Brazil: immediate, unconditional abolition, without a transition period. As for the 1871 law, he stated, it was just a blatant lie, because with only the measures enacted by this law, it would be necessary to wait "two centuries" for the country to be "purified" of slavery (Schoelcher 1881). In addition, Schoelcher said that the emperor of Brazil, known for his liberal ideas, should feel humiliated by his status as ruler of the last sovereign nation of the civilized world to reign over slaves. This statement by Victor Schoelcher would be used repeatedly by Brazilian abolitionists, who had been in direct contact with the French abolitionist.

What were Louis Couty's arguments to defend the process of gradual emancipation against the abolitionist view? In correspondence with Victor Schoelcher—which was included in his book *L'Esclavage au Brésil*—Couty first tried to convince him that the law of 1871 was not a lie. Brazil had already almost completed the process of emancipation, by enforcing the law and with the cooperation of the slave owners: in 30 years, there would be no slaves in Brazil (Couty 1881, 11).

However, Couty knew that this argument was not enough, nor would the prediction that immediate abolition would bring economic ruin. Victor Schoelcher had already argued that the economic crisis was nothing but a specter conjured up by the defenders of slavery everywhere. While not wanting to label Couty as proslavery, Schoelcher identified those of Couty's arguments that were the same as those of the slave owners (Couty 1881, 15). Although he admitted that his knowledge of Brazil was not as complete as that of Louis Couty, the abolitionist leader called upon the Brazilian abolitionists to help him: "I'll only remind you that the Brazilians are very far from sharing your fears, as they already formed an abolitionist partnership to accelerate the path of emancipation as laid out in the law of 1871" (in a letter from Victor Schoelcher to Louis Couty, in Couty 1881, 15).

But Couty sought to strengthen his defense, serving up an argument that was increasingly employed by supporters of progressive emancipation: that idleness of blacks after the abolition would represent a danger to the economy and society. The French doctor devoted several pages to prove this thesis, putting together a large number of examples, often contradictory and incorrect, regarding the "laziness" of blacks (Couty 1881, 62–66). Moreover, liberation based on savings was presented as the "easiest thing in the world" and if it didn't happen more often, it was because slaves were not working enough (Couty 1881, 9, 22, 70–71).[14]

Despite having made several references to the economic activities of former slaves in his book on Brazil, Louis Couty ignored these examples completely to argue that freedom for blacks would mean idleness. Certainly, Couty knew of the work of freed men and knew that idleness among freed slaves was an exception. However, what was at stake was the continued work on large plantations, since despite defining Brazilian slavery by its softness, Couty admitted that the field work was quite hard, "the only true slave labor" (Couty 1881: 24–25, 46–47). He should also have admitted that, for the freed men, freedom could not mean continuing to work on the large plantations. And indeed, he understood that the dream of the slaves on the large plantations was to have a plot of land to clear and then "cultivate beans, manioc, corn, and raise pigs." However, Couty stated, this dream would not bring foreign income to the State; thus, abolition would trigger a crisis of the plantation sector, on which the state was dependent (1881: 5, 7, 29). But Victor Schoelcher had already warned in his correspondence that such an economic crisis could not justify the continuation of slavery, because Brazil was not the only country to face this problem.

So why should the Brazilians be entitled to more time to solve these problems? This economic and social crisis had been a danger in all slavery-based countries, and the small differences among them were not sufficient to justify the slow pace of the Brazilian process. To address this point, Couty used an argument that, in the nineteenth century, held a central role in the formation of Brazil as a nation. Brazil should be entitled to more time because it was working on a project that no other country would undertake until the late nineteenth century: harmony between the races. Emancipation had never been a central issue in Brazil, because the free black man would become equal to white men, able to reach the highest ranks within the bureaucracy (Couty 1881: 7–9, 20, 24–29, 32–33, 69–71). In contrast, immediate abolition prevented the process of progressive transformation of the slave into a free man. Brazil should have time to make this transition peacefully, without the repressive measures that both the United States and the West Indies had to adopt against blacks following abolition (Couty 1881: 26). But Brazil could claim this because, unlike all other countries, it had not been affected by racial prejudice.

If this argument could be used to show Brazil in a less unfavorable light, however, it was not enough to justify a more distant deadline to complete abolition. After all, why did the possibility of social mobility for the newly freed men justify the postponement of abolition? How could the absence of racial prejudice in Brazil help to avoid the economic downturn, if Louis Couty had already stated that the black man would surrender to indolence after being given his freedom?

Couty did not attempt to respond to these questions. In any case, the idea of a country "without racial prejudice," where the "liberated didn't encounter insurmountable barriers," seems to have seduced Victor Schoelcher: "In any case, thanks to your letter, I am happily aware that Brazil hasn't experienced absurd and disastrous prejudice based on color, the deadly wound of our colonies. . . . Due to this, emancipation, albeit delayed by few years, will certainly always have a result worthy of the nineteenth century" (in a letter from Victor Schoelcher to Louis Couty, in Couty 1881, 15).

Among the French journalists and travelers analyzed in this article, the only one to directly oppose this type of argument was Elisée Reclus. In the 1860s, he recognized the positive aspect of Brazilian legislation, which unlike American law "didn't lock slaves into an unsurpassable cycle of servitude," thus generating an impassable gap between white and black. However, he felt that for the future of the country the relevance of this fact "could not in any way be an excuse for Brazilian slavery which, by its nature, is identical to the divine Anglo-American institution" (Reclus 1862, 388).

Probably Couty—like many other French and Brazilians in the nineteenth century—truly believed in the absence of racial prejudice in Brazil. Having embraced the most racialist theories of the period, including polygenism, he nonetheless considered racial relations in Brazil to be quite harmonious, simply because blacks and whites shared certain spaces. Indeed, in this respect, Couty had the support of many other travelers, who also strengthened and spread the idea of racial democracy in Brazil, or in the terms of that time, of "harmony between the races" (cf. Ribeyrolles 1861, 2, 64; Assier 1867, 310; Liais 1882, 218; Berenger 1879, 442; Aimard 1888, 256; Moustier 1885, 8; Allain 1886, 322; Leclerc 1890, 60).

In these travel accounts, the idea of racial harmony was associated with certain issues: the large number of mixed-race people, the presence of blacks and mestizos in prominent positions, and the absence of segregationist laws. However, this idea was also linked to a certain view of nonwhites, because frequently the authors who more emphatically supported the theory of harmony between the races were also those who vigorously defended the racialist theory of the inferiority of non-Europeans (Couty 1881, 68; cf. Santos 1999, 288–303).

Indeed, the only travelers who opposed this way of thinking were the *quarante-huitards* Charles Expilly and F. Dabadie, because according to them, despite the large number of mestizos and the absence of segregation laws, racial prejudice indeed still existed in Brazil (Expilly 1862, 200–01, 237, 292, 330; Expilly 1863, 59, 251, 254–57; Dabadie 1858, 375). But in 1882, they already belonged to the past, even if Emmanuel Liais and Gustave Aimard still strove to refute their writings (Liais 1882, 209–10; Aimard 1888, 96).

Thus, during this second half of the nineteenth century, travel reports were an increasingly important source of information—supposedly reliable and original—about the countries that appeared to be possible destinations for capital and a European labor force. And it is possible to clearly distinguish two camps of opinion concerning race relations in Brazil, slavery, and the law of 1871. In this sense, French travelers and journalists should not be seen as mere spectators, but as key players in the formation of "European opinion" regarding the process of emancipation in Brazil. As we review the discussions of the 1871 law by French travelers and publicists, we can say that the French supported the policy of gradual emancipation, and thus became powerful allies of the Brazilian government regarding this controversial international issue—including their assistance against the propaganda campaign by the "enemies of Brazil" during the 1860s. However, their main contribution, legitimizing the process of gradual emancipation, cannot allow us to forget the role played by French opponents of gradual emancipation. Analysis of the international scenario preceding the enactment of the law of 1871 should incorporate and emphasize the *quarente-huitards'* campaign against slavery in Brazil, which had wide repercussions in Europe.

Therefore, neither Brazil nor Europe can be understood as having a single social and political perspective on Brazilian slavery, and in that sense, we should avoid referring to "European influence" as if it presented a single perspective. On one hand, we find Louis Coury and Emmanuel Liais, who in France stood against the changes of the French Revolution, and in Brazil against the permanence of slavery; on the other, Charles Expilly, F. Dabadie, Elisée Reclus, and Victor Schoelcher defended the Revolution of 1848 in France, and the immediate abolition in the Brazilian Empire. Just as there was no single "Brazilian opinion" about the races, slavery, and emigration, neither was there consensus in Europe. In this sense, the notion of public opinion should be considered within the context of a network of conflicting debates and writings—constantly revisited—to which travelers, journalists, diplomats, and many others contributed.

Notes

1. Actually, the institution of slavery underwent significant changes after the enforcement of the 1850 law. One of the most important, the internal slave trade, grew considerably, which led to opposition to this continuation of slavery. Besides the regional concentration of slaves, some historians have identified a social concentration of slave ownership (Mattos 1998). This concentration of slave ownership would have reduced the number of owners directly interested in the continuation of slavery. Undoubtedly, the domestic trade also generated significant changes in the living conditions of slaves. If, in the selection of slaves, the slaves'

preferences or their family ties had been, in some cases, taken into consideration at the time of sale, the growth of the internal slave trade ended this consideration in practical terms.

The separation of families and the disregard of bonds of friendship were not the only consequences of domestic trade: slaves also experienced changes in the pace of work, which resulted in an increased number of crimes committed by slaves (Mattos 1998; Chalhoub 1990). On the other hand, the end of trade also led to initiatives by those planters who relied on the reproduction of their own stock to improve the living conditions of slaves. Ricardo Salles believes that conflicts arising from differences in conduct during the emancipation process can be explained in part by different expectations with regard to the growth of the slave population. The major opposition to the *Ventre Livre* "Free Womb" bill in the Paraíba Valley region may have resulted from the expectations that Vale farmers would have about the natural growth of the slave population (Salles 2008).

2. In 1855, the government helped to create the Central Association of Colonization (*Associação Central de Colonização*), based in Rio de Janeiro, which sought to centralize the operations of regional companies and establish contracts with European emigration agencies that recruited settlers.

3. In 1853, the imperial government granted lots and interest-free loans to the Mucuri Company, headed by Teófilo Otoni, for the settlement of European immigrants in the Mucuri Valley in the state of Minas Gerais. In 1856, this company, through the Central Settlement Association, established contracts with European emigration agencies. The government paid a fee to these agencies for each settler recruited; three-quarters of that fee would be transferred to the settler for travel expenses. The settlers, Swiss, French, and German, were recruited in large numbers. In January 1859, while traveling in the state of Minas Gerais, the German naturalist met a number of these settlers who had been recruited by the Mucuri Company. They were in terrible condition, "lying helpless . . . , devastated by disease" (Reclus 1862, 400). Avée Lallemant wrote to the emperor for help. "On March 2, 1859, a steamship sent especially by the emperor arrived with the order to 'bring the sick and the unfortunate'" (Reclus 1862, 403). In his report, published in 1860, Avé Lallemant described these events to discourage the emigration of Germans, and Europeans in general, to Brazil. For its part, the Mucuri Company claimed that the European emigration agencies sent the settlers before facilities were ready.

There were also conflicts at the Ibicaba farm in the state of São Paulo in 1856, where the settlers were established according to the partnership system that was adopted by most coffee planters in the western part of São Paulo between 1852 and 1856. A large number of European settlers were recruited by the Vergueiro Company or directly by other owners in Europe. During 1855 and 1856 there were several conflicts between the settlers and planters in São Paulo state. The conflict in Ibicaba attracted the attention of the central government as well as the authorities of the settlers' countries of origin. As most of these settlers were of Swiss origin, the Helvetian Confederation sent consul J. J. Von Tschudi in 1859 to appraise the status of Swiss settlers established in São Paulo province.

4. A decree on January 15, 1855, under the government of Napoleon III, created a special commissioner's office for emigration in France. This measure, as well as several others taken between 1855 and 1861, opposed emigration with "multiple formalities and difficulties" (cf. Chevalier 1947, 129–33).

5. It is difficult to calculate the extent to which Charles Expilly's activities contributed to reducing the number of French immigrants to Brazil. During the nineteenth century, French emigration to the Prata region, near Uruguay and Argentina, was considerable, but this was not the case for Brazil.

6. J. Von Sturtz was consul in Brazil for ten years. He supported initiatives by Hermann Blumenau in Santa Catarina province in 1848, where there were colonies based on small farms. On the other hand, he completely opposed the emigration of Germans to those colonies that contracted settlers in partnership agreements (Expilly 1864a, 91).

7. Mr. Arnaud, a lawyer and businessman in Marseille, was hired by the Brazilian legation in Paris in June 1866—at the request of the Ministry of Foreign Affairs—to write an article against Charles Expilly. Similarly, the article "Don Solano Lopes et la Guerre du Paraguay," written by Mr. Xavier Raymond, was published in the *Revue des Deux Mondes* to challenge Elisée Reclus's position in the same publication; cf. M. R. E., Missions Diplomatiques, Paris, 226/4/14; M. R. E., Missions Diplomatiques, Paris, 225/2/9.

8. In relation to the Paraguayan War, Charles Expilly wrote two books, *La Verité sur le conflit entre le Brésil, Buenos Ayres, Montevideio et le Paraguay* in 1866 and *La Politique du Paraguay, identité de cette politique avec celle de la France et de la Grande Bretagne dans le Rio de la Plata* in 1869, in which he defended Paraguay against "the oppressive, slave-based Brazilian state—an enemy of civilization."

9. The chronological information in Gustave Aimard's report refers to 1878 as well as 1886 and, moreover, is not consistent with the data in his biography; about the "Gustave Aimard Case," see Santos (1999).

10. These letters were written and published in the years 1867 and 1868.

11. Sidney Chalhoub drew attention to the possible relationship between the crimes committed by slaves and the promulgation of the Free Womb law (1990). Similarly, Ademir Gebara sought to demonstrate the importance of slave resistance in this context by writing in the *Jornal do Comércio* e *Correio Paulistano* about crimes committed by slaves in the province of São Paulo. He also mentioned the discourse by the defenders of the law of 1871 regarding the dangers of a slave revolt, even though he admitted it could be considered simply rhetorical in nature. Ademir Gebara also mentioned a report by the British diplomats (January 1866) with references to a "feeling of revolt among slaves and a sense of fear among the elite" (Gebara 1986, 43–49). Undoubtedly, a quantitative approach to slave-based crime with a broader chronological scope would contribute greatly to the reworking of these explanations.

12. If, in 1855, Charles Expilly referred to the role of slave rebellions in the approval of the law of 1850, there is no reference whatsoever to this factor with regard to the Free Womb law in reports and articles by French travelers and journalists.

13. I base the notion of racialism on the definition by Tzvetan Todorov (1989).

14. Regarding the few opportunities for slaves to earn their freedom by working, see Queirós Mattoso (1994, 214–22).

Works Cited

Aimard, Gustave. 1888. *Le Brésil nouveau.* Paris: E. Dentee.

Alencar, José. 2009. "Ao Imperador: Novas cartas políticas de Erasmo. Segunda carta. (Sobre a emancipação)." In *Cartas de Erasmo*, edited by José Alencar. Rio de Janeiro: Academia Brasileira de Letras, 275–294.

Allain, Emile. 1886. *Rio de Janeiro, quelques données sur la capital et sur l'administration du Brésil.* Paris: Bibliothèque de Deux Mondes.

Assier, Adolphe. 1867. *Le Brésil contemporain: Races, moeurs, institutions, paysages.* Paris: Durand et Lauriel.

Berenger, Paul. 1879. "Le Brésil en 1879." *Revue des Deux Mondes* (Paris), janvier: 434–57.

Cardoso, João de Menezes e Souza. 1875. *Theses sobre a colonização do Brasil.* Rio de Janeiro: Typographia nacional.

Chalhoub, Sidney. 1990. *Visões da liberdade: Uma história das últimas décadas da escravidão na corte.* São Paulo: Companhia das Letras.

Chevalier, Louis. 1947. "L'Émigration française au XIXème siècle." *Études d'histoire moderne et contemporaine.* Paris: Hatier, 129–33.

Cochin, Auguste. 1871. "L'Abolition de l'esclavage au Brésil." *Revue des Deux Mondes,* 711–17.

Conrad, Robert. 1972. *The Destruction of Brazilian Slavery, 1850–1888.* Berkeley: University of California Press.

Couty, Louis. 1881. *L'Esclavage au Brésil.* Paris: Guillaumin.

Dabadie, F. 1858. *A travers l'Amérique du sud.* Paris: Sartorius.

Expilly, Charles. 1862. *Le Brésil tel qui'il est.* Paris: Denter.

———. 1863. *Les femmes et les moeurs du Brésil.* Paris: Charlieu et Hillery.

Expilly, Charles. 1864a. *La Traite, l'émigration et la colonisation au Brésil.* Paris: A. Lacroix, au Bureau de la *Revue du Monde Colonial asiatique et américain.*

Expilly, Charles. 1864b. *Du Mouvement d'Emigration par le port de Marseille.* Marseille: Typographie-Roux.

Falloux, Comte de. 1884. *Auguste Cochin,* 4th ed. Paris: Emile Perrin.

Gebara, Ademir. 1986. *O Mercado de Trabalho Livre no Brasil.* São Paulo: Ed. Brasiliense.

Leclerc, Max. 1890. *Lettres du Brésil.* Paris: Librairie Plon.

Liais, Emmanuel. 1882. *L'Espace Céleste ou description de l'Univers, accompagné des récits des voyages entrepris pour en compléter l'étude.* Paris: Garnier Frères.

Lyon, Max. 1880. *La question sociale au Brésil.* Paris: E. Capiomont.

Mattos de Castro, Hebe. 1998. *Das cores do silêncio: Os significados da liberdade no sudeste escravista.* Rio de Janeiro: Nova Fronteira.

Michaux-Bellaire, Léon. 1876. *Considérations sur l'abolition de l'esclavage et sur la colonisation au Brésil.* Paris: Guillaumin.

Michel, Ernest. 1887. *A travers l'Hémisphère sud ou mon second voyage autour du monde: (Portugal, Sénégal, Brésil, Uruguay, République Argentine, Chili, Pérou).* Paris: Victor Palmé.

Moustier, Renaud de, Cte. 1885. *Une étape à Rio de Janeiro.* Paris: Jules Gervais.

Queirós Mattoso, Kátia de. 1994. *Etre esclave au Brésil, XVIème-XIXème siècles.* Paris: L'Harmattan.

L. R. 1872. "L'Abolition de l'esclavage au Brésil." *Revue maritime et coloniale,* no. 32: 148.

Reclus, Elisée. 1862. "Le Brésil et la colonisation: provinces du littoral, les noirs et les colonies allemandes." *Revue de Deux Mondes* (Paris), 375–414.

Ribeyrolles, Charles. 1861. *Brazil Pittoresco.* 2 vols. Paris: Lemercier.

Salles, Ricardo. 2008. *E o Vale era o escravo—Vassouras, século XIX: Senhores e escravos no coração do Império.* Rio de Janeiro: Civilização Brasileira.

Santos, Cláudia 1999. "*Les Voyageurs français et les débats autour de la fin de l'esclavage au Brésil (1850–1898).*" Unpubl. PhD diss., Paris IV—Sorbonne.

Schoelcher, Victor. 1881. "Banquet commémoratif de l'abolition de l'esclavage: Discours de M. Schoelcher." Journal *La République Française,* le 7 mai.

Todorov, Tzvetan 1989. *Nous et les autres: La Réflexion française sur la diversité humaine.* 2 vol. Paris: Seuil.

CONTRIBUTORS

Yann Moulier Boutang is professor of economics at the University of Technology of Compiègne, France, and associate professor at the Sino-European University of Technology at Shanghai University. He is the author of *Cognitive Capitalism* (2012), *L'Abeille et l'économiste* (2010), and *Athusser, A Biography (Part One, 1919–1956)* (2002), and also the director of the journal *Multitudes*.

Rachel Caé holds a master's degree in history from the Universidade Federal do Estado do Rio de Janeiro. She currently teaches history at public schools in Rio de Janeiro, Brazil.

Enrico Dal Lago teaches American history at the National University of Ireland, Galway. He is the author of *Agrarian Elites: American Slaveholders and Southern Italian Landowners, 1815–1861* (2005); *American Slavery, Atlantic Slavery, and Beyond: The U.S. "Peculiar Institution" in International Perspective* (2012); and *William Lloyd Garrison and Giuseppe Mazzini: Abolition, Democracy, and Radical Reform* (2013).

Keila Grinberg is associate professor of history at Universidade Federal do Estado do Rio de Janeiro. She is author of several books and articles in Portuguese, English, French, and Spanish. She recently published, with Sue Peabody, *Free Soil in the Atlantic World* (2014).

Wazir Mohamed is associate professor of sociology at Indiana University East. He is author of "Peasant or Proletarian: Emancipation and the Struggle for Freedom in British Guiana in the Shadow of the Second Slavery" in *The Second Slavery: Mass Slaveries and Modernity in the Americas and in the Atlantic Basin* (2014).

Inés Roldán de Montaud is full research scientist in history at the Spanish National Research Council. Previously, she was a research scholar at the London School of Economics, 1992–1993. She has been an associate professor on the Faculty of Arts of the Universidad de Alcalá (Madrid) since 1997. Roldán de Montaud's publications include *La Restauración en Cuba: el fracaso de un proceso reformista* (2000); *La Banca de emisión en Cuba, 1856–1898* (2004); *Las Cajas de Ahorros de las provincias de Ultramar, 1840–1848; Cuba y Puerto Rico* (2010); and, as editor, *Las Haciendas públicas en el Caribe hispano en el siglo* (2008).

MARIANA MUAZE is a member of the department of history of Universidade Federal do Estado do Rio de Janeiro. She holds a PhD in history from Universidade Federal Fluminense. In 2007, she was one of the winners of the Arquivo Nacional prize and the Jorge Zahar prize for the book, *Memórias da Viscondessa: família e poder no Brasil Império* (2008).

JOSÉ A. PIQUERAS is professor of history at Universitat Jaume I (Castellón, Spain) and author of *La esclavitud en las Españas. Un lazo transatlántico* (2012). He is editor of *Trabajo libre y coactivo en sociedades de plantación* (2009), coeditor of *State of Ambiguity: Civic Life and Cultural Form in Cuba's First Republic* (2014), and coeditor of the journal *Historia Social.*

DANIEL ROOD is assistant professor at the University of Georgia, teaching U.S. and Atlantic World history. His most recent publication is "Bogs of Death: Slavery, the Brazilian Flour Trade, and the Mystery of the Vanishing Millpond in Antebellum Virginia" in the *Journal of American History* (2014).

CLAUDIA SANTOS is professor of history at Universidade Federal do Estado do Rio de Janeiro. She is author of *Narratives of Travel and Writing of History: The French Case in the Brazilian Abolitionist (1850–1899)* (2013).

DALE W. TOMICH is deputy director of the Fernand Braudel Center and professor of sociology and history at Binghamton University. He is author of *Slavery in the Circuit of Sugar: Martinique and the World Economy, 1830–1848* (1990); *Through the Prism of Slavery: Labor, Capital, and World Economy* (2004); and various articles on Atlantic history and world-economy.

INDEX